R J HA

For their advice upon relevant sections of *R J Harris's Moon Gardening* thanks must go to Dr Ray Mathias, Head of Science Communication and Education, John Innes Centre, Dr Serge Six, MD, Mr Bob Parker and Mr Brian L Dunsby, Secretary and Public Relations Officer, John Innes Manufacturers Association. For their endlessly supportive endeavours Mrs Olive Harris and Mrs Diana Summers, also, must be thanked — Mrs Harris for her photographic work in respect of the manual's companion website, and Mrs Summers for copy editing and proof reading. Thanks must go, as well, to Mr and Mrs David Willis for their fundamental aid, and to the users of the manual since its publication in July 2002 and the visitors to the manual's website. During a seven-year period these kind folk generously offered their comments on and reactions to the publisher's plans for the manual and to the sample pages of it that have been displayed in the website for critical discussion. Especially, Mr and Mrs George Robinson's permission to refer to Tresillian estate and its horticultural projects must be acknowledged.

R J Harris's
MOON
Gardening

The West Country head gardener's way
of growing fine vegetables, with 100 tips
and 109 panels of associated information

For beginners at gardening
For beginners at moon gardening

Reportage and compilation: WILL SUMMERS

*a really
useful book
from*

✔

Really Useful
Books

R J Harris's Moon Gardening: is published by
Really Useful Books, Shrewsbury, Shropshire,
SY3 8HT, **+44** 01743 246469,
reallyusefulbooks@boltblue.com, a division of
The Really Useful Partnership

First published in Great Britain by
Really Useful Books July 2002
First impression of first edition July 2002
Second impression February 2003
Third impression June 2003
Fourth impression April 2005
Fifth impression September 2005

First impression of second edition February 2007

British Library Cataloguing in Publication Data

A catalogue record for this book is available from the British
Library

ISBN 978-0-9542394-1-1

Design by Perfect Graphics. Typeset in Bookman and Avant
Garde by Keyboard Wonders

Printed and bound in Great Britain by
The Cromwell Press, Trowbridge, Wiltshire.

CONTENTS

See the final pages for a full index

Where it is appropriate, instructions regarding soil preparation and plant management are repeated throughout the manual to save the user the inconvenience of cross-referencing. The whole is presented within a detailed context of moon gardening and of crop rotation designed according to the R J Harris way of vegetable gardening.

R J HARRIS is a professional horticulturist who grows vegetables, fruit and flowers with the help of three of horticulture's oldest and least-used tools: the moon; knowledge of plants' ability to help each other to thrive or to perish; knowledge of how gardeners worked before the arrival of today's technology. He was discovered nationally by BBC2's *Garden Stories*, and was, until recently, the head gardener of three major horticultural undertakings: the 20-acre Tresillian estate near Newquay, Cornwall; an adjacent 70-acre conservation area; one of Cornwall's largest tourist attractions. Tresillian is now a consolidated, 200-acre estate in non-commercial ownership. Cornishman R J Harris remains its head gardener.

Mr Harris began his career as an apprentice in the mid 1950s. He has practised in the public and the private sectors, his studies of the moon's influence on the management of plants dating from the 1960s.

He is a poet, a story-teller, a local radio broadcaster, a show judge and the chairman of several of the West Country's horticultural societies. He has introduced moon gardening to a number of television programmes. He has advised on the horticultural aspects of costume dramas filmed for the cinema and for television.

A special charge on him has been the recovery from dereliction and the restoration to its original state of Tresillian's Victorian walled, kitchen garden. Standing in the shoes and occupying the minds of those who were head gardeners before him, he pursues a programme of research into yesterday's plants and yesterday's ways with them. As word has spread of his efforts, the garden has become a Mecca for writers, publishers, producers, educationists and students at all levels of horticultural training.

Upon a number of fundamental, practical levels his restoration work does not emulate the practice of his Victorian predecessors. They dared admit no constraint in their fight to send up to the big house nothing other than a comprehensive supply of unblemished produce and flowers. Anticipating the onset of pests and diseases, they did not hesitate to order the application of poisons that were harmful to humans, animals, birds and insects. He has not revived that example.

With a half-century-long career behind him — and with having witnessed 20th-century gardening's limitations and penalties — he is of sufficiently senior status to be able to jettison the practices that he sees as undesirable, whether they be of the past or of the present. He applies in their place his own combination of positive organic horticulture (seeing that as more than solely a rejection of what, patently, is undesirable), compatible planting and inherited knowledge of the influences of the moon's phases as they were understood and interpreted by the Romans, the Greeks and the Romanies.

This manual is about that combination. It is for the beginner in gardening and for the beginner in moon gardening. It is the product of more than seven years of talks with a retired journalist whose working life has granted to him the time and the opportunity to do little more, horticulturally, than contain the maraudings of a series of suburban patches.

WS: March 2002

Make a basic, Tresillian-style, crop-rotated vegetable garden, manage it with the help of the moon, and grow crops the quality of which is no longer available from the shops. Do so in four annual stages.

The Victorian walled, kitchen garden, the ornamental beds and borders, the soft- and hard-fruit trees and bushes, the woods and

For the newcomer to vegetable and moon gardening, the supremely important reason to take a close interest in the *Aquadulce Claudia* broad bean is that cultivating it provides the perfect moment, the perfect opportunity, to begin to convert to domestic vegetable production according to head gardener R J Harris's convictions about and knowledge of crop rotation, the moon's influence, companion planting and the advantages that stem from applying the soil-management practices of bygone years and bygone horticulturists.

This perfect moment is created by the fact that the centuries-old *Aquadulce Claudia* must be sown in the Autumn, and that the Autumn is the best time to start to apply the methods that hallmark the R J Harris way of vegetable gardening.

coppices of the 200-acre Tresillian estate in Cornwall are an expression of head gardener R J Harris's system of soil preparation and improvement, seed sowing, seedling and plantlet propagation, and plant, bed and border management. The vegetable beds, in particular, express his understanding and exploitation of the relationship that exists between each of the moon's four quarters and Earth's water table. Influencing the whole of his approach is his revival and study of the ways and customs of gardening, which, nowadays, are largely forgotten or abandoned.

With the help of the broad bean, prepare to crop rotate.

Of the several antique and modern broad beans that are grown in Tresillian's walled, kitchen garden, the variety that estate head gardener R J Harris recommends is the essentially gardener-friendly, longpod type that is known as *Aquadulce Claudia*. This is a broad bean with an exceptionally long pod (hence 'longpod'). It has a smooth, green exterior and a pale-green interior lined with white fur. It carries a cargo of about six large, cream-coloured, firm, flavoursome beans.

Autumn-sown, Winter/Spring-cultivated, early-Summer harvested, the *Aquadulce Claudia* is valued by Mr Harris partly because it provides him — as it has done for many past generations of head gardeners — with some of the first of the heavy-weight produce of the vegetable-garden's new season.

He values it, equally, because its tiny, delicately-hued flowers furnish some of the first blossom of the new year, heralding the glories that are to come.

Mr Harris's principal reason, however, for recommending the *Aquadulce Claudia,* is a three-part and horticulturally practical reason: *a)* it incurs the least risk of attack by the broad-bean grower's major enemy, the destructively rapacious blackfly. Moreover, when the blackfly onslaught begins (as begin it must; organic gardening knows no way to prevent this very nasty insect's arrival), the attack is of the lightest and the most successfully dealt with; *b)* like all of the many members of the vast legume family, the broad bean possesses roots which deposit a valuable cost- and labour-free tranche of nitrogen in the soil. The bonus creates the ideal medium for the nitrogen-hungry crops that take over from Tresillian's *Aquadulce Claudia* to open the way to that holy grail of all vegetable gardeners, year-round production. Of these, that most under-rated citizen of the vegetable world, the cabbage, is the head gardener's favourite; *c)* each year, the Autumn-sown broad bean launches a new set of Mr Harris's two special vegetable beds upon their four-year cycle of crop rotation.

This and the next chapter, *CABBAGES*, are also primers of many of RJ Harris's basic methods.

The seeds of the *Aquadulce Claudia* are available at most garden centres as from August or September. More often than not, Mr Harris buys his via mail order from Kings Seeds at Colchester in Essex (see *SUPPLIERS*).

He sows them in a precisely-measured, rect-

1

Before embarking upon head gardener R J Harris's style of moon-aided, crop-rotated vegetable gardening, establish and, in time to come, hold firmly to a policy on the disposal of waste vegetable matter. As a result, expect to use time and mental and physical effort when gardening more economically.

At the earliest moment, decide upon one of two courses.

1 during the initial four years of the garden conversion, dispose of the garden's *non-weed* plant waste in the bottom of the trench that always awaits completion as a deep-trench bed in one of the four crop-rotation Areas. Also, turn arising grass turfs upside down in the bottom of the same trench. With effect from the fifth year, when no trench awaits completion, store the material in garden sacks until it is required for deep-trench-bed purposes. At the same time, dispose of the whole of the arising annual and perennial weeds and all household vegetable waste securely away from the garden, where it can have no influence upon the garden's performance

2 place the annual weeds and their roots in the garden's compost bin or heap (adding to them non-weed garden vegetable waste and household vegetable waste). Dispose of the arising perennial weeds and their roots securely off site, where they can do no harm.

The first is Mr Harris's preferred course. For that reason, it is the waste-vegetable-management method that is advocated by this manual.

angular section of one of his single-dug beds in the Autumn of the first year of that bed's four-year life span. This is just after the making of the bed in September, when the nutrients and moisture of its 30cm or so thickness of buried, fully-composted, well-strawed animal manure are untapped.

Adjacent to the broad-bean-bearing section of the new single-dug bed are other rectangular sections, which are earmarked for the Spring commencement of one or more of his wide and varied range of first-year, single-dug-bed-specific vegetables (listed in *ROTATION*).

Alongside the freshly-created, first-year, single-dug beds are freshly-created, first-year, deep-trench beds. These differ from the single-dug beds in design, construction and purpose, and each is furnished in each of its four years of production with its own year-specific vegetables (also listed in *ROTATION*).

The two bed types are located within a self-contained area, which occupies a quarter of Tresillian's kitchen garden. The three other quarters within the kitchen garden's four 10-metre-tall, fruit-tree-bearing, red-brick walls are similarly equipped, each set of beds at the time of the broad beans' Autumn sowing commencing the second, third or fourth year of its four-year life span.

The four areas are divided from each other and bounded by broad, hard-surfaced paths laid down when the garden was installed in the mid 1800s to maintain the people of the big house (Tresillian is Cornish for *House in the Sun*) in vegetables, herbs, fruit, flowers and the plant matter that was required in those days for now-forgotten

2

practical uses and applications.

At the centre of the four areas, where the service paths cross, is a herb garden.

Diagram 1, page 14, gives an impression of this typically Victorian layout.

Supporting the four crop-rotating areas is a continuation of the estate's founding gardeners' intensive employment of seed beds, cold frames and cold and heated greenhouses. To-day, as in those early staff members' times, these essentials for volume production are sited within or just outside the garden's walls.

The instructional content of this manual is based upon and derives from the supervision of the four crop-rotated areas by head gardener R J Harris and his staff.

To prepare to cultivate the broad bean that is known as *Aquadulce Claudia*, and, by these means, to embark upon the head gardener's combination of moon gardening, four-year crop rotation, companion planting and

R J Harris holds that weeds have no place in the correctly-managed garden, whether in the ground or out of it. For that reason, where he is in charge of the soil, he does not produce vegetable-waste compost. Neither does he opt for holding *weed* material in bags in readiness for the next renewal of a deep-trench bed, of which the walled, kitchen garden of the Tresillian estate always possesses many. His experience has taught him that certain weed seeds and roots survive and even prosper when buried at a depth beneath the surface of the ground. Hence, his is the professional's view — that home-made compost is to be abjured because of the risk of its inevitable weed-seed content. Additionally, he positively prefers the ready-made, traditional, animal-derived soil conditioners. For him, they are accompanied by and create none of what he sees as the time-, energy- and cost-consuming production, management and application problems that are inextricably associated with the composting and employment of waste-vegetable matter.

To those whose commitment to home-made, waste-vegetable compost is unshaken by the head gardener's views, Mr Harris advises, "Site your compost bin where the stuff inside it can be kept moist, and let the material age for at least one year before using it. And if your bin is smaller than ten-foot square by six-feet high, with an empty one of the same size alongside for turning purposes, give up. Only that amount of volume is likely to generate enough heat to kill the weed seeds."

The head gardener notes that there are gardeners, an irreverent corps, who compost all vegetable matter at any stage of its growth, and who argue: "So what if the weed seeds germinate when the compost is turned into the ground.

"Take out the young weeds before seed-setting time and the result is yet more material for the compost bin"— to which they add — "and don't tell us that a few young weeds in the bed and uprooted as soon as they are large enough to be held between thumb and forefinger rob the resident vegetables and flowers of any significant amounts of moisture and nutrients."

"No two gardeners or gardens are alike," responds Mr Harris. "That is one of the marvels of gardening."

3

Challenged, head gardener R J Harris would almost certainly acknowledge that of all of the manually-operated tools held in Tresillian's tool store, the hoe, probably, is the one that confers the most benefit upon garden and gardener. "It is also the one that is the most overlooked," says Mr Harris, "which is a pity when you consider how much good it can do — especially where the vegetables grow.

"To me, it is one of *the* indispensable tools, and the garden in which it is never used — and there must be thousands of those up and down the country — is a garden which never gets the chance to find out what its full potential is."

Mr Harris lists the rewards that accrue from applying the hoe to a bed's surface: "Almost total weed prevention, for a start, because the disturbance caused by running the hoe through the surface of the soil once per week without fail makes it well nigh impossible for the weed-seeds to germinate. No young weeds means no food for the slugs and the snails, so giving them no reason to linger where the new seedlings are sprouting. No weed growth means the bed's nutrients and moisture are available in their entirety to the developing plants. And, importantly, hoeing turns up moistened earth. That adds moisture to the top few inches of surface for the benefit of the developing roots' systems."

The head gardener urges that the hoe be applied in the late afternoon or early evening in preference to any other time of the day.

"That is when conditions are cooler," he says, "and so there is the least evaporation of moisture from the hoed soil. As a result, there is increased return in moisture recovery for a given amount of effort.

"And," he adds, "in any event, what better leaning post is there to put your weight on when pausing to mop your brow and look at the results of your labours and tell yourself what a good job you are doing?"

many of the gardening ways of times past and gardeners long gone

1 note that the conversion to R J Harris's style of vegetable gardening occupies four years

2 note that when the four-year project is applied to virgin land, its basis is as follows

■ **FIRST YEAR**
One quarter of the ground that is earmarked for conversion is equipped with one of Mr Harris's single-dug beds and one of his deep-trench beds. It is committed to first-year-specific vegetable production. It is known as the Year 1 Area.

The unemployed, adjacent three-quarters of the earmarked ground is launched upon general, manual, weed clearance

■ **SECOND YEAR**
An adjacent quarter of the ground that is earmarked for conversion is equipped with one of Mr Harris's single-dug beds and one of his deep-trench beds. It is committed to first-year-specific vegetable production. It is known as the Year 2 Area. The Year 1 Area is in its second year. It continues with second-year-specific vegetable production. The unemployed, adjacent one-half of the earmarked

ground continues with general, manual, weed clearance

■ THIRD YEAR

An adjacent quarter of the ground that is earmarked for conversion is equipped with one of Mr Harris's single-dug beds and one of his deep-trench beds. It is committed to first-year-specific vegetable production. It is known as the Year 3 Area. The Year 1 Area is in its third year. It continues with third-year-specific vegetable production. The Year 2 Area is in its second year. It continues with second-year-specific vegetable production. The unemployed, adjacent one-quarter of the earmarked ground continues with general, manual, weed clearance

■ FOURTH YEAR

The adjacent fourth and final quarter of the ground that is earmarked for conversion is equipped with one of the head gardener's single-dug beds and one of his deep-trench beds. It is committed to first-year-specific vegetable production. It is known as the Year 4 Area. The Year 1 Area is in its fourth and final year. It continues with fourth-year-specific vegetable production. The Year 2 Area is in its third year of production. It continues with third-year-specific vegetable production. The Year 3 Area is in its second year. It continues with second-year-specific vegetable production. Now, all four of the quarter-sized areas of the earmarked ground are converted to crop rotation according to the R J Harris system. The general, manual, weed clearance is complete

3 note that the ground that is earmarked for development into the four Year Areas accommodates also a seed bed. See *Diagram 1*, page 14. The seed bed is established at the same time as the Year 1 Area. There is no provision for herb growing

4 note that, at the end of the fourth year, the Year 1 Area completes its four-year cycle. In the following year (the fifth year of moon gardening), it embarks upon a new four-year cycle with the aid of a renewed single-dug bed and a renewed deep-trench bed

5 note that, as from the end of the fourth year, this is the continuing pattern of vegetable production. Annually, an Area reaches the end of its four-year life span and is renewed by being equipped with a renewed single-dug bed and a renewed deep-trench bed

TIP 1

→ **Do not attempt the quite impracticable task of creating and planting up at one and the same time all four of the Year Areas. At first thinking, it may seem to be a good, if physically demanding, idea. It is not. The four areas must be started one after the other, annually, throughout the four-year period. If they are not, the nutrients of their beds diminish at the same rate, making possible each year only the crops that are specific to that year. The crop range and variety that is provided annually by the correctly out-of-step Year Areas becomes unattainable, and a highly important reward of crop rotation is lost.**

(PERMANENT PATH)

YEAR 2 AREA

Year 2 Area's single-dug bed in the first year of its four-year life span

Autumn-sown broad beans — located here to the right of a temporary, trodden path (all such paths shown as a grey strip) — are the Year 2 Area's first-year, single-dug bed's first crop. Space remains to the left of the temporary, trodden path for a later-sown, first-year, single-dug-bed crop

Year 2 Area's deep-trench bed in the first year of its four-year life span

(PERMANENT PATH)

YEAR 3 AREA

Year 3 Area's single-dug bed in the first year of its four-year life span

Autumn-sown broad beans — located here to the right of a temporary, trodden path (all such paths shown as a grey strip) — are the Year 3 Area's first-year, single-dug bed's first crop. Space remains to the left of the temporary, trodden path for a later-sown, first-year, single-dug-bed crop

Year 3 Area's deep-trench bed in the first year of its four-year life span

(PERMANENT PATH)

(PERMANENT PATH)

Year 1 Area's deep-trench bed in the first year of its four-year life span

YEAR 1 AREA

Year 1 Area's single-dug bed in the first year of its four-year life span

Autumn-sown broad beans — located here to the left of a temporary, trodden path (all such paths shown as a grey strip) — are the Year 1 Area's first-year, single-dug bed's first crop. Space remains beyond the temporary, trodden path for a later-sown, first-year, single-dug-bed crop

Year 4 Area's deep-trench bed in the first year of its four-year life span

YEAR 4 AREA

Year 4 Area's single-dug bed in the first year of its four-year life span

Autumn-sown broad beans — located here to the left of a temporary, trodden path (all such paths shown as a grey strip) — are the Year 4 Area's first-year, single-dug bed's first crop. Space remains beyond the temporary, trodden path for a later-sown, first-year, single-dug-bed crop

N

(PERMANENT PATH)

SEED BED

Its role is the same, year after year

It raises seedlings and plantlets

It can be aligned with any of the four sides of the total crop rotation area

(PERMANENT PATH)

6 note that when the four-year conversion project is applied to an existing vegetable garden, production ceases for three years in the ground that is outside the planned Year 1 Area. That ground lies unused, awaiting incorporation into the four-year conversion project. It is subject only to the general weed-clearance programme

7 note that when the four-year conversion project is applied to a flower/shrub garden, the existing plants are maintained, diminishing in number throughout the four-year period as, progressively, the four Year Areas for crop rotation are installed

8 resolve that the first year of the conversion to crop rotation is to commence in a September

9 **during the months prior to the chosen September**, examine the ground that is

Diagram 1
The plan highlights the position in the moon-garden-to-be during the opening months of the first year of the four-year garden-conversion project. The Year 1 Area bears Autumn-sown broad beans marking the starting point of the four-year, crop-rotation cycle that is based upon the R J Harris system. The Year 2 Area is added at the start of the second year of the four-year garden-conversion project, the Year 3 Area at the start of the third year and the Year 4 Area at the start of the fourth year.

In the fifth year, the Year 1 Area's beds are renewed, and the Area embarks upon its next four years of crop rotation. It then becomes known as the Year 5 Area. This general pattern extends as the seasons come and go, each season bringing an Area renewal and renaming according to the number of the current year.

The plan is not to scale. It is not a plan of Tresillian's Victorian, walled, kitchen garden.

available to be converted to the head gardener's way of gardening. Do so the moment that weather and soil conditions permit. Much thinking and detailed planning are required, and the process is best not hurried

10 ensure, as a result of the examination, that to be able to accommodate one of R J Harris's single-dug beds and one of his deep-trench beds in each of the four Year Areas (as well as, additionally, the necessary service paths), the space to be converted is either

— at least 900cm wide and 1430cm long, its 900cm width aligning east to west.
[*Considerations:* **1** — *these are the dimensions of the layout that is shown by Diagram 1. It is the layout that underlies the whole of this manual's instruction, being preferred by the head gardener;* **2** — *each of the four Year Areas is of a standard size: 300cm wide and 490cm long. The service path is 100cm wide;* **3** — *the seed bed is 700cm long and 50cm wide. Its 50cm width renders it workable with ease from the service paths that bound each of its two long sides. This reduces to the minimum the physical effort demanded of the gardener;* **4** — *a decision not to raise seedlings and plantlets in a seed bed in the open garden renders a seed bed unnecessary. Hence, it can be dispensed with. As a result, a reduced return from the*

4

This manual presumes that its user commands sufficient raw, uncultivated ground for the creation of an R J Harris-style vegetable garden. In truth, few gardeners are so blessed. For most, the site referred to as the garden has long been equipped with paths, beds and plants. Having, often, an history of successfully vanquished past owners, it is fully capable of staying as it is despite the current proprietor's intentions, ambitions and best efforts. Even when that is not the case, the reshaping of what exists can look to be too daunting, too expensive, too time-consuming a task.

"The advantage of my kind of crop rotation," Mr Harris points out, "is that it takes four years for the conversion to be completed. During that period, things are done one leisurely step at a time, each bringing only short-term, limited, not too demanding disruption."

The head gardener suggests: "First understand the principles and practices of this other way of gardening. Then decide how elements of it could be applied with as little disturbance as is possible to what is already there.

"In short, get as many of the benefits of crop rotation and moon gardening as can be got, and know that, as a result, the already-formed garden is a fitter, better-looking, more productive place.

"Keep in mind, too," he adds, "the very great importance of it all.

"We are no less exposed and vulnerable to Nature's uncertainties and mankind's greed-driven desires and wiles than were our distant forebears. Their ability to extract food from the ground — and they were very good at that — could well, once again, become a key to the survival of the individual and of that individual's family."

R J Harris way of horticulture is to be expected]

or

— at least 690cm wide and 1850cm long, its 1850cm length aligning east to west. [***Considerations: 1*** — *each of this space's four Year Areas is of the standard size: 300cm wide and 490cm long;* **2** — *the seed bed is 490cm long and 50cm wide. The service path is 100cm wide;* **3** — *the four Year Areas and the seed bed are in line, positioned side by side. They are separated by service paths and surrounded by a perimeter service path;* **3** — *the 690cm width of the overall layout is dictated by the 490cm length of the individual Year Area plus the 100cm width x 2 of the perimeter service path]*

or

— at least 500cm wide and 2610cm long, its 500cm width aligning east to west. [***Considerations: 1*** — *each of this space's four Year Areas is of the standard size, 300cm wide and 490cm long;* **2** — *the seed bed is 300cm long and 50cm wide. The service path is 100cm wide;* **3** — *the four Year Areas lie end to end; the seed bed is at their top or tail. The five are separated by permanent service paths and are surrounded by a perimeter service path;* **4** — *the 500cm width of the* *overall layout is dictated by the 300cm width of the individual Year Area plus the 100cm width x 2 of the perimeter service path]*

11 note that an alternative is to locate the four Year Areas and the seed bed throughout the available ground at unrelated points, each within its own 100cm-wide, perimeter path.
*[**Considerations: 1** — of the alternative Area dispositions, this is the least satisfactory, so it is not considered within the general discussion of this manual; **2** — to such an arrangement, if it must be utilised, Mr Harris's methods and principles can be applied with no loss of effectiveness despite there being, almost certainly, a loss of efficiency in the overall management of the total garden]*

12 note that, ideally, the 300cm width of each Year Area is aligned east to west. This is the case no matter which of the four discussed layouts is adopted.
*[**Consideration:** the single-dug bed and the deep-trench bed of the individual Year Area extend across the east-to-west, 300cm width of the Area. As a result, almost all of the beds' rows of plants also align east to west (notable exceptions are the onion row and the pea row. See ONIONS and PEAS). Hence, the sun almost always brings benefit to both sides of a given row throughout the day, not first one side in the morning and the other side in the afternoon. An added benefit is that, for this reason, one east-to-west row cannot cast a shadow upon an*

adjacent, parallel row, and cannot be in the shadow of that row]

13 note that the stated dimensions are of the smallest spaces that most would consider to be viable for open-air, in-bed vegetable production. They are proposed in order to provide a basis for instruction and discussion, and to acknowledge that the majority of the United Kingdom's domestic gardens are small. They cater, also, for the fact that four-year crop rotation applied efficiently and comprehensively demands more space than does conventional vegetable gardening

14 decide whether or not to increase the dimensions stated above in order to bring

TIP 2
➜ **September is the optimum month in which to lay out the four Year Areas and to begin to develop the Year 1 Area even when there is no sowing until Spring of the first year of conversion. September can be relied upon to provide comfortable weather/soil conditions for bed installation. The pause as Winter passes enables the two bed types to become fully settled. As a result, the surface of the deep-trench bed develops a helpfully rain-collecting depression. On both beds young weeds appear. They are easily extracted prior to sowing/planting, bringing about a one-generation reduction of the weed population by non-poisonous means.**

into production a greater available space. If the dimensions are to be increased, decide what they are to be, record them, and, from this point on, substitute them for this manual's proposed dimensions. Subsequently, apply the revised dimensions to the proposed sowing/planting schemes

15 observe, in connection with this, a cardinal R J Harris rule. This is that whilst any vegetable-producing bed's stated length may be increased, its width may not. [**Consideration:** *this is because beds that are wider than those that are recommended impose increased demand upon the gardener's resources of strength, energy and manual dexterity. Lengthened beds impose no such demand*]

16 ensure, as far as possible, that the space selected for conversion (be it existing garden or undeveloped ground or a combination of the two) is

— fully exposed to the sun

— fully exposed to the rain

— not subject to chance or temporary over-shadowing by tall structures or tall plants

— not affected by the roots of permanent planting such as bushes, shrubs or trees

— protected, if possible, from high winds

— easily accessible by a gardener equipped with tools and/or wheeled equipment

5

The head gardener insists that, whenever and wherever possible, the beds that carry his above-the-surface developers such as broad beans be no more than wide enough to house two parallel rows — whether single- or double-rank rows. Then, any point within a bed's width is reachable by hand or by long-handled tool from the paths on either side of the bed without excessive physical effort.

Harvest time, in particular, gains benefit from this simple and yet not immediately obvious thinking. Those who have planted four or five parallel rows of strawberries in a bed running alongside a garden path know what physical hell awaits them when they stretch out from the path to explore the depths of rows four and five and slightly beyond.

"And, of course, all of this caters for the rule that the bed's surface — any bed's surface — must never be trodden, knelt or leaned upon," says R J Harris.

— endowed with a top-soil layer at least thick enough to accept a trench which is one spade's blade deep before sub soil, industrial hardpan, native rock or other undesirable material is struck

and decide to

— take whatever steps it is possible to take to enable the selected ground to equal or draw close to the above standards, and to accept the conditions that are unchangeable

— learn to garden in the presence of the unchangeable

conditions, and to convert those conditions into opportunities for a varied style of gardening offering challenges and rewards. [*Considerations:* **1** — *shade, for example, can be seen as doing nothing more 'harmful' than delaying ripening and, thus, extending the period of a given harvesting. Often, this can relieve the pressure upon the kitchen;* **2** — *an advantage of R J Harris's revival of the beds of old is that, once established, their locations never move. Hence, the excavation and then removal from site of undesirable material such as sub soil to make a trench for the deep-trench bed is undertaken only once. The advantage attaches to the single-dug bed to a lesser degree*]

17 ensure that accessible, additional space is available upon which to site and manage leafmould bins and/or heaps, and for the composting and storage of mixed farmyard manure and/or horse manure

18 note that the ideal sites for the bins and/or heaps are as cool as possible and as exposed as possible to the rain.
[*Considerations:* **1** — *these are the sites at which there is the least moisture evaporation due principally to the prevailing low ambient temperature;* **2** — *insufficient moisture results in unsatisfactorily composted material. In the extreme, an absence of moisture prevents vegetable matter, whatever its*

kind and origin, from composting and causes it to become largely useless tinder; **3** — *at Tresillian, the coldest and, hence, most moisture-conservant site is adjacent to the wide expanse of the external, northward-looking face of one of the four tall, boundary walls of the kitchen garden. Here are located Mr Harris's manure and leafmould heaps and bins, in company with the kitchen garden's and the estate's ancillary offices and storerooms*]

19 note that the head gardener views home-made waste-vegetable compost as unnecessary to the style of gardening that utilises the old ways of crop rotation and bed construction

20 **as soon as possible prior to the September of the chosen first year of the garden conversion**, drive twenty-four 100cm-long canes each 30cm into the topsoil of the earmarked ground to position

— the rectangles of the Year 1, 2, 3 and 4 Areas and the seed bed

— the permanent paths of the chosen vegetable-garden layout

21 link the canes with coloured (for visibility) plastic (for long life) garden line placed at ground level and gently tautened. See *Diagram 1*, page 14

22 cap the tops of the twenty-four garden canes, for safety's sake. Use purpose-made plastic caps bought at a garden centre, or large

19

corks suitably pre-drilled, or very small, well-washed glass jars up-ended onto the canes' tops

23 ensure that

— each of the corners of the six laid-out rectangles is 90° square

— the opposite sides of each of the six rectangles are of equal length

24 ensure that the 300cm width of each Year Area is aligned so that it is in an east-to-west direction

25 insert a label into one corner of each of the outlined Year Areas to identify the Year 1 Area, the Year 2 Area, the Year 3 Area and the Year 4 Area. Identify the seed bed in the same way. Use plastic labels marked with a weatherproof marker

26 purchase

● a card-index box

● a set of A-to-Z index cards to fit into the card-index box

● a pack of lined cards to fit into the card-index box

and place the A-to-Z index cards inside the card-index box

27 write

YEAR 1 AREA

in the top, left-hand corner of one of the purchased, lined cards

28 file the YEAR 1 AREA lined card in the card-index box. Place it behind the Y index card

29 write

YEAR 2 AREA

in the top, left-hand corner of one of the purchased, lined cards

30 file the YEAR 2 AREA lined card in the card-index box. Place it alphabetically and numerically behind the Y index card

31 write

YEAR 3 AREA

in the top, left-hand corner of one of the purchased, lined cards

32 file the YEAR 3 AREA lined card in the card-index box. Place it alphabetically and numerically behind the Y index card

33 write

YEAR 4 AREA

in the top, left-hand corner of one of the purchased, lined cards

TIP 3
➜ **Bear in mind the old, old way of deciding what was the ideal width of the vegetable-garden service path. Could one under-gardener squatting on the path and working on an adjacent bed leave a sufficient width of path space behind him (always a him; never a her) for another to be able to pass by without inconvenience to self, squatter or either's associated equipment? This was when gardens were large enough for such common-sense thinking. It is the kind of perfection that is within the reach of very few nowadays, alas.**

34 file the YEAR 4 AREA lined card in the card-index box. Place it alphabetically and numerically behind the Y index card

35 write

AREAS

in the top, left-hand corner of one of the purchased, lined cards

36 write on the AREAS lined card

See YEAR 1 AREA

See YEAR 2 AREA

See YEAR 3 AREA

See YEAR 4 AREA

37 file the AREAS lined card in the card-index box. Place it behind the A index card

38 write

SEED BED

in the top, left-hand corner of one of the purchased, lined cards

39 file the SEED BED lined card in the card-index box. Place it behind the S index card

40 write

BED, SEED

in the top, left-hand corner of one of the purchased, lined cards

41 write on the BED, SEED lined card

See SEED BED

and file the BED, SEED lined card in the card-index

box. Place it behind the B index card

42 write

BEDS

in the top, left-hand corner of one of the purchased, lined cards

43 write on the BEDS lined card

See SEED BED

and file the BEDS lined card in the card-index box. Place it alphabetically behind the B index card

44 close the card-index box and lodge it, its contents and the lined cards where they are not subject to interference, for continued use at a later stage

45 **still as soon as possible prior to the September of the first year of the garden conversion**, decide whether the surface of the 100-cm-wide permanent path is to be of compacted earth, stone sets, bricks, concrete, gravel or pebble. [*Consideration: timber decking of any type is not suggested as a possible alternative. It has a limited life. Its materials and installation can be costly. Supremely, its surface is dangerously slippery in wet conditions*]

46 note that the compacted earth surface, whilst cost-free, is, almost certainly, grass- and weed-ridden. [*Considerations: 1 — the grass/weed growth that characterises the earth-surfaced path need present no maintenance problems*

Contact R J Harris at *rjh@moongardening. fsnet.co.uk*. if further explanation is required.

6

*C*rimson Flower is Mr Harris's favourite broad bean for Spring sowing when the broad bean has to be sown at that time in the Tresillian estate. The head gardener is aware that it and the other Spring-sown broad-bean varieties usually bring with them the need to combat serious blackfly infestations. This can be a messy, thankless, time-consuming task involving the use of purchased, sprayed-on pest killers (although, not for the head gardener, who rejects practices of this kind).

The planting method is precisely as for *Aquadulce Claudia*, with the moon and the other key stages being programmed to cater for March, April or May sowings (commencing with whichever month brings workable soil and warmed conditions).

The head gardener always bears in mind the Spring/Summer broad-bean blossom's delightful scent. If possible, and if his four-year rotation system permits, he positions it so that it is close to where Tresillian's garden seats are located. Then its scent can be enjoyed at leisure, and to the full.

within the context of R J Harris's approach to beds' management. The deliberate absence of vertical containment timber boarding (a method favoured by many gardeners) around the head gardener's two kinds of bed is an advantage. It makes possible the mowing of the paths across the whole of their width without impedence, so that there is no development of the grass/weed fringe that is

a characteristic of (and is encouraged by) vertical timber edging. The fringe requires to be dealt with by a hand fork, with, inevitably, a disturbance to the path's surface. Otherwise, it requires physically-demanding hand clipping, to prevent it from becoming tall, unsightly, seed-bearing and bed invasive; **2** — the devotees of bin-made waste-vegetable compost regard the weed growth that can be harvested from earth-surfaced paths as legitimate compost-bin vegetable matter. They accept readily the disciplines involved in cutting the weeds before seeds are set. For these gardeners, amassing sufficient vegetable matter is a constant challenge, and no cut leaf, no cut non-woody stem or item of kitchen waste is to be ignored]

47 note that a surface of stone, brick or concrete combines longevity (not always an unmixed blessing, given the considerations of future ground availability and employment) with relatively high financial and/or physical cost. [***Considerations: 1*** — *the impecunious urban gardeners of the 1930s (which is to say, most of the gardeners of those days of high unemployment and almost no state-supported social safety nets — to whom a farthing spent on gardening was always a farthing too far), mixed one part of common cement with four parts of any kind of sand and added water to make a stiff mortar. They covered the compacted,* *closely-mown, grass-surfaced path with bricklayers' trowelfuls of the mortar positioned close to, and yet not touching, each other. Each trowelful was pressed to about 4cm in thickness with a small piece of timber board the instant it was deposited. It was then trimmed to crazy-paving shape with the trowel. Progressively, the overall result was that of unmortared crazy pathing; **2** — an advantage of this extremely low-cost surfacing method was that the job could be done a bucketful of mortar at a time, and could be an occasional task spread over as many days or weeks as best suited the gardener and the demands of the garden. It brought instant as well as progressively increasing benefit. Also, its advancement being measured by the bucket, it entailed no left-over and, hence, wasted materials. Another benefit was that it entailed none of the physical effort demanded by conventional path laying, and none of conventional path laying's disruption to the garden; **3** — a further practical advantage was that the 'crazy paving' could be lifted with ease, 'stone' by 'stone', when garden re-organisation called for that. Unspoiled, usable top soil was revealed by this process; **4** — grass/weed growth between the closely-set 'stones' was controlled easily by regular mowing; **5** — care was taken to use clean materials and implements. The 1930s gardeners knew that if any of these was contaminated accidentally by earth, conditions would be created within the hardened mortar that encouraged moss growth. The result, eventually, would be moss covered 'stones' bringing unsightliness and a slippery surface]*

48 note that a gravel or pebble path requires, ideally, to be timber-framed, bringing an increase in financial cost and installation complexity. [***Consideration:*** *"Not a wise choice," comments Mr Harris. "The stuff is is likely to get everywhere, especially into the beds. Controlling it creates extra work"*]

49 **still as soon as possible prior to the September of the chosen Year 1 of the garden conversion**, install the length of service path that surrounds the four sides of the site of the Year 1 Area and the four sides of the site of the seed bed

50 remove the garden canes and garden lines that outline the Year 1 Area and the seed bed. Clean them and return them to store. [***Consideration:*** *they are made redundant by the presence of the finished sections of the service path*]

51 retain the canes and lines that outline the sites of the Year Areas that are not surrounded by service paths. Retain the canes and lines that indicate the as yet undeveloped service paths

52 continue path installation in advance of each Year Area being brought into cultivation. Thus, spread the overall path-laying demand throughout the four-year conversion to crop-rotation. [***Consideration:*** *R J Harris's overall recommendation is, "Hard paths. But, of course," he adds, "laying down truly permanent paths — even those of the '30s — commits the garden to being laid out*

7

For the professional horticulturist, one of many secrets of success is the systematic recording of employed techniques and resources, and of the resultant performances of affected plants. Professional gardeners have known this for a very long time. Indeed, ever since social history became respectable (there was a time when few of the explorers of the past would ever have deigned to drop their gaze below levels royal), the social historians have been adding to today's knowledge of a steadily increasing number of yesterdays by delving into and analysing the innumerable and often far from legible journals, diaries, bills, delivery notes, planting lists and programmes of the head gardeners of the 1700s, 1800s and early 1900s.

These very expert senior staff members maintained their records not for the fun of it — and certainly not for posterity's benefit. Record keeping of this kind was stultifying work offering few moments of excitement. These latter-day specialists reached for pen and ink pot at the end of the long, tiring work day to protect their reputations and to safeguard their jobs. Both, they knew, depended upon never repeating mistakes, always capitalising upon success, and having written evidence to fall back upon instead of their employers' (and their own) memories.

Only the written word, made secure in safeguarded volumes, could be relied upon to pinpoint the crucially important gardening moments throughout the often numerous seasons of their professional lives.

R J Harris's records go back to his apprentice days in the 1950s. Then, they were inspected regularly by the Cornish head gardener under whom he trained. Little escaped that disciplinarian's eye, and woe betide the young Harris if his writings were judged to be inadequate.

for the crop-rotation way. Once that is the case, there is no going back without bother, untidiness and, perhaps, expense. The matter must be considered fully first of all"]

53 observe, so far as is possible, a pre-determined horizontal or near-horizontal level from the very start of path-laying.
*[**Considerations: 1** — the perfectly horizontal path and the continuation of that path as it is extended simplifies the tasks entailed in achieving a perfectly horizontal ground level throughout the four Year Areas; **2** — for most*

gardeners, this order of perfection is well-nigh unattainable. It pays, however, to strive for it]

54 take whatever steps are necessary in the Year 1 Area to achieve a more-or-less level surface.
*[**Considerations: 1** — as a matter of good practice, involved in levelling must be no more than the most minor of top-soil removals. In general, the distance between the top soil's surface and the surface of the sub soil beneath it must not suffer the order of marked reduction that is likely when hillocks are removed, or when soil is*

excavated from one place and deposited in another in order to fill a marked depression. Certainly, no attempt must be made by such means to convert a general slope into a more-or-less level surface; **2** *— at the same time, there is no objection to emulating R J Harris's performance when, newly appointed, he arrived in Tresillian's derelict walled, kitchen garden in the late 1980s to find that top soil had been removed by the vehicle load, leaving scarcely-covered sub soil in key places. He imported tons of surface earth from nearby building sites (where the house builders were only too pleased to be rid of it), had it spread where it was required and beyond, and advantageously created a kitchen-garden-wide, overall layer of first-quality growing medium, which was thicker than that that existed originally. The example underlines that whilst reducing the depth of top soil is certain to reduce the likelihood of fully productive vegetable cultivation, increasing the depth evenly and comprehensively can only bring improvement;* **3** *— care must be taken not to increase the depth of the soil that is over the roots of established trees and other permanent plants. The relationship between the levels at which permanent plants establish their roots and the surface of the ground above those roots is an important one. It has influence upon the plants' ability to find required volumes of moisture and, hence, nutrients, and to co-habit mutually supportively with the creatures of the soil. The gardener needs to understand but one thing about the permanent roots/surface relationship: "Do nothing that may drastically change it," warns the head gardener. "It*

could cause the slow dying of an affected tree or bush. And, probably, you would not notice what was happening until it was too late"]

55 drive two metre-long garden canes each 30cm into the ground, one opposite the other, to indicate in the path-encircled Year 1 Area the site of the single-dug bed that is shown in *Diagram 1*, page 14. Make the site 300cm wide to match the 300cm width of the Area. Make it 330cm long. Position the 330cm length within the Area's 490cm length. Note the east-to-west alignment of the 300cm width of the site of this single-dug bed

56 cap the tops of the two canes, for safety's sake

57 link the two canes with garden line placed at ground level. Gently taughten the garden line

58 write

   SINGLE-DUG BED
   YEAR 1 AREA

upon a weatherproof, plastic garden label. Use a weatherproof marker. Insert the label into one corner of the site of the single-dug bed

59 write

   SINGLE-DUG BED, YEAR
   1 AREA

in the top, left-hand corner of one of the purchased, lined cards. File the card in the card-index box. Place it alphabetically behind the S index card

60 write

BED, SINGLE-DUG,
YEAR 1

in the top, left-hand corner
of one of the purchased,
lined cards

61 write on the BED, SINGLE-
DUG, YEAR 1 lined card

See SINGLE-DUG BED,
YEAR ONE

and file the BED, SINGLE-
DUG, YEAR ONE lined card
in the card-index box. Place
it alphabetically behind the
B index card

62 retrieve the BEDS lined card
from the card-index box

63 add to the BEDS lined
card's contents

See SINGLE-DUG BED,
YEAR 1

and re-file the BEDS lined
card in the card-index box.
Place it alphabetically
behind the index card B

64 drive two metre-long garden
canes each 30cm into the
ground in the Year 1 Area.
Position one opposite to the
other, to indicate the site of
the deep-trench bed that is
shown in *Diagram 1*, page
14. Make the site 100cm in
width. Make it 300cm in
length, to match the 300cm
width of the Year 1 Area.
Position the 100cm width
within the Year 1 Area's
490cm length, as is shown
in *Diagram 1*

65 cap the tops of the two
canes, for safety's sake

66 link the two canes with
gently taughtened garden
line placed at ground level

67 write

DEEP-TRENCH BED,
YEAR 1 AREA

upon a weatherproof, plastic
garden label. Use a
weatherproof marker

68 insert the label into one
corner of the site of the Year
1 Area's deep-trench bed

69 write

DEEP-TRENCH BED,
YEAR 1

in the top, left-hand corner
of one of the purchased,
lined cards

70 file the DEEP-TRENCH BED,
YEAR 1 lined card in the
card-index box. Place it
behind the D index card

71 write

BED, DEEP-TRENCH,
YEAR 1

in the top, left-hand corner
of one of the purchased,
lined cards

72 write on the BED, DEEP-
TRENCH, YEAR 1 lined card

See DEEP-TRENCH BED,
YEAR 1

and file the BED, DEEP-
TRENCH, YEAR 1 lined card
in the card-index box. Place
it alphabetically behind the
B index card

73 retrieve the BEDS lined card
from the card-index box

74 add to the BEDS lined card's
contents

See DEEP-TRENCH BED,
YEAR 1

and re-file the BEDS lined
card in the card-index box.

Place it alphabetically behind the B index card

75 note that in *Diagram 1*, page 14, the inserted four garden canes and the two lengths of garden line that connect them also outline a 60cm-wide and 300cm-long earth service path. This temporary path separates the site of the deep-trench bed from the site of the single-dug bed.
[**Considerations: 1** — *the four canes and two lines are kept* in situ *throughout the Year 1 Area's four-year life span also to preserve the locations of the single-dug bed and deep-trench bed. This knowledge is required throughout the four years;* **2** *— the path is used as seldom, and as little, as*

possible, for the reasons that are stated later]

76 outline the two beds of the Year 2 Area. Do so as the two beds of the Year 1 Area are outlined

77 make the Year 2 Area's overall outline a mirror image of the Year 1 Area's overall outline to facilitate deep-trench digging in the Area (see the *DEEP-TRENCH BED* installation instruction and *Diagram 1*, page 14).
[**Consideration:** *the Year 2 Area is required in a fully-outlined state during the first year of the Year 1 Area because the site of its deep-trench bed has a particular role to play (explained later) during the Year 1 Area's first year*].

BROAD BEANS: preparing to sow

With the four Year Areas of the vegetable-garden-to-be outlined in sketch form, with the detail of the Year 1 Area and of the Year 2 Area fully outlined, and with the inauguration of a card-index-based system of recording progress as the garden-conversion project goes forward (and whilst **still during the months prior to the first September of the Year 1 Area**)

1 purchase two packets of the seeds of the longpod broad bean that is known as *Aquadulce Claudia*.
[**Consideration:** *the retailed packet of* Aquadulce Claudia *contains 35-to-40 seeds. The required two double-rank, broad-bean rows sown in the Year 1 Area (see* Diagram 1, *page 14), contain 64 plants. Hence, two packets of seeds are*

required to meet the sowing needs of the broad-bean section shown in Diagram 1, *page 14*]

2 check to ensure that the seeds are dated as being suitable for sowing during the coming few months. Make the check at the time of purchase. Then hold one seed packet upright, so that the seeds inside it fall to the bottom of the packet

3 place the packet upon a flat surface, its reverse side uppermost

4 write neatly in a print-free space at the top of the reverse side where the seeds have been bought, and when

5 turn over the packet and write very boldly on its front the

8

Whilst *Aquadulce Claudia* is the head gardener's preferred broad bean, two other longpod types win his approval — principally because they, also, are over and done with before any serious arrival of the blackfly. Even if still *in situ* when that dread thing happens, both of them are Winter-hardened by that time and, hence, unattractively tough for even the sharpest of blackfly jaws.

One of the two is *Sutton Dwarf.* The other is *Witkiem.*

At 45cm high, *Sutton Dwarf* is self-supporting and good at crouching low in order to avoid Winter's worst. It requires not even the end-of-row stakes that the *Aquadulce Claudia* sometimes demands. Mr Harris points out that It has three disadvantages: 1) its first appearance above ground requires that it be protected by cloches should the Autumn/Winter weather conditions be over-severe. For those who garden where the climate is not friendly and who desire simplicity in their gardening, that could be reason enough to avoid it; 2) it sprawls, occupying much ground surface; 3) its pods each contain only three-to-four beans.

It can be sown as the *Aquadulce Claudia* is sown, but in single-rank — not double-rank — rows. The single-rank rows are spaced 90cm apart, to leave room for hoeing and harvesting.

Witkiem is very similar to *Aquadulce Claudia,* and possesses many of that type's virtues. It lacks the *Aquadulce Claudia*'s venerable history.

Both, taken young, can be eaten raw in the pod. Both, when more mature, are good when podded and briefly steamed. Both freeze well and easily. Suffolk Herbs supplies them (2006). See *SUPPLIERS.*

---

figure 1. Take care not to write over the seeds within the packet and, in the process, inflict damage upon them

6 do the same in all almost all respects with the other *Aquadulce Claudia* broad bean seed packet, boldly marking the figure 2, not 1, upon its front. [**Consideration:** *leave these essential tasks until later and when away from the point of purchase, and, in all probability, memory fades, and inaccuracy of recorded information is a result, with unhelpful consequences*]

7 file the two marked-up *Aquadulce Claudia* seed packets in the card-index box. Place them in number order and alphabetically behind the A index card

8 write

   CLAUDIA, AQUADULCE

in the top left-hand corner of one of the purchased, lined cards

9 enter upon the CLAUDIA, AQUADULCE lined card

   See AQUADULCE CLAUDIA 1 & 2

and file the lined card in the card-index box. Place it behind the C index card

10 write

   BROAD BEANS

in the top left-hand corner of one of the purchased, lined cards

11 enter upon the lined card the inscription

See AQUADULCE
CLAUDIA 1 & 2

12 file the lined card in the
card-index box. Place it
alphabetically behind the B
index card

13 write

BEANS, BROAD

in the top left-hand corner of
one of the purchased, lined
cards

14 enter upon the lined card

See BROAD BEANS

and file the lined card in the
card-index box. Place it
alphabetically behind the B
index card

15 write

SEEDS

in the top left-hand corner of
one of the purchased, lined
cards

16 enter upon the lined card

See AQUADULCE
CLAUDIA 1 & 2

and file the lined card in the
card-index box. Place it
alphabetically behind the S
index card

17 close the card-index box and
hold it, its contents and the
lined cards in reserve, for
continued use at a later
stage

18 lodge the card-index box in a
cool, dark, dry place, where
it is not subject to
interference

19 **during the first and the
second moon quarters of
September in the first year
of the conversion**, begin to

The moon's quarters are
referred throughout this
manual as the first, second,
third and fourth quarters.
This renders the four parts
of the moon's month-long
progression from birth to
death and then, instantly,
rebirth, immediately applicable to horticulture's needs.
Hence, in any pocket diary
(the most convenient and
lowest-cost source of the
current lunar quarter dates),
substitute first, second,
third and fourth for New
Moon, First Quarter, Full
Moon and Last Quarter. Note
that each date in the diary is
of the first day of the quarter.

install the head gardener's
single-dug bed in the Year 1
Area. See *SINGLE-DUG BED*,
page 123, for an installation
instruction. See also
Diagram 1, page 14

20 **by the start of the
September moon's third
quarter**, complete the
installation of the single-dug
bed.
[***Consideration:*** *the reasons
for working with the three
lunar quarters are explained
in the single-dug bed
installation instruction*]

21 replace in one corner of the
new, 330cm long by 300cm
wide single-dug bed the
almost certainly disturbed
weatherproof, plastic label
bearing the legend

SINGLE-DUG BED
YEAR 1 AREA

written in weatherproof
marker

22 note that the surface of the single-dug bed is raised above the level of the adjacent service paths. Note that the difference between the two levels equals the length of a garden spade's blade.
[**Consideration:** *the feature is accounted for in SINGLE-DUG BED*]

23 note that the sides of the single-dug bed are sloped slightly

24 retrieve from the card-index box the SINGLE-DUG BED, YEAR 1 AREA lined card. Find it placed alphabetically behind the S index card

25 enter upon the SINGLE-DUG BED, YEAR 1 AREA lined card the single-dug bed's commencement and completion dates

26 re-file the SINGLE-DUG BED, YEAR 1 AREA lined card alphabetically behind the S index card

27 retrieve from the card-index box the YEAR 1 AREA lined card. Find it placed numerically behind the Y index card

28 enter upon the YEAR 1 AREA lined card the date of the Year 1 Area's commencement. For this, use the date of the single-dug bed's commencement

29 re-file the YEAR 1 AREA lined card numerically behind the Y index card in the card-index box.
[**Consideration:** *when the three further single-dug beds are created in the Year 2, Year 3 and Year 4 Areas,*

they, also, are related by means of marked-up, weatherproof, plastic garden labels to the alphabetically/ numerically-filed, lined cards that are created for them for holding in the card-index box]

30 insert two metre-long garden canes each 30cm into the earth opposite each other and link them with gently taughtened garden line placed at ground level across the 300cm width of the Year 1 Area's single-dug bed. Position the garden line so that it divides the single-dug bed into a 170cm deep broad-bean section and an adjacent unemployed 160cm-deep section

31 site the 170cm-deep broad-bean section so that one of its 300cm-long sides is bordered by a permanent service path. See *Diagram 1*, page 14

32 avoid treading upon the surface of the newly-installed, single-dug bed. Make no impact upon its sloped sides

33 write

    BROAD BEANS SECTION, YEAR 1 AREA

upon a weatherproof, plastic garden label. Use a weatherproof marker. Insert the label into one corner of the 170cm-deep, broad-bean section of the Year 1 Area's single-dug bed

34 note that the adjoining 160cm-deep section of the Year 1 Area's single-dug bed accommodates a broad-bean-section-bordering,

The moon's quarters are referred throughout this manual as the first, second, third and fourth quarters. This renders the four parts of the moon's month-long progression from birth to death and then, instantly, rebirth, immediately applicable to horticulture's needs. Hence, in any pocket diary (the most convenient and lowest-cost source of the current lunar quarter dates), substitute first, second, third and fourth for New Moon, First Quarter, Full Moon and Last Quarter. Note that each date in the diary is of the first day of the quarter.

60cm-wide, temporary path for use only when no other means of access to the bed's surface is available

35 note that, beyond the temporary path, the 100cm-deep strip of the single-dug bed is available for other first-year-specific, single-dug-bed-specific plants. See *ROTATION*.
[***Considerations:* 1** — *where the prescribed 170cm depth of the broad-bean section is judged to be insufficient to produce a desired volume of broad beans, and where bed lengthening is not possible, sow an extra double-rank row of broad beans in the 100cm-deep strip of the single-dug bed. Maintain the 170cm depth of the broad-bean section. See* Diagram 1, *page 14. "Better two beds each of which is easy to manage from adjacent paths*

than one bed so wide that it turns planting, hoeing and harvesting into a misery," comments Mr Harris; **2** — *note that, for variety's sake, the additional row may be better employed growing another of the Year 1-specific, first-year-specific, single-dug-bed-specific crops*]

36 **at the start of the September moon's third quarter**, position tread boards on the 60cm by 300cm temporary path that bounds the single-dug bed's broad-bean section. See *Diagram 1*, page 14. Preserve the sloped edges of the single-dug bed.
[***Considerations:* 1** — *a lack of tread-board protection gives rise to damage by the gardener's weight to the structure of the top soil. It also results in the compression of the underlying layer*

TIP 4
➔ **Gardening is made less physically demanding and more enjoyable when its major projects are broken down into a number of small, self-contained tasks each offering the satisfaction that stems from achieving a pre-set goal. Hand tools play a part in this, and those whose days of the strength and dexterity of youth are but a memory (such as this reporter) should note that most of the conventional hand tools of gardening come in two categories: those for the ladies and those for the gentlemen. The former are markedly smaller, lighter and easier to handle than are the latter. Elderly gentlemen benefit when they take advantage of this.**

of animal manure. As well, untidiness is created by the mess that is inherent in bare, usually moist, earth being trodden upon time and again; **2** — head gardener R J Harris recommends: "Use boards, troublesome though that may be. In any event, the well-run garden should have these useful items as standard equipment. They do not have to be massive and unwieldy and heavy"; **3** — a 2440mm x 1220mm (8' x 4') x 25mm sheet of marine 1088 plywood divides neatly into eight conveniently light-weight, warp-resistant, 1220mm-long (4'-long) 'boards' at low cost. Any builders' merchant (such as Jewson) readily takes an order for this kind of material by telephone and does the necessary sawing and delivery. "Removing the saw marks from the edges of the boards with glass paper, and rounding the edges slightly at the same time, is a good idea," comments Mr Harris. "Muddy earth is the more easily cleaned off"; **4** — pressure-preserved timber is an alternative, in metre-long planks each having a width of 30cm and a thickness of 25mm. Such timber is well-nigh everlasting when fully cleaned and stored in dry conditions after use in the garden. All builders' merchants supply it. 'Tanalised' is a proprietary process to specify when ordering pressure preservation (current at the time of writing: 2006); **5** — untreated elm or green oak is the eco-friendly choice, not having been treated with chemicals. It is also the most expensive choice and the least easy to source]

37 break up the large clods of earth lying upon the broad-bean section's surface. Use a hoe. Use the full length of the hoe's handle and, thus, be able to adopt a generally upright, less tiring, stance. Work, principally, from the permanent paths that border the broad-bean section of the Year 1 Area's first-year, single-dug bed. [**Consideration:** the clods were left on the bed's surface deliberately when the bed was created with the aid of a garden spade]

38 work from the tread boards on the temporary boundary path as little as possible. [**Consideration:** this minimises the slight compaction that takes place beneath the boards. As a general rule, use positioned tread boards as seldom as possible. See Diagram 1, page 14]

39 resolve never to place foot upon the surface of the broad-bean section

40 resolve never to place foot upon the 100cm-deep, non-broad-bean section of the single-dug bed. [**Considerations: 1** — a result of treading upon the top soil's surface is locally-compressed earth. Each foot-shaped depression blocks air penetration. Without air penetration, fertility-enhancing warmth and moisture are locked out; **2** — each foot-shaped depression acts as a reservoir. Water collects in it and creates a habitat for those insects that the garden is better without; **3** — the structure of the top soil is destroyed when the

9

The R J Harris way with broad-bean production entails the encountering of few of the horticultural nightmares that haunt the pages of some books on vegetable gardening. His single-dug bed and deep-trench bed, and his management of the two, generate plants the health and vigour of which generally see off most of the well-known pests and diseases. This is due, in part, to the nutrients that are built into the two bed types. It is due, also, to the head gardener's overall policy of avoiding problems, if possible, not attempting to solve them. An example is his preference for the broad bean that develops in the weather conditions that are hostile to the bean's principal and deadliest enemy. So is his readiness to uproot and banish the problematic plant rather than devote time and, almost always, money, to trying to remedy its ailments or to make good its deficiencies.

Admittedly, this expresses the attitudes of the professional — and indicates the inescapable pressures that are always upon the professional. Even so, in Tresillian's walled, kitchen garden, the overall financial and environmental reward is that of a poisons- and patented-medicaments-free zone (which, consequently and not unimportantly, is a haven for the beneficial insects). Adopting the underlying R J Harris policy ensures that these advantages are obtainable in any garden, no matter what its size and purpose.

bed's surface is trodden upon. This has an adverse impact upon the friendly creatures of the soil. Structure and creature activity are as essential to the enhancement of soil fertility as are air, warmth, moisture and the husbandry of the responsible gardener]

41 break up, further, the reduced clods on the surface of the broad-bean section. Use a garden rake. Move the soil backwards and forwards with the full length of the rake's tines. Criss-cross the soil's surface in the process. Use the full length of the rake's handle. Aim for a rake-tine depth of very coarse earth crumbs, evenly laid out

42 de-earth the rake frequently, to keep its tines unblocked all of the time

43 remove from the bed's surface the stones that are so large that they are trapped by the rake's unblocked tines. Place these stones in a convenient container. Lodge the container to one side, where it cannot impede operations

44 follow on, if possible, with R J Harris's preferred four-tined cultivator. Use it as if it were a rake. Achieve a finer breaking down of the broad-bean section's surface particles. [***Considerations:*** 1 — *of the several manually-operated cultivators that are available at Tresillian, the head gardener and his staff use the long-handled tool that has three, four or five long, curved tines. In practised hands, the three-tined cultivator provides a*

The moon's quarters are referred throughout this manual as the first, second, third and fourth quarters. This renders the four parts of the moon's month-long progression from birth to death and then, instantly, rebirth, immediately applicable to horticulture's needs. Hence, in any pocket diary (the most convenient and lowest-cost source of the current lunar quarter dates), substitute first, second, third and fourth for New Moon, First Quarter, Full Moon and Last Quarter. Note that each date in the diary is of the first day of the quarter.

its rains and frosts. This penetration, head gardener R J Harris believes, creates the conditions that increase soil fertility and introduce a measure of pest control]

46 **still at the start of the September moon's third quarter**, dress the raked-level surface of the broad-bean section with 60g to the square metre of fish-blood-and-bone fertiliser (306g for the size of the broad-bean section that is under discussion). Rake in the fertiliser lightly and gently. [***Considerations: 1*** *— as the moon's third quarter commences, the satellite planet's gravitational pull upon planet Earth peaks and begins to reduce. Earth's*

coarse tilth, the four-tined a less coarse tilth, and the five-tined a fine tilth; **2** *— having more widely-spaced tines than the rake, the four-tined cultivator leaves the essential small stones in situ in the affected bed]*

45 do not extend the finely-crumbed surface to the unemployed remainder of the single-dug bed (unless an additional row of broad beans is planned, beyond the bordering 60cm-wide temporary path). In this remainder, maintain the rugged, ploughed field appearance that resulted from spade digging when the single-dug bed was installed. [***Consideration:*** *the head gardener holds that Winter requires the coarse, lumpy, open texture that is attained by spade digging in the Autumn if it is to succeed in penetrating the surface with*

TIP 5
➔ Gloves for gardening can be bought in an extensive range of styles and for a wide range of prices. Mr Harris's long time in horticulture has taught him that the best glove for gardening is distinguished by two features: 1) it is made of a single piece of material, and, hence, does not impose sown-together seams upon any part of the hand — which can be painful; 2) it can be turned inside out and is then washable without difficulty in soap and hot water (or, better, in a domestic washing machine) and, when washed, dries quickly. The industrial work glove, coloured red and moulded in plastic-like material, is the only glove that meets these criteria. It has the added advantage that it is low in price and, hence, can be discarded with an easy conscience when worn out.

water table begins to fall, released by the reducing gravitational pull; 2 — the water table continues to fall during the whole of the third and the fourth of the moon's quarters; 3 — this provides a fortnight or so of reducing water-table pressure upon the top soil. This, in turn, creates a drawing-in effect within the top soil. This encourages the maximum dissemination within the new broad-bean section's top soil of the nutrients of the applied fish-blood-and-bone fertiliser; 4 — the reverse is the consequence when fish, blood and bone fertiliser is applied at the end of the moon's fourth quarter. Then, the fertiliser releases its nutrients against the upward pressure caused by the water table beginning to rise in response to the increasing gravitational pull of the moon's first and second quarters. The fortnight or so of the adverse influence thus created inhibits the comprehensive distribution of the fish, blood and bone's nutrients]

47 return to the section's surface any scatterings of soil that have spilled onto the permanent path.
*[**Consideration:** misplaced earth left upon the hard surface of a path creates an environment for moss and weed development, as well as an unsightly and potentially slippery surface. As a general truth, the maintenance of neatness and tidiness in the vegetable-producing garden encourages improved crop quality and, overall, the more efficient use of resources]*

48 restore the smooth appearance of the section's surface, if that is necessary. Use a rake

49 rehabilitate the sloped edges of the section, if that is necessary. Use the flat of a garden spade

50 cover the whole of the surface of the broad-bean section with pieces of fine-mesh wire net to protect it from cat interference

51 replace the BROAD BEANS SECTION, YEAR 1 AREA and YEAR 1 AREA plastic labels, if that is necessary

TIP 6
➔ **Consider tailoring the application of R J Harris's horticultural system according to the size of the area that is available within the garden as a whole for the cultivation of vegetables and their allied plants. In the process, accept that the return that Mr Harris achieves at Tresillian, where he is the head gardener, may not be attainable, and that a diminished return must be accepted and is to be preferred to no return. As example, if space limitations so dictate, establish just one single-dug bed and use it during the four-year period of Mr Harris's crop-rotation system. Then renew it for a further four years. Be guided by the lists to be found under *ROTATION* in selecting the vegetables to grow in it each year. Equally, major on a deep-trench bed and accept what that provides annually during its four-year life span prior to renewal — again, being guided by *ROTATION*.**

52 replace the broad-bean section's two boundary-marking, capped canes and linking garden line, should they have been disturbed

53 remove the tread boards from next to the broad-bean section of the first-year, single-dug bed. Put them to one side, for cleaning and storage at a later stage

54 take the removed stones, tread boards and employed tools off site

55 clean the equipment and the tools. When they are dry, return them to store

56 store the stones for use in future stone-demanding projects in the garden. [**Considerations: 1** — *cost-conscious gardening aims always to conserve useful resources. Large stones can be an irreplaceable ingredient in garden projects, and merit the small amount of storage space that they occupy when conserved;* **2** — *the stones that slip through the rake's and, if it is used, the cultivator's, unblocked tines, and are left in the bed, are of the size that is needed by the bed. They aid drainage. They act as a moisture-retaining mulch. During the warm months they release by night the heat that they absorb during the day, relatively warming the bed and its contents;* **3** *— the stones that are gathered by the rake's and the cultivator's regularly de-earthed tines, and are collected for storage, are positively too large to be wanted in the bed;* **4** *— generally, if no stone removal*

from a bed is desired, use a hoe when a bed's surface is worked upon. Its shape prevents it from trapping stones of any crucial size]

57 write

BROAD BEANS SECTION, YEAR 1 AREA

in the top left-hand corner of one of the purchased, lined cards

58 enter upon the BROAD BEANS SECTION, YEAR 1 AREA lined card the date of the section's installation. For this, use the date of the treatment with the fish, blood and bone fertiliser. Record, also, the weight of the applied fertiliser

59 file the BROAD BEANS SECTION, YEAR 1 AREA lined card in the card-index box. Place it alphabetically behind the B index card

60 write

BEANS, BROAD, YEAR 1 AREA SECTION

in the top left-hand corner of one of the purchased, lined cards

61 enter upon the BEANS, BROAD, YEAR 1 AREA SECTION lined card the inscription

See BROAD BEANS SECTION, YEAR 1 AREA

and file the lined card in the card-index box. Place it alphabetically behind the B index card

62 retrieve the SINGLE-DUG BED, YEAR 1 AREA lined card from the card-index box. Find it placed

alphabetically behind the S
index card

63 enter upon the SINGLE-
DUG BED, YEAR 1 AREA
lined card the date of the
broad-bean section's
installation. For this, use
the date of the treatment of

the bed's top soil with the
fish, blood and bone
fertiliser

64 re-file the SINGLE-DUG
BED, YEAR 1 AREA lined
card in the card-index box.
Place it alphabetically
behind the S index card.

BROAD BEANS: sowing

The stage has been reached at which the four Year Areas have been outlined in sketch form, and the detail of the Year 1 Area and the Year 2 Area has been fully outlined. A card-index-based, information-storage system has been inaugurated in support of this, designed to record progress as the garden conversion journeys from its starting point to completion in four years' time. Accompanying these developments, the Year 1 Area's single-dug bed has been installed, and the bed's broad-bean section has been fed with fish, blood

and bone fertiliser. In conse-quence, the single-dug bed is launched — along with the Year 1 Area as a whole — upon the first year of its four-year life span. To move the conversion forward

1 **at the start of the October moon's second quarter** in the first year of the Year 1 Area and of the garden conversion, place three clean, dry, paper envelopes on a table top in clean conditions

2 write

— on the front of one of the three envelopes

AQUADULCE CLAUDIA
FIRST SOWING

— on the front of another of the envelopes

AQUADULCE CLAUDIA
SECOND SOWING

— on the front of the third envelope

AQUADULCE CLAUDIA
SURPLUS SEEDS

3 retrieve the two packets of *Aquadulce Claudia* from the card-index box. Find the packets behind the A index card

4 hold each packet upright, so that its seeds fall to the bottom

> The moon's quarters are referred throughout this manual as the first, second, third and fourth quarters. This renders the four parts of the moon's month-long progression from birth to death and then, instantly, rebirth, immediately applicable to horticulture's needs. Hence, in any pocket diary (the most convenient and lowest-cost source of the current lunar quarter dates), substitute first, second, third and fourth for New Moon, First Quarter, Full Moon and Last Quarter. Note that each date in the diary is of the first day of the quarter.

of the packet. Manage this as gently as possible

5 place the two packets flat upon the table top

6 hold the base of one packet gently, yet firmly, against the table top with one hand placed over the seeds

7 slit open the top of the packet. Use a very sharp, preferably pointed, kitchen knife. Do not use scissors. Do not create jagged edges to the cut paper of the packet's top

8 handle the packet with very great care in order to preserve its uncrumpled, uncreased, pristine condition

9 do the same with the other seed packet

10 empty the two packets' broad-bean seeds onto the table top. Do so gently

11 place the neatly cut-open, empty seed packets to one side, in a clean location

12 gather together the 64 seeds that are required for sowing in the broad-bean section of the Year One Area's first-year, single-dug bed

13 divide the 64 broad-bean seeds into two quantities, each of 32

14 place one quantity of 32 seeds in the paper envelope marked AQUADULCE CLAUDIA, FIRST SOWING

15 place the other quantity of 32 seeds in the paper envelope marked AQUADULCE CLAUDIA, SECOND SOWING

10

Autumn/Winter-sown broad beans go into the ground in Tresillian's walled, kitchen garden at monthly intervals between October and January, furnishing the longest possible season for this kind of broad bean.

"We could sow in February as well," says head gardener R J Harris, "but the harvest then would be far too great."

The sowing is done even when deep Winter forces the gardeners to stay away from the beds. Trays, individual pots and modules are filled with John Innes No 2 potting compost and seeded and posted in cold frames.

With the compost kept moist and the frames properly ventilated and protected against the cold, the broad beans are ready for planting out — at the start of each moon's second quarter — the moment that soil/weather conditions make it possible.

The harvest is gathered in between April and July. It is succeeded by cabbage plantlets, which are April/May/June-sown in a seed bed or in trays and modules filled with John Innes No 2 potting compost.

---

16 place the surplus of the broad-bean seeds in the paper envelope marked AQUADULCE CLAUDIA, SURPLUS SEEDS

17 handle the seeds as little and as gently as possible throughout the whole of the above procedure.
[*Considerations: 1 — the broad-bean seed is a large*

seed. It is sufficiently robust to accept considerate handling without bruising or being crushed and, as a result, being rendered sterile; 2 — this is a general truth, and may be applied to all large seeds; 3 — it cannot be applied to the very fine seeds. Fine seeds must never be touched by the fingers. They bruise or crush easily and unnoticeably. Damaged by these means, they may be unable to germinate; 4 — fine seeds are sown into the ground with the aid of a purpose-built dispenser. This is a simple tool, considered by head gardener R J Harris to be an essential tool. It can be filled without contact being made between finger tips and seeds. It is available at low cost at any garden centre]

18 seal the three envelopes containing the broad-bean seeds

19 fold the envelopes marked AQUADULCE CLAUDIA, SECOND SOWING and AQUADULCE CLAUDIA, SURPLUS SEEDS, so that they are of a size to fit into the card-index box

20 file the two envelopes in the card-index box. Place them alphabetically behind the A index card

21 re-file the two now empty, cut-open seed packets in the card-index box. Place them alphabetically and in number order behind the A index card. Preserve their pristine condition

22 place the envelope marked AQUADULCE CLAUDIA

The moon's quarters are referred throughout this manual as the first, second, third and fourth quarters. This renders the four parts of the moon's month-long progression from birth to death and then, instantly, rebirth, immediately applicable to horticulture's needs. Hence, in any pocket diary (the most convenient and lowest-cost source of the current lunar quarter dates), substitute first, second, third and fourth for New Moon, First Quarter, Full Moon and Last Quarter. Note that each date in the diary is of the first day of the quarter.

FIRST SOWING in a convenient pocket, from which it can be retrieved easily

23 **still at the start of the October moon's second quarter**, remove the anti-cat, wire-net pieces from the surface of the Year 1 Area's first-year, single-dug bed's broad-bean section. Place them to one side, where they cannot impede operations

24 peg a garden line onto the broad-bean section's surface 20cm in from the edge of the nearest permanent path and traversing the section's 300cm length. See *Diagram 1*, page 14

25 peg another line parallel to the first and 20cm from it

26 excavate a 20cm-wide, 8cm-deep channel between the

two garden lines and along the whole of their 300cm length. Use a narrow-bladed garden spade. Work from the permanent path

27 deposit the excavated soil neatly onto the section's surface for the whole length of the far line and at a slight remove from that line.
[**Consideration:** *the 'slight remove' guards against accidental spillage back into the channel as the soil is excavated*]

28 ensure that the two long sides of the 8cm-deep channel are vertical

29 remove the garden lines. Place them to one side, where they cannot impede operations

30 insert a 30cm-long marker stick 15cm into the soil and 15cm from one end of the channel, close against one of its two sides

31 insert a 30cm-long marker stick 15cm into the soil and 15cm from the other end of the channel, close against the same side

32 repeat with two more 30cm-long marker sticks. Position these close against the other side of the 20cm-wide channel. Insert a total of four marker sticks at these four points

33 cap the tops of the four marker sticks, for safety's sake

34 produce the envelope marked AQUADULCE CLAUDIA, FIRST SOWING

35 extract fourteen seeds from the envelope. Place the seeds gently in the palm of one hand

36 fold over the envelope, to secure its contents. Re-pocket it

37 post one of the fourteen seeds at one end of one side of the channel, 20cm from the end of the channel

38 post the remaining thirteen seeds after the first seed along the same side of the channel. Space the fourteen seeds 20cm apart

39 produce the envelope marked AQUADULCE CLAUDIA, FIRST SOWING

40 extract thirteen seeds from the envelope. Hold the seeds gently in the palm of one hand

41 fold over and re-pocket the envelope

42 post one of the thirteen seeds at one end of the unsown side of the channel, 30cm from its end

43 post the remaining thirteen seeds after the first seed along the same side of the channel. Space the thirteen seeds 20cm apart.

44 note that the result is staggered seeds' postings, so that, within the channel, each seed faces a blank space at the opposite side of the channel.
[**Consideration:** *this ensures*

that almost all of the double-ranked plants support each other as they grow tall. They do so almost entirely without the aid of supportive stakes and string]

45 produce the envelope marked AQUADULCE CLAUDIA, FIRST SOWING, unfold it and extract from it the remaining five broad-bean seeds. Hold the seeds gently in the palm of one hand. Re-pocket the empty envelope

46 post the five seeds in a row at one end of the channel, centrally between the two rows of posted seeds and commencing 20cm from the end of the channel. Space the seeds 10cm apart. [**Consideration:** *the 10cm spacing ensures that transplanting the resultant plantlets later on for row-repair purposes (should that be necessary) presents no difficulty caused by too-close sowing]*

47 insert a 30cm-long marker stick 15cm into the soil after the fifth posted seed, 10cm away from it. Site the stick in the centre of the channel

48 cap the top of the marker stick, for safety's sake

49 backfill the channel with the displaced soil. Use the back of a rake as a scoop. Or use the hands, wearing gloves. Do either with great care. Work from the service path

50 cover the seeds with an 8cm thickness of soil. In the process, do not dislodge the seeds from their postings

51 compress the sown, filled-in channel's top very gently and slightly with the back of a rake. In the process, create a shallow, rain-collecting depression along the length of the double-rank row. Position the depression comfortably between the two hidden, single rows forming the double-rank row

52 ensure that the five capped marker sticks are not dislodged from where they are inserted into the soil

53 mark one end of the newly-sown double-rank row with a plastic, weatherproof label recording with a weatherproof marker what kind of seed has been

TIP 7

➔ **A less arduous way to sow broad-bean seeds:** *a)* **site the garden line on the bed's surface as instructed;** *b)* **insert a capped marker stick at each end of it;** *c)* **add another garden line 20cm away from the first and parallel to it;** *d)* **insert a capped marker stick at each end of the extra line;** *e)* **guided by the two garden lines, excavate with a trowel the 27 8cm-deep seed holes that are 20cm apart and the five 8cm-deep seed holes that are 10cm apart;** *f)* **stagger the 27 holes' positions in the two rows in relation to each other;** *g)* **drop a seed into each hole;** *h)* **return to the start and fill in the holes. The method calls for less physical effort than when first channelling with a garden spade. Filling the seed holes last of all reduces the risk of 'blanks' being left in the sown, double-rank row.**

11

The broad bean that is planted in October and November, and provides a harvest before any serious arrival of the blackfly in the following mid-Spring, was first mentioned in Britain in the mid 1800s by Suttons, the seeds' merchants. This firm's catalogues of the time referred to it as *Aquadulce* and identified it as being one of the longpod varieties.

It was known and valued centuries before Suttons came into existence, being recognised in mediaeval times as a prime source of high-quality protein for horses during the winter — when hay and grass were scarce — and for hungry peasants at any time (for whom, when there was no alternative, it was a storable, when dried, substitute for meat). The aristocracy regarded it with the contempt and suspicion that they reserved for all non-meat foods. In the process, ironically, they were the losers in the race for life-sustaining nutrients (among them, from the broad bean, carbohydrates and three of the principal vitamins in addition to good-quality protein).

Probably, the early Egyptians must be thanked for this important legume, and the Romans for adding it to the diet of the Celtic tribes that they conquered, absorbed or persuaded into submission.

In Victorian days, the bean's delicate blossom, considered to be a thing of no little beauty, was prized for cosmetic purposes. Its petals were distilled into a lotion, which was applied to the complexion and thought to be a beneficial enhancer.

inserted into the ground, and when.

[***Considerations: 1*** *— for the week prior to this first sowing of the broad-bean seeds, commencing at the start of the moon's first quarter, the moon's gravitational pull begins to increase. It continues to increase until the end of the moon's second quarter. Throughout this moon-waxing fortnight or so, Earth's water table rises in response to the increasing moon pull. In doing so, it exerts upward presssure. A result is that the moisture content of the top soil is concentrated, making increased moisture available to the newly-sown seeds;* **2** *— the combination of increasing moisture and increasing pressure provides the seeds of these above-the-surface developers — sown at the start of the moon's second quarter because they are above-the-surface developers — with the optimum germination conditions. Later, the applied fish-blood-and-bone fertiliser helps to provide the optimum seedling-development conditions*]

54 straddle improvised, fine-mesh, wire-net arches over the new double-rank row

55 position the arches between the ends-of-row capped marker sticks and over the single capped marker stick

56 overlap the arches, one end upon the other, so that no gaps occur between them. By these means, protect the broad beans' young, tender, green shoots, when they appear, from bird attack

57 rehabilitate the single-dug bed's sloped edges, if that is necessary. Use the flat of a garden spade

58 replace the cat-resistant wire-net pieces — recut and reshaped, if necessary — upon the whole of the surface of the unoccupied remainder of the broad-bean section

59 remove the garden line and the other employed equipment and materials from site. Clean them. Return them to store

60 retrieve from the card-index box one of the two empty, cut open *Aquadulce Claudia* seed packets

61 slit apart one of the packet's two long sides and its remaining, unslit narrow side

62 use a very sharp, preferably pointed, kitchen knife to do so. Do not use scissors. Execute unjagged cuts in the paper of the packet

63 retrieve from the card-index box and slit open in the same way the other empty *Aquadulce Claudia* seed packet. Achieve the same pristine result

64 open out the packet marked with a bold figure 1, converting it into a folder

65 reveal the folder's two white, blank inner surfaces

66 record on the left-hand blank, inner surface of the seed packet the date of the purchase of the broad-bean seeds. Record, also, where the seeds were bought. [**Consideration:** *find both items of information on the reverse of the packet*]

67 add to this information

— the date of the October sowing, and that 32 seeds were sown in a double-rank row

— that the seeds were sown in the broad-bean section of the first-year, single-dug bed during the first year of the Year 1 Area

68 inscribe in such a way that space remains on the left-hand surface and the right-hand surface for the further entry of information about the *Aquadulce Claudia* broad bean's career in the Year 1 Area

69 refold the packet so that its original front and back faces are visible

70 file the two now fully cut-open seed packets in the

TIP 8
➜ **Do not make seed holes with a dibber instead of excavating with a trowel to sow seeds in the broad-bean section of the Year 1 Area's first-year, single-dug bed. The dibber severely compacts the bottom of the hole that it makes. This creates a collection point for moisture. Sown seeds and inserted plant roots are less than happy to be immersed in water. At worst, they rot. Notably, many a failed seed potato owes its demise to the water gathered at the bottom of the dibbered hole into which it has been dropped.**

43

12

TO ESTABLISH HOW MANY BROAD-BEAN SEEDS
IT IS SENSIBLE TO SOW, GARDENING THE R J HARRIS WAY

decide what weight, in grammes, of broad beans is required per week for domestic consumption

add to this the weight of any other weekly consumption

multiply the result by 52, to establish the weight of the broad-bean requirement for one year

divide the result by 850. This is the average weight of broad beans, in grammes, that a single, successful *Aquadulce Claudia* can be expected to produce. The harvest from a single, successful *Aquadulce Claudia* is between 750g and 1000g of de-podded beans

add five seeds per double-rank row of plants for row-repair purposes. The result is the total of broad-bean seeds to be sown

then

reduce the required weight of broad beans when the 300cm broad-bean-section length proposed in this instruction is seen to be insufficient, and

accept that the constraints imposed by the garden's size are unalterable. (The 300cm length of the broad-bean section of the planned single-dug bed accommodates 64 fully-grown plants producing at least 45,900g of de-podded broad beans. See *Diagram 1*, page 14)

or

reduce the broad-bean section's length from 300cm, if that is judged to produce too large an harvest

or

accept an over-sized harvest from the size of broad-bean section proposed in this instruction, trusting to the freezer, friends and/or relatives to ensure that no beans go to waste

or

lengthen (but not widen) each of the four proposed Year Areas if the garden permits, when a greater harvest is required than this instruction advocates.

card-index box. Place them appropriately behind the A index card

71 retrieve from the card-index box the BROAD BEANS SECTION, YEAR 1 AREA card. Find it placed alphabetically behind the B index card

72 record on the BROAD BEANS SECTION, YEAR 1

AREA card the date of the October sowing of the *Aquadulce Claudia*

73 refile the BROAD BEANS SECTION, YEAR 1 AREA card in the card-index box. Place it alphabetically behind the B index card

74 **during the second moon quarter of October,** the moment that the October

The moon's quarters are referred throughout this manual as the first, second, third and fourth quarters. This renders the four parts of the moon's month-long progression from birth to death and then, instantly, rebirth, immediately applicable to horticulture's needs. Hence, in any pocket diary (the most convenient and lowest-cost source of the current lunar quarter dates), substitute first, second, third and fourth for New Moon, First Quarter, Full Moon and Last Quarter. Note that each date in the diary is of the first day of the quarter.

broad-bean sowing is complete, begin to install the head gardener's deep-trench bed in the Year 1 Area. See *DEEP-TRENCH BED*, for an installation instruction. See *Diagram 1*, page 14, in addition

75 by the start of the October moon's third quarter, complete the installation of the deep-trench bed. [**Consideration:** *the reasons for adhering to the two lunar timings are explained in the installation instruction. They are not relevant to the present stage of the general discussion*]

76 replace in one corner of the new, 300cm long by 100cm wide deep-trench bed the almost certainly disturbed weatherproof, plastic label bearing the hand-written legend DEEP-TRENCH BED, YEAR 1 AREA

77 note that the surface of the deep-trench bed is level with the adjacent service paths. Note that this surface sinks as the settlement of the bed's contents takes place during the coming months. This creates a valuable, rain-collecting depression

78 retrieve from the card-index box the DEEP-TRENCH BED, YEAR 1 AREA lined card. Find it placed alphabetically behind the D index card

79 enter upon the DEEP-TRENCH BED, YEAR 1 AREA lined card the deep-trench bed's commencement date and completion date

80 re-file the DEEP-TRENCH BED, YEAR 1 AREA lined

TIP 9
➔ There is aother way to ensure an absence of blanks when trowelled-out broad-bean seed holes are being seeded: *a)* park one seed on the bed's surface adjacent to each hole; *b)* stand back and check that each hole is accompanied by a seed; *c)* drop the seeds into the holes, working, methodically, left to right or right to left, one row at a time; *d)* go back to the first hole to be seeded and earth in, one hole after the other; *e)* in each case — again, methodically — first check that the hole being filled in is occupied; *f)* retain a few seeds in one hand, to be able to make good a missing seed without having to turn away to seek a supply and, in consequence, risk losing sight of where correction is required.

The moon's quarters are referred throughout this manual as the first, second, third and fourth quarters. This renders the four parts of the moon's month-long progression from birth to death and then, instantly, rebirth, immediately applicable to horticulture's needs. Hence, in any pocket diary (the most convenient and lowest-cost source of the current lunar quarter dates), substitute first, second, third and fourth for New Moon, First Quarter, Full Moon and Last Quarter. Note that each date in the diary is of the first day of the quarter.

card alphabetically in the card-index box

81 **at the start of the November moon's second quarter**, place the tread boards upon the temporary, earth path that abuts the broad-bean section and traverses its 300cm width. Ensure that the broad-bean section's boundary-establishing garden line remains *in situ*. See *Diagram 1*, page 14

82 remove the anti-cat, wire-net pieces that protect the surface of the broad-bean section. Leave *in situ* the wire-net arches that protect the October sowing

83 repeat the October sowing in almost all respects, including the recording of key information in the card-index system. Observe the following differences

— omit the fish, blood and bone application.
[*Consideration: the September feeding of the broad-bean section prior to the October sowing is considered to be sufficient, also, for the November sowing. "The biggest danger with feeding the soil," Mr Harris comments, "is over-feeding. It cannot be corrected. Under-feeding can. That is why it is always better to under-feed, just as it is always better to under-water. Best of all, of course, is to get the quantities right in the first place"*]

— use the Second Sowing envelope of *Aquadulce Claudia* broad-bean seeds. Find it under the A index card in the card-index box

— position the double-rank row parallel to and 90cm from the October-installed double-rank row. Observe that, in consequence, the November double-rank row is positioned 20cm away from the edge of the broad-bean section and

TIP 10
➔ **When the forecasters promise a savage November, sow the *Aquadulce Claudia* in September and then in October. Create the single-dug bed one month earlier. Observe the moon quarters that the head gardener prescribes. The general effectiveness of the bed is in no way diminished by an earlier construction. Also, the four-year crop rotation programme affecting the earlier-installed, single-dug bed is as described. See *ROTATION*, for the range of crops that the single-dug bed supports.**

the adjacent tread-board-covered, temporary path

— label the November row with a plastic, weather-proof label stating what has been sown and when

— use wire-mesh arches to protect the row from the pigeons. Place fine-mesh, wire-net pieces to protect the unsown surface of the broad-bean section from the neighbourhood's cats

84 fill the 170cm depth and 300cm length of the broad-bean section by these overall means with two protected, double-rank rows of *Aquadulce Claudia* containing, in total, 64 seeds

85 leave *in situ* the tread boards that are positioned over the temporary, earth path alongside the broad-bean section

86 retrieve from the card-index box the sealed, paper envelope marked AQUADULCE CLAUDIA, SURPLUS SEEDS. Find it behind the A index card

87 transfer the surplus seeds to the kitchen store cupboard. Retain them for future use as food, not seeds. [***Considerations: 1*** *— soak the surplus seeds in water for at least twenty-four hours prior to adding them to any stew-type or casserole-type dish that is being assembled for oven or hob-top preparation. Discard the water that has been used for soaking. It may contain harmful toxins;* **2** *— these are seeds that must not be relied upon to germinate if sown in the Year 2 Area's broad-bean section in the Autumn of that Area's first year*].

BROAD BEANS: managing

With the *Aquadulce Claudia* fully sown — and with **a)** the four Year Areas of the garden-to-be outlined in sketch form, **b)** the detail of the Year 1 Area and the 2 Area fully outlined and **c)** the Year 1 Area's first-year single-dug bed and deep-trench bed installed — manage the broad-bean section of the Year 1 Area's first-year, single-dug bed with the aim of ensuring that its plants flourish and are able to produce the optimum harvest. At the same time, augment the minerals of the soil of the broad-bean section in readiness for the head gardener's recommended follow-on crop, which is cabbage. To achieve these two aims

1 **one week after the October sowing of the broad-bean**
seeds **(and, hence, well before the November sowing)** — and working as much as possible from the adjacent permanent path — remove the protective wire-net arches from above the double-rank row of October-sown seeds

2 remove the wire-net pieces that protect the surface of the unoccupied area of the broad-bean section from interference by the neighbourhood's cats

3 place the arches and the wire-net pieces where they cannot impede operations

4 tie a garden line between one pair of the capped marker

13

Potash lack in broad beans is signalled by the appearance of pale brown spots upon the plants' leaves. Mr Harris compensates for the lack by applying comfrey solution (one part of comfrey stock to twelve parts of water) to where the plants emerge from the soil and to the adjacent area. He does so in the cool of the evening, not in the heat of the day, knowing that hot plants experience growth check when they or their host soil are doused with cold water. He uses a can fitted with a fine rose, to reduce splashing upon the plants.

The garden that is in its initial year of R J Harris's way of gardening is very unlikely to have home-grown comfrey with which to make stock, not having yet developed it.

"Ignore the brown spots until you can take action," advises Mr Harris. "The world will stay in one piece. Lose no time, though, in getting a few comfrey plantlets into the ground so that stock making can begin as soon as possible.

"Then be equipped to correct organically the next time the problem shows itself."

the top soil with the hoe's blade. See *Panel 3*

7 avoid applying the hoe directly above the sown seeds (which are only 8cm beneath the surface of the ground). Be guided by the two garden lines where not to hoe

8 avoid, also, applying the hoe above the five row-repair seeds sown at one end of the double-rank row. The single capped marker stick indicates where this very short, single row of seeds ends

9 weed the surface above the seeds by hand. Place all of the hoe- and hand-extracted weeds in a garden bucket for disposal, later, off site. [**Consideration:** *there is a risk that dislodged weeds retaining their roots are as good as replanted when left to lie upon the bed's surface*]

10 hoe the surface of the remainder of the broad-bean section. Use the inner garden line that is above an October-sown row of seeds and the permanently-positioned section-boundary garden line as indicators of where to hoe and where not to hoe. Take the hoe to a greater depth in this area. At this stage, no sown seeds are at risk of being disturbed

sticks and over a single row of hidden, October-sown seeds. Tie with care. Do not disturb the inserted, capped marker sticks in the process

5 repeat with another garden line over the other row of hidden, October-sown, broad-bean seeds

6 hoe carefully between the two garden lines. No more than ripple beneath the surface of

11 work from the tread boards only if that is unavoidable

12 remove from the earth's surface any large stones that are revealed by the hoe. Place them in a garden bucket

13 remove the two garden lines from above the October-sown seeds. Ensure, in the process, that the five capped marker sticks remain firmly *in situ*

14 place the two garden lines to one side on the permanent path, where they cannot impede operations

15 replace the row-protective wire-net arches and the surface-protective pieces of wire net

16 clean the hoe and the garden lines. Return them to store

17 dispose of the bucket of weed growth securely off site

18 add the garnered stones to the store of re-usable stones

19 retrieve the BROAD BEANS SECTION, YEAR 1 AREA lined card from the card-index box. Find it placed alphabetically behind the B index card

20 enter upon the BROAD BEANS SECTION, YEAR 1 AREA lined card the date of the first hoeing

21 re-file the the BROAD BEANS SECTION, YEAR 1 AREA lined card in the card-index box. Place it alphabetically behind the B index card

22 repeat the hoeing at weekly intervals until the second sowing, in November, has taken place. Then, apply the hoe, weekly, to the fully-sown broad-bean section. Be aware constantly of the presence of four rows of sown seeds posted only 8cm

beneath the section's surface and indicated by four adjusted garden lines

23 hoe only when soil and weather conditions permit. Work from the tread boards only when doing so is unavoidable, and only for as short a period as is possible

24 leave the tread boards *in situ*, once they are applied, to render the repeated hoeings less onerous

25 ensure that when hoeing does not take place, the protective wire net remains *in situ*, to continue to fend off the neighbourhood's cats

26 inspect daily, as from December of the first year of the Year 1 Area, for the first polished, dark-green, spear-like, October-started broad-bean shoot to break the surface of the broad-bean section's top soil

27 retrieve from the card-index box the modified *Aquadulce Claudia* packet marked with a bold 1 (or 2, if the first packet's inner surfaces have been filled)

28 enter in the modified seed packet the date of the emergence of the first *Aquadulce Claudia* shoot

29 re-file the modified seed packet in the card-index box. Place it alphabetically behind the A index card

30 be alert for the first broad-bean shoot to be joined by other shoots, until the complete, double-rank row of the October sowing declares itself fully

31 continue the daily inspection, looking for the first October shoot to develop four leaves. When this is seen, take it as a signal that the seedling has developed to plantlet stage

32 retrieve from the card-index box the modified *Aquadulce Claudia* packet marked with a bold 1 (or 2, if the first packet's inner surfaces have been filled)

33 enter upon one of the two inner surfaces of the seed packet the date of the first development from broad-bean shoot to broad-bean plantlet. Re-file the modified seed packet in the card-index box. Place it alphabetically behind the A index card

34 continue the daily inspection, looking for the moment when all, or almost all, of the October shoots develop four leaves and so become plantlets

35 remove the protective wire-net arches in step with the October shoots achieving plantlet stage.
[*Considerations:* **1** — *omit this, and the upward-reaching plantlets become entangled in the wire net of the arches;* **2** — *a few of the developing shoots may remain just short of full plantlet stage when most of their fellows in the row have attained or, possibly, exceeded that development. Despite this, remove the protective arches that are over these laggards. It is better to place a few seedlings/plantlets at risk from the birds (for only a*

very short period, in any event) than to place their much more numerous neighbours at risk from the wire net of the arches]

36 remove the capped marker sticks from the October sowing. Detach and clean the caps. Clean the sticks. Flatten the wire netting of the protective arches. Return all to store

37 leave the other wire-net arches and wire-net pieces *in situ* to continue to protect the other areas of the section

38 note where gaps occur in the two single rows forming the October-sown double-rank row of broad-bean plantlets. These are the consequence of sterile seeds or failed germination

39 fill each gap in the double-rank row in the following way, weather conditions and ground conditions permitting. If they do not, wait until they do

TIP 11
➔ **Charity plant sales often offer potted comfrey plantlets. Snap up three or four of these at the earliest opportunity and insert them at unused points in the garden to secure a cost-free, organic plant/bed feed and/or plant medicament. A first-year, garden-conversion start is essential, to begin to obtain an annual supply usually some three or four years after planting out. Be warned: comfrey has very deep roots, and is extremely difficult to remove once it is mature.**

(acknowledging, at the same time, that 'permitting' may equate to less than comfortable soil/bed conditions in which to work)

— water, gently, the soil around the five row-repair plantlets grouped at one end of the October-sown, broad-bean, double-rank row

— wait for at least two hours, so that the soil may absorb fully the added water

— excavate a small, shallow, square hole where one of the gaps occurs in the double-rank row. Use a narrow-bladed, sharp knife to do so

— make, gently, four cuts into the moistened soil around the base of one of the spare broad-bean plantlets. Use the narrow-bladed knife to do so

— lift out, gently, the plantlet rooted in a tiny block of soil. Use the flat of the knife as a lifting/ supporting instrument. [*Consideration: the tiny block in which the plantlet is rooted does not break apart, thanks to the preliminary, thorough moistening of the soil*]

— place the block of soil into the excavated hole. Ensure that the original earth mark on the plantlet's stem is on a level with the surrounding ground surface

— earth in the block of soil, gently. Use the flat of the knife to do so

— repeat the transplanting until all of the gaps in the two single rows have been filled

40 leave the unused row-repair plantlets, if any, *in situ*. [*Consideration: positioned at the end of the double-rank row, these 'unnecessary' plants-to-be can be seen as providing bonus broad beans at harvest time*]

41 reinstate, gently, the disturbed soil from where the transplanted plantlets have been moved

42 use the permanent path as much as possible, throughout. Use the tread boards as little as possible

43 retrieve from the card-index box the modified *Aquadulce Claudia* packet marked with a bold 1 (or 2, if the first packet's inner surfaces have been filled)

44 enter upon one of the two inner surfaces of the seed packet the number of failed *Aquadulce Claudia* seeds

45 re-file the modified seed packet in the card-index box. Place it alphabetically behind the A index card

46 draw up earth at the two sides of the double-rank row when all of the October sowings are fully at plantlet stage. Form a broad ridge which is at least 20cm in width along the length of the row. Use a rake. Do so very, very gently

47 make the ridge as high as the plantlets, so that they are fully covered by the carefully raked-up soil. [*Considerations: 1 — this offers protection should Winter and Spring be exceptionally harsh. It also*

encourages extra root formation. The plantlets continue to extend in height, despite the presence around them of the all-enveloping, protective, earth packaging; **2** *— the earthing-up creates a shallow trough on each side of the double-rank row. The trough collects rain and directs it down to the young plants' roots]*

48 embark upon the earthing up only when the soil is workable. If it is not, wait until it is

49 extend the management of the October sowing to the November sowing as the November-sown seedlings develop into plantlets. Embrace in this the weekly hoeing, the row repair, the earthing up and the related record-keeping in the card-index system

50 maintain the anti-cat wire-net pieces on the surface of the broad-bean section throughout, whenever hoeing does not take place

51 remove the wire net when the plants are of a generous height. At this stage they are of no interest to the birds, and serve to deter the visiting cats. Flatten and clean the wire net pieces. Return them to store

52 be alert, as the weather conditions improve, for the slightest sign of blackfly on the highest part of each broad-bean plant's stem. Inspect daily after the arrival of the first broad-bean pods

53 inspect, especially, when ants are seen hurrying

busily from ground level to bean plants' tops.
*[**Consideration:** the ants travel to protect the blackfly and, if permitted to do so, to herd it over the pasture of the plant's whole being. By these means, the blackfly population increases and spreads, and the affected plant becomes increasingly shrouded in a blackfly blanket. The ants' reward for their husbandry is the sustenance that they gain by 'milking' the blackfly]*

TIP 12
➜ **Potato water — safe, organic, cost-free — is Mr Harris's favourite remover of blackfly when it is too late for surgery. The water in which potatoes are boiled or steamed is accumulated in screw-top jars and stored in the Harris refrigerator. It remains usable for about one week. After that, it is thrown away — creating no difficulty, for there is a constant supply of it. When spraying time arrives, the water is passed through a muslin-cloth strainer to remove solid matter, transferred undiluted to a pump-up sprayer, and sprayed onto the all-too-visible black creatures. Its otherwise harmless potato-starch content cloaks the flies and renders them incapable of clinging onto the bean plant. They fall to the ground, where predators await them. Spray at the end of the day. Then, the affected plant has cooled and has become less vulnerable to the shock of the temperature drop that is caused by the dousing with the cold liquid. Potato water deals also with greenfly and whitefly.**

14

The horticultural writer, the late Laurence D Hills, threw light upon the blackfly problem in his *'Month-by-Month Organic Gardening: The Green Gardener's Calendar'* (Thorsons Publishing Group). He reported that once, before farming's policies and practices changed, the black-fly over-Wintered its eggs in the farm hedgerows, and that each newly hatched generation migrated to the domestic gardens in the Spring in time to catch the soft, green growth which, unfailingly, it found there.

This age-old pattern had been changing ever since the hedgerows started to be removed in order to win enlarged fields for evermore extensive monoculture, and the pest had been driven to both lay and over-Winter its eggs in suitable garden shrubs such as the ubiquitous *Virburnum*.

Combat this seriously unwelcome development, the writer suggested, by encouraging the tits to keep the eggs company. Attract these relentless hunters into the garden by hanging bacon rind from branches during January, February and March, he advised. Hang short, thin strips just large enough to support no more than two birds at one time.

Thus, a hungry queue would be created, which would forage as it waited, reducing the size of the coming season's blackfly population.

Remove the fat after March, Mr Hills warned. Tits made bad company for tender flower buds.

54 cut off, immediately, those portions of the plants' tips that are seen to be carrying the slightest of black specks. Use sharp secateurs or scissors. Do so gently and neatly. Achieve each amputation with a single, firmly-executed cut. Make the size of each removed portion as small as possible.

55 drop the blackfly-bearing pieces into a plastic bag as they are removed from the plant. Knot the bag tightly the moment the job is done. Dispose of the bag in the kitchen rubbish bin. [*Considerations: 1 — the blackfly can feed only on the broad-bean plant's most tender parts. These are the affected plant's stem tip and then the tips of its youngest pods and leaves; 2 — a removal of the portion of the stem tip the moment that it is attacked — and the whole of the only slightly affected pod or leaf — prevents the blackfly from spreading throughout the plant;*

TIP 13

➔ **The water that is used to cook potatoes is of value in the kitchen as well as in the garden that suffers from blackfly attack. Its role as a vegetable stock is well known. Less familiar is its role as a replacement for water when bread dough is mixed — whether by hand or by bread-making machine. Its vitamin C content, gleaned during the cooking of the tubers, strengthens the bread flour's proteins. A result is a higher rise during the proving stage, and a larger loaf with an improved flavour. The loaf also has a more open texture, which can be a boon to the maker of wholemeal bread.**

The question '*Is it or is it not a good idea to pinch out the tops of the broad-bean plants when they are fully-grown*' continues to be debated in horticultural literature, and, probably, will remain unanswered for as long as broad beans are grown in the kitchen garden.

'Pinching out' sees the top of the fully-grown plant's stem being carefully cut off with scissors or secateurs down to the first pair of leaves "and no lower," warns R J Harris. "It is imperative that these two tiny leaves be left on the plant when the cutting has been done."

The technique undoubtedly generates the earlier production of pods — and, in the larger picture of gardening practice, offers yet another demonstration that Nature *will* compensate, come what may and at no matter what cost. Feeling that its life is under threat (for that is the message that is sent to it by the removal of a part of its body matter), the de-topped broad-bean plant hurries seed production to counter the threat to its species's chances of survival. In general, threatening the life of any seed/fruit-bearing plant wins a larger harvest, for the plant compensates by increasing its seed production.

A further benefit is advanced by the pinching-out lobby. De-topping the stem removes the very part of the plant that the blackfly seeks out and settles upon when it arrives. When that ultra-tender stem section is not present, it is argued, the blackfly has no choice but to go else-where to roost and to feed.

Against this, it is reasoned that, left *in situ*, the tip of the plant's stem acts very helpfully as a warning beacon. It is where the blackfly always appears first and, thus, is most easily seen and most easily dealt with by means of a single snip or organic spraying.

Further, it is pointed out that when a stem tip is not present as a landing pad, the blackfly, maddened by hunger and/or herded by ants, is capable of occupying the tips of the nearby new leaves and young pods instead — often causing a larger initial infestation than when the stem tip is available. To correct this, there is no choice but to cut off the affected leaves and young pods. This further harmfully reduces the plant's body matter.

All in all, R J Harris favours leaving the broad-bean plant in a whole state and the secateurs on the rack on the wall of Tresillian's potting shed.

"In any event," he says, "it is one job less, and that is worth something.

"Mind you," he notes, "if you are so inclined, the pinching out can benefit the cook pot.

"Right up to just after the first world war all of the cut-off tips of the broad-bean plants were carefully bagged and taken to the kitchen at the end of the day.

"Bear in mind that they had no aphids on them, because of the timing of the pinching out.

"In the kitchen, they were washed and then cooked as if they were spinach.

"They were a bonus at that early time of the year, for they made a very welcome and delicate vegetable substitute."

3 — *instant reaction to the blackfly's and its shepherding ants' arrival also results in the plant losing as little as possible of its body matter to the secateurs*]

56 retrieve from the card-index box the modified *Aquadulce Claudia* packet marked with a bold 1 (or 2, if the first packet's inner surfaces have been filled)

57 record on the modified seed packet the date of the blackfly's arrival. Record, also, when and what steps began to be taken to counter the pest. Subsequently, maintain a record of the result of taking action

58 re-file the modified seed packet in the card-index box. Place it alphabetically and in number order behind the A index card.

BROAD BEANS: harvesting

As the rotation-oriented, moon-garden-to-be's first harvest time approaches, **a)** the four designated Year Areas that are to form the fully-converted garden have been outlined in sketch form, **b)** the detail of the Year 1 and Year 2 Areas has been filled in, **c)** the Year 1 Area's single-dug bed and deep-trench bed have been installed, **d)** both beds are in the first year of their four-year life span, and **e)** the greater part of the single-dug bed has been developed into a broad-bean section, which now bears rapidly-maturing *Aquadulce Claudia* plants almost at their maximum height of about 90cm and bearing pods laden with very young, barely-formed beans. At this stage — May, approximately, of the first year of the garden conversion — the remainder of the Year 1 Area, the fully-outlined Year 2 Area and the sketched-in Year 3 Area and Year 4 Area are unemployed and undeveloped.

To move on the Year 1 Area to its next first-year-specific, single-dug-bed specific crop, the cabbage

1 continue the anti-blackfly vigilance and surgery (or spraying, if it is too late for surgery) for as long as pods are on the broad-bean plants

2 excavate — at this increasingly kindlier time of the season, and whilst waiting for the *Aquadulce Claudia* to mature in their pods — the metre-wide, metre-deep, 300cm-long trench in the Year 2 Area that will be required for that Area's deep-trench bed when the Area commences the first year of its four-year life span. This will be in the second year of the garden conversion. See *DEEP-TRENCH BED*, for an instruction. Also, see *Diagram 1*, page 14

3 cover the dug trench with a lid, so that no living creature can fall into it accidentally

4 write

DEEP-TRENCH BED, YEAR 2 AREA

in the top, left-hand corner of one of the purchased, lined cards for the card-index box

5 record on the DEEP-TRENCH BED, YEAR 2 AREA lined card the date of the excavation of the trench for the Year 2 Area's deep-trench bed

6 file the DEEP-TRENCH BED, YEAR 2 AREA lined card in the card-index box. Place it alphabetically behind the D index card

7 write

BED, DEEP-TRENCH, YEAR 2 AREA

in the top, left-hand corner of one of the purchased, lined cards

8 enter on the BED, DEEP-TRENCH, YEAR 2 AREA lined card

See DEEP-TRENCH BED, YEAR 2 AREA

and file the BED, DEEP-TRENCH, YEAR 2 AREA lined card in the card-index box. Place it alphabetically behind the B index card

9 retrieve the BEDS lined card from the card-index box

10 add to the BEDS lined card's contents

See DEEP-TRENCH BED, YEAR TWO AREA

and re-file the BEDS lined card in the card-index box. Place it alphabetically behind the B index card

11 seize the opportunity presented by the current more amenable weather conditions to make the first removal of weed growth from where any or all of the Year 2 Area and the outlined Year 3 Area and Year 4 Area occupy virgin ground. Uproot every detected weed and dispose of it securely off site

12 repeat the activity monthly as the first year of the Year 1 Area's four-year life span

progresses. Aim to extract new weeds by hand at the earliest possible stage of their development

13 maintain the *status quo* where the four-year conversion to crop rotation is applied to a conventional garden. De-weed thoroughly where existing plants remain, as the conversion advances

14 continue to hoe the Year 1 Area's first-year, broad-bean section's surface weekly, as the weather conditions permit, to combat weed germination and development, and to maintain dampness in the top soil

15 insert a plant-high-plus-30cm stick 30cm into the ground at each end of each of the four single rows in the two double-rank rows of the broad-bean plants. Avoid the plants' roots as the stakes are driven into the ground

16 tie to the stakes any end-of-row plants that evince a tendency to flop. Tie with soft string

17 consider whether or not there is plant congestion at the ends of the two double-rank rows, caused by the extra ten seed sowings

18 cut off at ground level any plants that cause the congestion. Leave their roots in the ground. Cut off as few plants as possible. Use sharp shears or secateurs

19 drop the removed vegetable matter into the bottom of the trench in the Year 2

16

Broad beans are known to moon gardeners as above-the-surface developers. So are peas and all of the many other members of the legume family. So is the cabbage family and the lettuce family and every plant — vegetable or otherwise — the principal part of which grows above the surface of the soil.

The classification is helpful, for the moon gardener knows that the seeds or plantlets of the above-the-surface developers are best placed in the earth when the moon-raised water table has increased the top soil's moisture content and is exerting upward pressure — at the start, in other words, of the second quarter of the moon of the chosen month of sowing or planting.

By the same token, the seeds of the below-the-surface developers (carrots, parsnips, potatoes, for example), find ideal conditions within the soil when the water table is at the commencement of its moon-attracted rise and is about to begin to increase moisture and pressure within the top soil. This is at the start of, or during the initial two or three days of, the first quarter of the moon of the chosen month of sowing or planting.

The differentiation between the two categories can be of significance, also, in the kitchen.

When not eaten raw, the above-the-surface developer requires exposure, briefly, to steam to be readied for the table as a perfectly-cooked dish offering maximum nutritional qualities and flavour. The below-the-surface developer requires to be immersed in cold water which is then brought to and held at boiling point until cooking is judged to be complete. This is when the non-steaming and non-boiling methods of food preparation are not employed.

In most of today's commercial kitchens the differentation is ignored. Professional chefs apply steam to both the above- and the below-the-surface developer to reduce cooking time, to preserve flavours and to reduce boiling's destruction of vitamins and minerals.

Truly, of course, the broad bean of any variety is at its best on flavour and nutritional levels when it is subjected to no cooking processes of any kind. For this, its pods must be picked when very young and containing scarcely formed beans. They must be topped and tailed, washed and, unopened, cut into three or four pieces and eaten raw as an ingredient in a dressed or undressed salad, or as a side dish.

This is possible only during the initial fortnight or so of the development of the bean plant's pods. Once formed, these mature rapidly and reach maximum development. Then, there is no choice but to harvest them. This is when their contents can become an overwhelming presence in the kitchen.

Fortunately, the broad bean freezes excellently and with ease. It has a long life when frozen, so that its appearances on the meal table may be spaced out during a period of at least twelve months before the next harvest begins to arrive.

Area that awaits completion as a deep-trench bed

20 replace the lid on the trench, for safety's sake.
[**Considerations: 1** — *the trench becomes an accumulator of the non-weed, soft, vegetable matter that arises as the season progresses. This matter is in a well-rotted state by the time the trench qualifies for completion as a deep-trench bed at the beginning of the Year 2 Area's first year (and at the beginning of the garden conversion's second year). It establishes an ideal foundation for the various materials that go to form R J Harris's deep-trench bed;* **2** — *this way of converting waste vegetable matter into a helpful product is the head gardener's equivalent to waste-vegetable compost making. He prefers the method because a range of time-consuming tasks is obviated. Also, he believes that there are disease and pest residues on waste vegetable matter, and that these are rendered harmless by the depth at which the matter is buried, eventually, and by the weight of the materials that are placed on top of it in the trench. No bin or heap can be trusted to achieve this order of beneficial destruction, he is convinced;* **3** — *the method reflects that Mr Harris's way of gardening grants no place for the use of bin/heap-made vegetable compost. Almost entirely, composted vegetable matter has no role in the head gardener's crop-rotated, lunar-oriented regime in the walled, kitchen garden at Tresillian. This does not prevent him from acknowledging that very many gardeners extract much pleasure from the various tasks and disciplines involved in creating home-made, waste-vegetable compost*]

21 judge *Aquadulce Claudia* development by gently easing one or two pods from a plant's stem each day or two and opening them and examining their contents

22 take these very young pods for eating raw in their whole state every day once it is seen that they contain very young beans

23 harvest from ground level, methodically ascending each plant's stem. Do so whatever the stage of maturity of the plucked pods.
[**Considerations: 1** — *denuded from the ground up,*

TIP 14
➔ **To freeze broad beans:** *a)* **de-pod the beans immediately after picking;** *b)* **spread a single layer of them on a baking sheet;** *c)* **place the loaded sheet in the freezer for a day or so;** *d)* **store the stone-like, frozen product in identified, dated, plastic bags. Keep the bags in the freezer. The beans are added into dishes such as casseroles and stews in their frozen state. They are used frozen when steamed as a separate vegetable. Nutritionally, the frozen bean is not quite the equal of the just-off-the-plant bean. Its flavour, too, may be judged to be diminished. The differences are so slight as to be of no significance.**

the broad-bean plant compensates by turning its energies to making more bean pods where the denudation has taken place, and to enlarging the very small, young pods remaining in its upper reaches; 2 — denuded in its upper reaches first of all, the plant turns its energies to enlarging the pods remaining at its lower levels. At the same time, it tends not to replace the picked pods. This results in a plant bearing fewer pods. Also, applying Nature's invariable law of compensatory reaction, the remaining pods over-quickly coarsen and become tough as they hasten towards full seed maturity. They then contain beans which rapidly become less than fit for use in the kitchen; 3 — harvesting aims never to permit the bean- or pea-bearing plant to bring its seeds to the stage of full maturity. This applies to all of the leguminous produce of the vegetable garden]

24 retrieve from the card-index box the modified *Aquadulce Claudia* packet marked with a bold 1 (or 2, if the first packet's inner surfaces have been filled)

25 enter in the modified seed packet the date upon which the first very young pods are taken, and their weight

26 re-file the modified seed packet in the card-index box. Place it alphabetically and numerically behind the A index card

27 harvest the fully mature pods the instant they are ready to be taken, whether or not they are required by the kitchen. Force the plants, by these means, to replace what has been removed until plant exhaustion brings an end to harvesting

28 transfer the harvested fully-ripened beans to the kitchen for de-podding and then serving and/or freezing. Do so the instant that the pods are off the plants. Do not permit them to linger in the garden or the kitchen, no matter how, finally, they are used. If delay cannot be avoided, refrigerate the beans in their pods until they can be processed

29 record in the modified *Aquadulce Claudia* seed

TIP 15

→ **To turn emptied broad-bean and pea pods to good account, wash them, drop them into a pan of boiling water, put a lid on the pan and simmer them gently for ten to fifteen minutes to produce vegetable stock. Allow the stock to become cold, bottle it and keep it in the refrigerator for use as the base for soups, casseroles, stews and gravies. Any 'waste' vegetable matter, such as carrot tops, outer cabbage leaves, onion skins, potato peelings, etc, is suitable for recycling in this way. Only the 'waste' from home-grown vegetables may be processed. Stock made with shop-bought vegetable material contains traces of the pesticides and herbicides with which their outer surfaces have been sprayed. Not even thorough washing rectifies this.**

packets in the card-index box the weight of the pods at each

harvesting. Record, also, the date of each harvesting.

BROAD BEANS: after harvesting

Leave the denuded broad-bean-plant stems *in situ* once they have been stripped of their pods. When all of the pods have been harvested

1 cut all of the denuded stems at ground level. Use sharp secateurs or garden shears. Leave the stems' roots in the ground and, thus, conserve their nitrogenous secretions

2 place the removed stems in the trench that awaits non-weed waste-vegetable matter in the Year 2 Area. Replace the trench's lid after each addition

3 use a hoe to empty the ex-broad-bean section's surface of weed growth

4 dispose of the weed material securely off site, conforming to the head gardener's weed disposal policy

5 record on the card-index system's modified *Aquadulce Claudia* packet marked with a bold 1 (or 2, if the first packet's inner surfaces have been filled)

— when the clearance of the broad-bean plants began

— when the clearance ended

— the total weight of picked, unpodded, mature beans

— comments on the seeds' and the plants' performance

6 record on the BROAD BEANS SECTION, YEAR 1 AREA card in the card-index box the date upon which the broad-bean section ended its life

7 retain the tread boards over the temporary path that is alongside the ex-broad-bean section for use when cabbage plantlets are transplanted to the section from the seed bed at the start of the July moon's second quarter. Refer to *CABBAGES*

8 note that at this ex-broad-bean, pre-cabbage juncture

— the four designated Year Areas and the seed bed that are to form the fully-converted garden have been outlined in sketch form with the aid of garden canes and garden lines

— the service path surrounding the Year 1 Area's four sides and the four sides of the site of the seed bed has been installed

— the detail of the Year 1 Area and the Year 2 Areas has been filled in

— the Year 1 Area's single-dug bed and deep-trench bed have been installed

— both beds are in the first year of their four-year life span

— the greater part of the single-dug bed has been developed into a broad-bean-producing section

— that section now awaits preparation for the arrival of cabbage plantlets (see *CABBAGES*)

— the remainder of the Year 1 Area, the fully-outlined Year

2 Area and the sketched-in Year 3 Area and Year 4 Area are unemployed and undeveloped

— the general weed clearance in the Year 2, 3 and 4 Areas has begun and is scheduled for continuation on a regular basis

— the trench for the Year 2 Area's deep-trench bed has been installed in the outlined Year 2 Area and has been brought into use for the first time as a non-weed, waste-vegetable-matter accumulator

— the whole of the 330cm length of the 300cm-wide single-dug bed is available for follow-on, first-year, single-dug-bed-specific crop development according to R J Harris's crop-rotation system

— the Year 1 Area's deep-trench bed, installed in October at the very beginning of the Year 1 Area's first year, is available for first-year, deep-trench bed-specific crops. See later in this manual and *ROTATION*

9 apply the cultivation and post-cultivation content of *BROAD BEANS* to each Year Area at the commencement of the first year of that Area's four-year life span.
[*Considerations:* **1** — *when, that is, Autumn-sown broad beans are scheduled as the opening crop of the new Area. When they are not, revised thinking, planning and activity are required, aided by consulting* ROTATION; **2** — *broad beans remaining as the launch point of the first year of each new Area, continue broad-*

bean-development record keeping. Progressively number the converted Aquadulce Claudia (and/or other) seed packets in the card-index system, so that the historical context of the recorded information is preserved

10 note that with the completion of the Year 4 Area's deep-trench bed, no trench awaits development into a deep-trench bed elsewhere in the fully converted vegetable garden. Hence, no trench is available as an accumulator of waste vegetable matter. For that reason, during and after the fourth and final year in the garden conversion, accumulate the arisings of waste-vegetable matter in plastic sacks. Store the sacks under cover. Use their contents when the next

TIP 16
➔ **Rice is the time-honoured accompaniment of the bean. Nutritionally, the two in combination have a value that is greater than the sum of their parts. Dishes globally testify to this — especially the low-cost but hugely satisfying rice and peas of Jamaica, for which fried chicken was invented (the 'pea' is a particular kind of Jamaican bean). For fully-matured, straight-from-the-plant, de-podded, briefly steamed broad beans, cheese sauce is the all-purpose, savoury saviour. Of course, the chief of the legume tribe is the soya bean. Its flavour is not to everyone's taste, but its innumerable culinary products and its industrial and commercial applications are legendary.**

trench for a deep-trench bed becomes available

11 note that in each Area the location of each of the two types of bed does not move as the bed is renewed. [**Consideration:** *the renewal of each bed's contents after each four-year period according to the head gardener's prescription ensures that the individual crop develops in what is the equivalent of previously unemployed medium. A major result is the perfect environment for cultivation*]

12 review the broad-bean data held in the card-index system before embarking upon fresh broad-bean cultivation. Note the lessons to be learned. Apply them

13 make a practice of accompanying the pursuit of moon-gardening success with the filing alphabetically in the card-index box of all purchased packets of seeds. Make a practice, also, of recording upon the purchased, lined cards each

fresh development in the vegetable garden

14 make a practice, importantly, of cross-referencing the recorded information, as a guard against memory lapse

15 avoid the storing of information about progress and developments in the converted vegetable garden in PC files instead of in a card-index system. [**Considerations: 1** — *a card-index box is not harmed by earth-encrusted fingers. This cannot be said of a computer's keypad;* **2** — *a seed packet or a card bearing essential information is more easily and less hazardously taken into the garden than is a PC or a laptop;* **3** — *the properly-safeguarded, old-fashioned card-index box is not subject to the kind of accidental loss of data to which the PC can be prone;* **4** — *the hand-written note releases information more readily than does the screen of a PC's monitor, especially in moments of gardening emergency*].

CABBAGES: seedlings and plantlets

To progress towards almost unbroken harvesting — the overall aim in the vegetable garden, no matter how production is achieved — the first year of the conversion to R J Harris's overall four-year, crop-rotational, moon-oriented method sees the Autumn-sown, broad-bean section of the first-year, single-dug bed in the Year 1 Area committed to an unrelated and compatible plant the instant that the broad beans come to an end (see the whole of *BROAD BEANS*).

There is no better unrelated and compatible plant than the cabbage.

Its hunger for the broad beans' nitrogen leavings in the soil is insatiable, and, irresistibly so far as any cost-conscious gardener is concerned, those leavings, being a gift from Nature, cost nothing.

Also, no better *food* is obtainable from the garden than the generally and quite unfairly scorned cabbage, which is highly placed nutritionally (its vitamin C content is greater even than that of lettuce) and is blessed

Apply to the *CABBAGES* chapter the anti-bird, anti-cat, tread-board, bed-edge-rehabilitation and top-soil-preparation disciplines that are prescribed in *BROAD BEANS*. Apply also the recommended stones-gleaning and tools/materials-cleaning/storage practices.

Respond to the need, during the four-year garden conversion, and as opportunity offers, to extend and complete the general service paths, and to apply manual weed clearance to the undeveloped Year 2, 3 and 4 Areas.

These fundamentals are referred to only briefly throughout the remainder of 'R J Harris's Moon Gardening'.

and can be available in the garden for almost all of the twelve months of the year.

In the first year of the Year 1 Area's single-dug bed — also the first year of the four-year garden-conversion programme — the key cabbage months are April and July.

In April, the cabbage seed is sown in the as-yet unused seed bed.

In July, the resultant cabbage plantlets begin to be moved to the single-dug bed's emptied broad-bean section.

The plantlets are of what the seedsmen refer to as Summer and Autumn Harvesting Cabbages. Among the many varieties that comprise this major stem of what is an extensive family is the excellent *Earliest of All*. It is this variety that the head gardener nominates for the purposes of this instruction.

He chooses *Earliest of All* because it is of a highly compact habit, and so requires less bed space when permanently planted out than do many of its cousins. Also, it offers a ball-like, not over-large, solid head, which lends itself to fine shredding for salad purposes. A bonus is that the head is contained within comparatively few outer leaves. These need not be discarded, no matter how much they stand testimony to the rigours of life in the cabbage patch. Thoroughly washed, they

with a weighty cargo of fibre. Equally, it possesses a minerals' range that is little short of a marvel — albeit, for many, a hidden, unappreciated marvel.

Added to these virtues must be its flavour range and its versatility in the kitchen.

The former is far greater than is commonly known, thanks to the innumerable cabbage types and to the determination of the seedsmen to be and to remain competitive. The latter stems from the fact that, when young, many of the cabbage varieties are as good raw as when cooked.

Equally, when correctly cooked, they require less cooking time than do most of the products of the vegetable garden.

Supremely, with correct management, the cabbage is easy to grow,

TIP 17
➜   **The best time to de-weed the undeveloped Areas of the garden-to-be is a day or two prior to the start of the moon's third quarter (Full Moon). Then, the top soil is at its most moist, thanks to the maximum pressure exerted upon it by the fully-raised level of Earth's moon-controlled water table. In consequence, the soil is at its most ready to release its hold upon the weeds' roots.**

convert well into cream of cabbage soup, cabbage and potato soup and vegetable stock.

Earliest of All falls within the lower retail pricing band at the garden centres, costing 70p-to-80p per packet (in 2006) of about 360 typically small seeds.

Once cabbage production as a component of crop-rotated cultivation has been mastered, and once the types known as Spring Harvesting Cabbages and Winter Harvesting Cabbages have been added, an endless exploration of the seemingly endless brassicas can be entered upon. Of great aid, in this connection, are the generally high-quality brochures issued annually by the better of the U K's seedsmen. Some of these are referred to in *SUPPLIERS.*

To be equipped in July with suitable cabbage plantlets, and to continue to advance the development of crop rotation and moon gardening

1 **in the September or the October that commences the first year of garden conversion, or just prior to those two months**, purchase one packet of *Earliest of All* seeds

2 begin to undertake broad-bean and Year-1-Area development in all of its parts and aspects at the same time, as is described in *BROAD BEANS.* Then pursue the broad-bean development until the broad-bean section is emptied and stands ready to become the cabbage section

3 **at the start of the second quarter of the April moon in the first year of the Year 1 Area's four-year life span**, empty the entire surface of the seed bed of weed top growth and weed roots. Work from the permanent service path that surrounds the bed. Use a

garden fork. Use the whole of the length of the fork's tines

4 ensure that no uprooted weed is left upon the surface of the seed bed and, thus, able to re-root itself

5 dispose of the collected weed matter securely off site, in accordance with head gardener R J Harris's policy on weed disposal

6 convert the surface of the seed bed to a levelled, fine tilth in readiness for seed sowing. Do so as when the broad-bean section of the Year 1 Area's single-dug bed was prepared for broad-bean-seed sowing. See *BROAD BEANS: preparing to sow*

7 insert two 30cm-long marker sticks 15cm into the seed bed's surface. Position one of them at the rear of the bed. Position the other opposite, at the front of the bed. Space both 15cm from one end of the bed

8 cap the tops of the two marker sticks, for safety's sake

9 place a short garden cane on the bed's surface across its 50cm width. Position it so that it touches the pair of marker sticks

10 retrieve from the card-index box the plain-paper envelope marked EARLIEST OF ALL. Find it behind the E index card

11 extract from the envelope the foil container of *Earliest of All* seeds.
[**Consideration:** *for an explanation of how and why*

17

Charles Darwin's interest in the evolution of life forms extended to, and embraced, the plant world, and in 1868, in his published *'The Variation of Animals and Plants Under Domestication'*, he wrote

'The principal kinds of cabbage existed at least as early as the 16th century, so that numerous modifications of structure have been inherited for a long period. This fact is the more remarkable, as great care must be taken to prevent the crossing of different kinds. I raised 233 seedlings from Cabbages of different kinds, which had purposely been planted near each other, and of the seedlings, no more than 155 were plainly deteriorated and mongrelised, nor were the remaining 78 all perfectly true. It may be doubted whether many permanent varieties have been formed by intentional or accidental crosses, for such crossed plants are found to be very inconstant.'

the foil container becomes transferred from its seed packet to a plain-paper envelope within the card-index box, see BROAD BEANS: preparing to sow]

12 hold the foil container upright. Gently flex it, and so loosen the contained seeds and encourage them to fall to the bottom of the container

13 cut off the top of the foil container. Use scissors, to achieve an unjagged cut.

[***Consideration:*** *this facilitates a smooth flow of the seeds as they are poured from the container, plus control over the speed of the flow of the poured seeds*]

14 funnel seeds from the *Earliest of All* foil container into a seed dispenser. Do so above a sheet of clean, dry paper placed upon the path, so that accidentally spilled seeds fall upon the paper. Ensure that, in the process, the seeds are not touched by the finger tips.
[***Consideration:*** *fine seeds are always sown into the ground via a purpose-built dispenser to obviate potentially damaging, sterility-inducing contact between seeds and fingers. The dispenser is a simple tool, considered by R J Harris to be essential. It costs very little at any garden centre*]

15 move two of the seeds spilled upon the sheet of paper upon the path so that they are side by side, and touching. Use any implement other than the finger tips to do so. If there has been no accidental spillage, funnel a few seeds from the foil container onto the sheet of paper

16 examine the two touching seeds closely against the white background of the paper. Gauge the length of their combined diameters. Make a mental note of it

17 funnel seeds from the sheet of paper into the seed dispenser

18 double over the foil container's top and replace the container in its envelope.

Fold over the top of the envelope, and pocket it

19 mark a drill in the seed bed's surface between the two marker sticks. Make it as deep as the combined diameters of two cabbage seeds. Use the tip of a trowel to do so, or of a fine dibber, or a defunct biro pen. Use the positioned garden cane as a ruler

20 remove the garden cane when the drill has been inscribed

21 dispense the *Earliest of All* seeds into the drill. Begin and end the sown row 5cm away from the inserted marker sticks. Sow thinly. Aim for seed postings in which individual seeds are 3cm from each other. [**Considerations: 1** — *the unnecessary and patently wasteful alternative is seeds laid down in a linear blanket. Achieving posted seeds is not difficult with seeds as large as, for example, those of the broad bean. With small seeds. such as those of the cabbage, the case is otherwise (although some seed dispensers have the ability to minimise the release even of very tiny seeds to a single seed at a time);* **2** — *hampering achieving the ideal is the rule that the small seed must not be picked up and deposited by the fingers or by any implement, for fear that it be crushed and, in consequence, rendered unable to germinate. All in all, the gardener can do no more than be aware of the ideal that is posted small seeds, and to strive to achieve it*]

22 ensure that the seed bed's surface is not leaned upon or trodden upon

23 empty the dispenser into the foil container once the sowing has been done. Do so above the sheet of paper placed upon the path

24 funnel spilled seeds into the foil container from the paper, if there has been spillage

25 double over the foil container's top. Place the container in its envelope. Pocket the envelope

26 brush earth gently from the bed's surface into the sown drill. By these means cover the dispensed seeds with the a layer of earth the thickness of which approximates to the diameter of a single cabbage seed

27 identify the sown row with an inserted weatherproof, plastic label marked *Earliest of All* and the date of the sowing. Mark the label with a weatherproof marker

28 cover the seed bed — immediately — with box-shaped, wire-net cages to stop the local cat population from converting the bed into a litter tray and to keep the birds at bay when seedlings show themselves above ground. Use the finest gauge of wire net, also to keep out the visiting cabbage butterflies. [**Considerations: 1** — *delay in doing this, and the task is likely never to be done. The bed's finely-raked surface draws the domestic pets as if*

it were a magnet. Dogs, also, are attracted to it; **2** — sixteen cages each 50cm (to match the width of the seed bed) by 80cm by 30cm in height totally cover the 50cm by 1280cm seed-bed; **3** — build plenty of folded wire netting into each cage, to achieve a robust structure]

29 ensure that the capped marker sticks remain *in situ* and undisturbed beneath the wire-net cages

30 note that at no stage has the seed bed been fed with any kind of fertiliser or manure. [***Consideration:*** *a seed being brought to seedlet and then plantlet stage in garden soil is likely to be inhibited if it is in the presence of added nutrients. Only when it is a permanently-posted young plant eagerly striving for adulthood does it require the kind of help that brings the quality of maturity that the head gardener expects — and which, often, is beyond unaided Nature's ability to supply*]

31 return the envelope containing the *Earliest of All* seeds in their foil packaging to the card-index box

32 at the start of the moon's second quarter in May, June, July and August, repeat the *Earliest of All* sowing in the seed bed. Place the four additional rows of sowings parallel to the initial row. Space the five rows 15cm from each other

33 finalise each monthly sowing with a thorough hand weeding of the seed bed.

[***Consideration:*** *the fragility of the seed bed's contents makes it unwise to apply a hoe or a similar tool to its surface, no matter how carefully and gently*]

34 know, prior to germination, where the invisible seeds lie by placing short garden canes between opposite marker sticks. Extract any growth that appears between two positioned, adjacent, parallel canes

35 position garden canes in the same way after germination, to differentiate between seedling growth and new weed growth. Ensure, by these means, that seedlings are not mistaken for young weeds, and removed

36 dispose of the collected weed matter securely off site, in accordance with Mr Harris's policy on weed disposal

37 position a small, clean, glass jar containing three or four anti-slug/snail pellets adjacent to each sown row. Place the jar so that it lies upon its side, with the

---

TIP 18
➜ **A more exact way to cover the seeds in a sown drill: pass top soil through a 6mm sieve and then dribble the result slowly through the finger tips onto the sown seeds. Restrict the flow of the sieved soil, so that it covers no more thickly than the thickness of an individual seed. A bonus is that the adjacent bed surface remains undisturbed. Scatter the sieve's contents over the bed's surface, to return the small stones to the soil.**

pellets nestling at the bottom of the jar. The pellets are preferably, but not necessarily, of the kind that does not harm the wild life. [**Considerations: 1** — *the slugs and the snails enter the jar to feed on the pellets. They die inside the jar;* **2** — *the anti-bird wire-net cages keep at bay the carrion-consuming birds and other fauna;* **3** — *no harm is done when the cages are not present. The carrion-consuming wild creatures are repelled by the enclosed space that is offered by the jars, and do not enter it;* **4** — *the small jar is not overly conspicuous and, sometimes, can be concealed by plant matter*]

38 position each anti-slug jar the moment that the seed sowing is done. [**Consideration:** *it must be accepted that the slugs and the snails always know well before the responsible gardener can possibly know that succulent shoots have appeared above the surface of the soil. They destroy in minutes that which has taken hours to achieve, and which has not been protected*]

39 examine the jars daily. Replace those containing dead slugs with fresh, pellet-charged jars. Clean out the removed jars into the kitchen refuse bin, wash them and hold them in readiness for re-use

18

"Consider," suggests the head gardener, "tackling the slug and snail problem by encouraging a hedgehog family and toads to take up residence in the garden.

"You can count on an almost slug/snail-free vegetable and flower cultivation once they are present.

"And you can get their help even in the most built-up of areas, for — like the fox — they have learned that the pickings in the town can be so much better than in the poisons-ridden, farm-racked countryside."

The key to acquiring these very special residents is habitat.

"Give them a place to live, and you'll have to shift out of the way smartly not to be trampled underfoot as they pack their bags and move in," advises Mr Harris.

"Loosely pile up small heaps of logs or stones in a decorative kind of way here and there. They become homes for all kinds of creepy crawlies, so they provide both food and living quarters. Then increase the volume of the habitat by develping a wild patch in the garden in an undisturbed spot. Permit the grass to grow to its natural height without cutting. Don't worry if the occasional weed gets a foothold. Dead-head it to prevent seed scatter. And forget water. Toads manage quite well without a special supply.

"Then, as the sun sinks, be watchful, and note that these eating machines also have entertainment value — particularly when Mr and Mrs H go for their evening perambulation trailing baby hedgehogs.

"Oh," R J Harris adds, "and don't worry about the household cat. It quickly learns about hedgehogs' spines, and that toads know how to turn themselves into extremely unpalatable meals."

40 replace the cages immediately after each sowing, hand-weeding and anti-slug-jar replacement

41 purchase more *Earliest of All* seeds, if they are required. Store them alphabetically in the card-index box

42 be alert for the first germination within the rows of sown cabbage seeds. This is likely to occur as from about three weeks after the first sowing

43 extract by forefinger and thumb the weak-looking seedlings. Stop doing this when a spacing of about 8cm between the remaining seedlings has been achieved

44 remove the extracted seedlings from site, so that they can offer no encouragement to the arrival of the disease known as cabbage clubroot

45 be alert for the first seedling to show five or six leaves, and to be between 10cm and 15cm high. Know that, at that stage, early plantlet status has been achieved

46 note that, at this time, the broad-bean section of the Year 1 Area's first-year, single-dug bed is very visibly populated with young, developing broad-bean plants (see *BROAD BEANS: managing, page 47*)

47 expect to begin to have available a supply of transplantation-ready cabbage plantlets with effect from the start of the July moon's second quarter

48 expect to have available too large a supply of cabbage plantlets. [**Consideration:** *this is a requirement. It ensures that cabbage plantlets of the necessary stamina and size for transplanting are available as and when they are needed. The reward is almost uninterrupted cultivation and almost continuously-employed, localised top soil*].

CABBAGES: planting out and managing

With *1)* the *Earliest of All* plantlets almost ready to be transferred from the protected seed bed to their permanent home in the Year 1 Area's ex-broad-bean section of the single-dug bed, *2)* the anti-slug jars on the seed bed efficiently managed *3)* the seed bed regularly de-weeded, and *4)* **the June moon's third quarter** just begun

1 remove the identifying label from the ex-broad-bean section of the first-year, single-dug bed in the Year 1 Area

2 de-earth and pocket the redundant garden label, for re-use later on

3 loosen the bared surface of the cleared ex-broad-bean section lightly with a garden rake

4 return to the depths of the soil any broad-bean roots that are brought to the surface by the garden rake's tines

5 remove from the surface any remaining weed growth.

19

Cabbage clubroot is to be taken seriously — indeed, so seriously that if experience shows that it is in the soil of the garden it is wise to adopt the R J Harris strategy of avoiding the intractable horticultural problem instead of trying to solve it. Decide not to grow any member of the cabbage family. For, clubroot spores in the garden's beds *a)* cannot be destroyed, *b)* cannot be removed, *c)* have a life span, it is reckoned, of about nine years. There are, it is true, one or two time-honoured ways of reducing the impact of the disease upon vulnerable root systems, Despite that, however, it is, beyond doubt, a merciless killer of all cabbages and all members of the cabbage family (except the radish, which escapes only because when correctly harvested it is not in the ground long enough to contract the disease).

Prevention is the only course.

Safeguard the seed bed by clearing the cabbage plantlets from it the moment they become plantlets. Do not permit them to linger and develop through adolescence to maturity. Being unmanaged and unprotected, they may attract clubroot's spores.

Strictly dispose of the removed cabbage plantlets and cabbage leaves off site. This is the material that does not find its way to the kitchen for culinary use. Do not place it into the trench that waits to be developed into a deep-trench bed (or into the compost bin, if that has a presence in the garden). Either way, there is a risk of it returning to the soil and creating clubroot-favouring pockets of growing medium.

During the four years of the garden-conversion programme rigorously and methodicall apply Mr Harris's annual weed-clearance policy. For clubroot is adept at living off certain common weeds and, thus, in the absence of the cabbage, at extending its otherwise potentially shortened life term. This ensures that once it arrives where there is no thorough and sustained annual weed clearance, it is likely to be ever present and ever ready to transfer at the advent of its preferred source of nutrients.

If, at the end of the season, weak, wretched-looking, unusable plants sitting on disgusting roots make it clear that prevention has failed, wait for at least ten years and until after ruthlessly applying weed clearance during all of that period. By that time, the beast may have starved to death. Note in the card-index box the date of the abandonment of cabbage cultivation, so that it is not left to the memory to gauge the passing of a decade.

Even then, two factors must be considered.

One, immoveably, is next door's garden. If that area sports a long-established weed population, continue to forget cabbage. It is likely that the disease waits there, alert for the insertion of the first cabbage plantlet in a cabbage section of a first-year single-dug bed.

The other is the unalterable fact that clubroot's spores are not destroyed when they pass through a cow's or a horse's digestive system. If this reality causes the manure within a given single-dug bed (or within a neighbouring deep-trench bed) to be infected, only the ten-year pause may bring reprieve — and, perhaps, not then. Of aid, here, to a limited extent, is the fact that the manure employed within the crop-rotated, R J Harris-style garden is renewed every four years.

Dispose of this securely off site, at a later moment

6 rake the surface of what is now the cabbage section of the Year 1 Area's first-year, single-dug bed to a fine tilth. Do so to no great depth, to preserve the relative compaction of the top soil's surface.
[**Consideration:** *the cabbage prefers to take root in, and does best in, firmed soil*]

7 dress the surface of the cabbage section evenly with 60g to the square metre of fish-blood-and-bone fertiliser (306g for the size of the cabbage section that is under discussion)

8 rake in the fertiliser gently. Re-firm the loosened ground with the head of the rake

9 cover the surface of the cabbage section with pieces of fine-mesh wire net to ward off cat disturbance

10 work from the permanent path as much as possible, Work from the positioned tread boards as little as possible

11 write

    CABBAGE SECTION

upon the ex-broad-bean, weatherproof, plastic garden label. Use a weatherproof marker

12 insert the label into one corner of the cabbage section

13 replace the cabbage section's two boundary-marking, capped canes and linking garden line, should they have been disturbed

14 take the removed stones, employed tools and surplus fertiliser off site

15 clean the equipment. Return it and the unused fertiliser to store. Store the stones for use in future stone-demanding projects in the garden

16 see *BROAD BEANS: preparing to sow* for the reasons for fertilising at the start of the third quarter of the June moon

17 **at the start of the July moon's second quarter**, remove the wire-net pieces from the surface of the cabbage section of the Year 1 Area's single-dug bed

18 place a garden line across the 300cm length of the surface of the cabbage section. Position it 25cm from the adjacent permanent path. Work from the permanent path in doing so. *See Diagram 1,* page 14

19 place a second garden line parallel to the first and 30cm away from it. Cap the four sticks holding the two

TIP 19
➔ **Refuse any gift of cabbage plantlets, no matter how well-intentioned the offer and apparently reliable its source. Do not buy cabbage plantlets from a garden centre, no matter how good the centre's reputation. Insert only your own grown-from-seed plantlets into the garden's vegetable beds, for these are the only ones that you can count upon to be the least likely to harbour clubroot's spores.**

garden lines in position, for safety's sake

20 remove the wire-net cages from the seed bed

21 hold the largest of the cabbage plantlets by its green-leaf top. Do so gently, and without applying undue pressure upon the leaves

22 ease the plantlet out of the seed bed. Use a hand fork, with the utmost care. Do not touch and, in consequence, possibly damage, the plantlet's root system as the system is exposed

23 measure the distance between the earth-surface mark on the plantlet's stem and the end of the plantlet's roots. Make a mental note of the distance

24 replace the plantlet's roots into the hole from which they have been withdrawn. Scatter earth upon the roots, to cover them temporarily

25 excavate nine planting holes 30cm apart along the first garden line that is upon the cabbage section's surface. Place the first hole 30cm from one end of the 300cm-long section's surface. Place the last hole 30cm from the other end of the section's surface

26 excavate six holes 30cm apart along the second garden line. Place the first hole 45cm from one end of the 300cm-long section's surface

27 use a narrow trowel to excavate the holes. Ensure that the depth of each hole is at least equal to the length of the removed plantlet's roots

28 note that in the two rows, opposite planting holes are staggered in relation to each other

29 retrieve the temporarily replaced *Earliest of All* plantlet from the seed bed. Hold it gently by its green-leaf top growth. Do not touch its roots

30 transfer the plantlet to the cabbage section. Do so with all speed, so that the plantlet's roots are exposed for as short a time as possible and, in consequence, suffer little or no dehydration

31 thread the plantlet's roots through the hole in the centre of a purchased cabbage collar

TIP 20
➔ **As a general practice, move plants at any stage of their development from one place in the garden to another at the very end of the day. Then, all in the garden is at its coolest and, hence, evaporation is at its lowest level. In consequence, soil and plants are at their most moisture-charged. In addition, the newly-inserted plants have the cool of the night ahead of them, not the rising temperature and increasing evaporation of the day. This gives them a sometimes crucial period during which to begin to recover from the trauma of the removal from a familiar habitat to an unfamiliar one.**

32 raise the collar up the plantlet's stem until it meets the plantlet's top growth

33 fold the collar upwards and around the top growth

34 hold the collar gently in that position in one hand, without over-compression

35 lower the plantlet's roots into the first planting hole of the first garden line until the plantlet's stem's earth line is level with the surrounding earth surface

36 firm in the roots gently with the other hand

37 smooth and level the surface of the earth around the embedded stem

38 permit the collar to fall flat upon the smoothed earth

39 ensure that the whole of the collar's under surface is in contact with the surface of the earth.

[***Considerations:* 1** — *cabbage collars are available at garden centres in packs of 30 or 40 at prices ranging from £1 to £2. They are available in a variety of diameters; buy those having the largest diameter;* **2** — *the collar masks the ground around the base of the plantlet and, thus, stops the maggots of the cabbage root fly from burrowing down to the plantlet's roots and taking up residence, to the severe detriment of the developing cabbage. The maggots develop from the eggs laid by the cabbage root fly, which settles upon the collar under the impression that it is settling upon the earth's surface;* **3** — *the cabbage root fly visits at least three times in the cabbage-growing season. In the organic garden it cannot be deterred. Only a physical barrier of the kind provided by the collar keeps its eggs and then its maggots where the predators can, and do, find them;* **4** — *the plantlet's stem thickens as it develops, more than filling the hole in the collar through which it is threaded. The developing plantlet does not suffer as a result of this. The thickening stem increasingly guarantees that, as the season moves forward, the cabbage root fly is unable to find ingress at the base of the cabbage's stem*]

40 plant out plantlets in this way until the fifteen planting holes have been filled

41 position anti-slug jars close to the plantlets. Afterwards, manage the jars daily. See

TIP 21
➔   A 5cm-long stem of rhubarb dropped into the planting hole before the young cabbage's roots are inserted is a well-tried way of averting an onset of clubroot. Sometimes the method works; sometimes it does not. The clubroot spore is an evilly intelligent, versatile, sophisticated organism, which is fond of mutating so that it can combat deterrents and target specific members of the cabbage family. Nothing is lost by taking the precautionary step. A bundle of rhubarb bought from the greengrocery counter costs little enough. The planting hole must be deepened by 5cm, of course.

20

The cultivation of the Winter Harvesting Cabbage and of the Spring Harvesting Cabbage — as the seedsmen refer to them — can be overlaid onto the cultivation of the Summer and Autumn Harvesting Cabbage, taking the crop-rotated vegetable garden into almost all-the-year-round cabbage production.

The Winter Harvesting Cabbage that the head gardener recommends is Kings Seeds' large-headed, white-hearted *Holland Late Winter*. It is ready for picking as from November. It is excellent raw or cooked. It stores well in the garden shed during Winter provided that it is protected from the frost.

Working in the first year of the garden-conversion programme, sow *Holland Late Winter* seeds in the seed bed (see *Diagram 1*, page 14) at the start of the May moon's second quarter. Sow all of the seeds in the packet at the one time. Late Autumn's and Winter's weather/ground conditions seldom lend themselves to successional planting out.

At the start of the June moon's third quarter, feed the 100cm-deep strip that is adjacent to the Summer and Autumn Harvesting Cabbage section of the first-year single-dug bed in the Year 1 Area with 60g to the square metre of fish, blood and bone fertiliser. (see *Diagram 1*, page 14)

At the start of the July moon's second quarter, move the *Holland Late Winter* plantlets to the 100cm-deep strip of bed. Space them 45cm apart in two parallel 270cm-long, east-to-west, 45cm-separated rows. Site the two rows centrally within the 100cm-deep strip.

Delay developing from the Year 1 Area's first year into its second year, allowing time for harvesting during November and beyond. Overall, the cultivation method — seed to harvested plant — is as described in this instruction in respect of the Summer and Autumn Harvesting Cabbage.

21

For Spring cabbage, sow Spring Harvesting Cabbage seeds in the seed bed in July or August during the first year of the Year 1 Area's four-year life span. Move the plantlets in October to the first-year single-dug bed in the Year 2 Area. Space them 30cm from each other in three parallel 270cm-long, east-to-west rows 30cm apart in the 100cm-deep strip that is adjacent to the sown broad-bean section of the Year 2 Area's single-dug bed. Kings's compact, pointed *April* is recommended (see *SUPPLIERS*). The cultivation method is as described in *CABBAGES*.

CABBAGES: seedlings and plantlets for an account of the use of anti-slug jars

42 place a blanket of fleece gently and very loosely over the whole of the cabbage section. Permit it to rest

lightly upon the newly-inserted, collared plantlets.
[***Considerations: 1*** *— the manmade, feather-light, white material known as commercial or*

industrial fleece is obtainable at most garden centres. It keeps the cabbage white butterfly at bay, preventing it from laying its eggs upon the leaves of the cabbage plants that it protects. If laid, the eggs develop into leaf-eating caterpillars. The fleece also serves as a cat deterrent; **2** — the butterfly's determination to lay its eggs is unremitting. It penetrates the smallest of apertures in order to reach its target, heedless that, subsequently, it almost certainly cannot find a way out of the enveloping covering, and must perish beneath it]

upon Earth. The table's pressure upon the top soil increases as it rises during the second quarter, peaking at the end of the quarter. This concentrates the available moisture, with the result that increased moisture is present in the top soil, driven into it by the increasing pressure. The combination of increasing pressure and increasing moisture supply encourages each plantlet's roots' system to absorb the nutrients-charged moisture. It does so when the young plant needs the encourage-ment more than at any other stage of its development]

43 secure the edges of the fleece to the ground with long, U-shaped, two-legged pins fashioned from light-gauge galvanised wire

44 ensure that downward pressure is not exerted upon the plantlets by the fleece

45 repeat all of the components of the July transplantations **in August and September.** Do so, each month, **at the start of the moon's second quarter.** Establish by these means a cabbage section in which are 43 plantlets in five parallel rows and spaced 30cm from each other in the rows. Each of three rows contains nine plantlets, and each of two, eight plantlets — the 43 transplanted at the rate of fifteen in July, fourteen in August, and fourteen in September. [**Consideration:** the start of the moon's second quarter coincides with the upward rising water table, drawn up by the enlarging moon's strengthening gravitational pull

46 replace the wire-net cages over the seed bed after each month's transference of plantlets

47 work principally from the permanent path that is adjacent to seed bed and cabbage section. Work as little as possible from the positioned tread boards

48 remove the surplus of the *Earliest of All* cabbage plantlets from the seed bed to the kitchen as soon as the cabbage section is fully stocked. In the kitchen, stir fry or steam the young leaves very quickly, or use them raw, as a salad ingredient. Dispose of their stems and attached roots in the kitchen garbage pail for disposal off site to continue the sustained drive to reduce to the minimum the risk of the arrival of cabbage clubroot

49 continue the cage protection of the seed bed whether or not it houses seedlings and/or plantlets. Do so to guard against cat disturbance to the surface of the bed

50 hoe weekly between the developing cabbage in the cabbage section, to obviate weed development and to raise moisture to the section's surface. Ensure that the anti-slug jars are

replaced and the fleece blanket is secured loosely over the plantlets immediately after each hoeing

51 hand weed the seed bed weekly, to obviate weed development. Ensure that the wire-net cages are replaced immediately after each weeding.

CABBAGES: harvesting

Harvest each cabbage just before, or as, it reaches maturity. Do so whether or not it is required by the kitchen. In the process

1 remove, each time, the most mature plant or plants. Leave the others *in situ*, to mature further.
[**Consideration:** *overall, the shorter the time that each brassica is in the ground the fewer the number of targets awaiting the ever-questing clubroot virus*]

2 remove the whole of each cabbage when it is harvested.
[**Consideration:** *total removal is essential as a component of sustained cabbage-clubroot prevention. The spores of the disease are attracted by the secretions of the cabbage's roots into the host growing medium. This process, and its attendant risk, is sustained for as long as cabbage stems draw sustenance from their bed*]

3 replace each harvested cabbage with an inserted lettuce plantlet (see *LETTUCES seedlings and plantlets*). Do so immediately. Maintain the rows established by the cabbages, to continue to simplify hoeing

4 harvest each lettuce the instant it reaches maturity. Do so whether or not it is required by the kitchen. Its next stage of development is seed setting. It arrives at that rapidly, upon which its flavour becomes bitter, and the product becomes unsuitable for culinary purposes.
[**Considerations: 1** — *lettuce can be cultivated anywhere in the vegetable garden at any time in the growing season. Hence, available areas of ground can be filled with it the moment that they become available, and for as long or as short a space of time as suits the gardener and the garden. For this reason, it pays to have a tray of transplantable lettuce plantlets always to hand (see LETTUCES seedlings and plantlets); 2 — lettuce makes so few demands upon the nutritional content of the soil that it may be permitted to fall outside the crop-rotation/moon oriented programme. To dedicate ground to its production can be judged, therefore, to be wasteful; 3 — in general, do not use radish as a follow-on crop after cabbage. It is related to the cabbage, and can attract cabbage clubroot*]

22

The spring onion, the lettuce and the radish are the head gardener's favourites for filling ground that is left empty by the deployment or removal of principal crops (with the radish being forbidden after cabbage, to reduce the risk of the spread of clubroot).

All three cope with any soil conditions and the smallest area of available soil. Hence, in Mr Harris's planning, they fall outside the crop rotation programme and are introduced at any time within the growing season into any empty places in any of the beds that he creates for specific crop developments.

He opts for catch crops from seeds sown in pots, trays or modules and developed to plantlet stage, instead of from seeds sown in the ground. Usable results are achieved more quickly. This is not simply an obviously good idea. It is a requirement. Ground that becomes available for a catch crop sometimes is not available long enough for development from seed to mature plant.

At Tresillian, the walled kitchen garden is constantly equipped with pots, trays or modules of catch-crop plantlets waiting to be planted out in permanent homes.

5 send the harvested, usable lettuces and cabbages to the kitchen or give them away

6 deposit the unusable, *seedless* lettuce and its roots to the Year 2 Area trench that awaits development into a deep-trench bed. Replace the trench's lid each time the trench has been used, for safety's sake

7 note that, by this time, the trench contains a respectable quantity of rotting, non-weed, vegetable matter

8 send the seed-bearing lettuce off site, for safe disposal

9 send the unusable cabbage off site for safe disposal. Bear in mind the threat of clubroot invasion that it could help to incur, if added to the Year 2 Area trench

10 discard the cabbage collars off site as they are removed from the stems of the harvested cabbage. Do not attempt to re-use them. Being deformed and having enlarged stem holes, they are ineffective as cabbage-fly barriers

TIP 22
➔ **The skilled, experienced gardener manages the sowing of the seeds of the three kinds of cabbage in such a way that the harvested end product, throughout the total cabbage-growing season, comprises cabbage ranging from youngsters to oldsters and including what have always been known as 'greens'. A part of this skill is knowing how to time the availability of plants at desired stages of development, so that the needs of both kitchen and garden are met as precisely as is possible. Achieving germination under glass and in trays or modules, and using cold frames, plays a role. No text is capable of describing adequately the disciplines that are involved, but the head gardener urges: "Try. And keep on trying. In time, you will get the hang of it."**

11 note that, more often than not, both lettuce leaves and cabbage leaves can be converted into excellent chilled or hot soup. This is no matter how severely time has dealt with them and what signs they show of the punishment inflicted upon them by their sojourn in the vegetable garden

12 make the final planting out of lettuce in September

13 **during the first and second moon quarters of September in the second year of the four-year garden conversion**, as cabbage/lettuce harvesting progresses, install the head gardener's single-dug bed and complete the deep-trench bed in the Year 2 Area. See *SINGLE-DUG BED and DEEP-TRENCH BED* for installation instructions. See *Diagram 1, page 14*

14 complete these two installations **by the start of the third quarter of the September moon**. [***Considerations:* 1** — *the Year 2 Area's first-year, single-dug bed is required at this time to be ready to receive the Spring Harvesting cabbage plantlets that await*

Producing the Spring, the Summer and Autumn and the Winter Cabbages throughout the year creates a problem in the crop-rotating garden the beds of which have the dimensions that are proposed in this manual. This is because of the golden rule that no cabbage may succeed another cabbage in the same soil more than once in at least four years — and then, ideally, only after the affected soil has been largely refreshed (as it is, in any event, when the head gardener's thinking and methodsof bed construction are applied).

The following makes the problem clear

THE YEAR 1 AREA, in its first year:

1) The Summer and Autumn cabbage arrives in the ex-broad-bean section of the single-dug bed after the broad beans have been removed. It stays there until the season ends and Winter closes in.

2) The Winter cabbage arrives in the 100cm-deep, next-door strip of the same bed (which has been unused, previously). It stays there until the season ends, and continues into Winter.

3) There is no possibility of Spring cabbage being cultivated during this first year of the Year 1 Area, no matter what the attendant considerations. This is because no seed bed exists in the period *before* Year 1 in which to deve-lop the required plantlets.

THE YEAR 2 AREA, in its first year:

1) The Spring cabbage arrives in the 100cm-deep strip that is adjacent to the Autumn-sown broad-bean section of the first-year single-dug bed. It stays there long enough to make its mark upon the soil. Its plantlets were produced in the seed bed during the Year 1 Area's first year.

2) The Summer and Autumn cabbage arrives in the ex-broad-bean section of

23

the first-year single-dug bed after the broad beans have been cleared away. It stays there until the season ends, and Winter closes in.

QUESTION.

What space is left, then, for the Winter cabbage during this first year of the Year 2 Area (and, of course, during the first year of the Year 3 Area and the Year 4 Area)? — considering that its plantlets, produced in the seed bed during the Year 1 Area's first year, are blocked out by the Summer and Autumn cabbage, and considering that they must not occupy the Spring cabbage's space when that space is made available by the harvesting of the Spring cabbage.

One solution is to increase the width of the single-dug bed beyond the proposed 300cm. In the Year 1 Area, during its first year, the extra space would house longer rows of broad beans, Summer and Autumn cabbage and Winter cabbage, as well as lettuce as a fill-in crop where possible. In the Year 2 Area, during its first year, the increased bed width would provide room for both Spring cabbage and Winter cabbage — each occupying its own, separate row length or section of ground. Of course, the increased single-dug bed width would bring in its train a consequent dimensional increase through-out all four of the Year Areas.

This would raise considerations of ground availability.

Another solution is not to increase the proposed 300cm single-dug-bed width, but to alternate Spring cabbage and Winter cabbage, growing the former during one year and the latter during the next, and so on. The Summer and Autumn cabbage would remain a constant.

No matter how the difficulty is resolved, one thing is clear. The golden rule — that cabbage may not succeed cabbage in the same place — must be observed.

*transplantation from the seed bed. This presumes that a decision has been made to aim for almost year-round cabbage production. The seeds of the Spring Harvesting Cabbage have been sown in the seed bed in July or August of the first year of the four-year garden conversion. See Panels 18 and 19; **2** — the Year 2 Area's deep-trench bed is required at this time so that it may have the whole of the coming Winter and Spring in which to become fully ready to receive its Spring-planted deep-trench-bed-specific, first-year-specific occupant/s]*

15 excavate in the Year 3 Area, at about this time, the metre-wide, metre-deep, 300cm-long trench of that Area's deep-trench bed. Cover the trench with a lid, for safety's sake. [***Consideration:*** *throughout the second year of the garden conversion, this trench awaits the waste, non-weed, vegetable matter that arises as the Year 1 Area's second year of cultivation and the Year 2 Area's first year of cultivation progress]*

16 draw a close to the harvesting of the Summer and Autumn Harvesting Cabbages, and of the lettuces, **in November at the latest.**

CABBAGES: after harvesting

On emptying the cabbage section of its cabbage and lettuce developments

1 clean and dry the fleece blanket. Return it to store

2 clean out and wash the anti-slug jars. Return them to store

3 remove and clean the tread boards that have been protecting the cabbage section's temporary path (or paths). Stand them to dry and then return them to store

4 note that when Winter Cabbage remains *in situ* in the Year 1 first-year, single dug bed after the clearance of Summer and Autumn Harvesting Cabbage and lettuce, the tread boards remain where they facilitate cabbage picking

5 **at the start of the November moon's fourth quarter,** at the commencement of the second year of the garden conversion, rough turn the Year 1 Area's ex-cabbage section's surface with a spade. Make its surface look like that of a ploughed field.
[*Considerations:* **1** — *at the start of the moon's fourth quarter, the moon's reducing gravitational pull permits Earth's water table to sink almost to its lowest level. As a result, the top soil is almost at its least charged with moisture*

24

Lettuce, like cabbage, is a victim of its own success. The range of lettuce types and categories that is available is bewilderingly diverse, and challenges both the seedsmen's ingenuity and the gardener's ability to make choices.

Whether or not this has always been so is in question, for there is general agreement that mystery surrounds the origins of the plant that, for a long period, was recognised and used as a member of the herb family. The ancient Greeks knew, ate and wrote about it. So did the Romans. Those implacable empire builders doubtless included its seeds in their food parcels to the remote islands that were to become Britain. Certainly, it was being mentioned by the English of mediaeval times.

Equally unrecorded is the period during which today's forms evolved. Of these, the cos type is notable. It hearts up, is tall, is less demanding of space and, arguably, offers some of the finest of lettuce flavours.

It happens also to be the most troublesome to grow.

The cabbage type is more gardener-friendly. It, too, hearts up well, although it hugs the ground and, spreading, is more demanding of space.

due to the easing of the upward pressure upon it by the falling water table. In this condition, it is at its easiest to spade dig; **2** *— this is a general truth. The third and fourth moon quarters bring the time of the least arduous working of the top soil, due to the reduction in moisture content;* **3** *— the drawing in* *effect of the easing pressure also encourages the absorption by the dug-over top soil of fertility-enhancing moisture and warmth*]

6 extend the rough spade turning to the whole of the Year 1 Area's top soil. Ensure, in the process, that the single-dug bed's layer of animal manure is not brought to the surface. Ensure, also, that lifted broad-bean roots are returned to the depths of the top soil

7 retain *in situ* the marker sticks that indicate where the single-dug and deep-trench beds of the Year 1 Area are located. [***Consideration:*** *at this juncture, the deep-trench bed has been as fully employed in vegetable production as has been the single-dug bed. It has produced one or other of the first-year, deep-trench-bed-specific vegetables listed in* ROTATION *and discussed elsewhere in this manual*]

8 leave the whole of the Year 1 Area to over-Winter, empty and untouched

9 note that the parts of the single-dug bed that house Winter Harvesting Cabbage at this time (and during the coming weeks of Winter) cannot be included in the pre-second-year soil turning with a spade. Leave it untouched until the pulling of Winter Harvesting cabbage is complete. Then continue to leave it untouched until Spring brings kindlier weather/soil conditions

10 note that the whole of the Year 1 Area's cabbage production programme is repeated in the Year 2 Area, accompanied — if it is possible: see *Panels 18, 19, 20* and *21* — by Spring Harvesting Cabbage sown during the first year of the garden conversion in the seed bed, and then moved on, as plantlets, to the Year 2 Area's single-dug bed

11 note that the catalogues of the reputable seedsmen offer information on the extensive range of cabbage types. Autumn is the time to secure these, for Winter provides the ideal moments in which to plan for what is to come, to make sowing/planting decisions, and to place orders for seeds. See *SUPPLIERS*

12 use Winter time to review the cabbage data recorded in the card-index system. Note the lessons to be learned from them. Apply the lessons.

LETTUCES: seedlings and plantlets

The need is to have in the garden, at any moment during the growing season and always to hand, a tray of lettuce plantlets ready to be planted out whenever unemployed ground in the converted vegetable garden of-fers itself. To create this invaluable aid

1 purchase two or three packets of the seeds of one of the easiest of all lettuces to acquire and to grow, *Webb's Wonder.* [***Consideration:*** *every retailed collection includes this familiar old reliable, which is large, frilly, crisp and cabbage-like.*

Quest for it whilst buying the broad-bean and the cabbage seeds. Expect to pay less than £1 per packet of 750 or 800 seeds (in 2006)]

2 check to ensure that the seeds are dated as being suitable for sowing during the coming year. Make the check at the time of purchase

3 incorporate the *Webb's Wonder* seeds in their foil container and their modified seed packet in the record-keeping system that is described throughout *BROAD BEANS*. Apply the system comprehensively to lettuce cultivation, as it is applied to broad-bean cultivation. Only brief reference is made in this chapter to this system

4 **in late May** (no moon-quarter involvement is entailed), retrieve from the card-index box the plain paper envelope marked WEBB'S WONDER. Find it behind the W index card

5 work under cover and place the paper envelope on a clean workbench top. Place alongside it sharp scissors, a seed dispenser, John Innes seed compost, a seed tray of the smallest available size, a 6mm garden sieve, two newspapers, a tea towel which is no longer required by the kitchen, and a filled can of water. Equip the can with a fine rose

6 loosely fill the seed tray with the John Innes seed compost

7 brush the hand across the top of the tray, lightly, to level off the seed compost

8 tap the base of the tray, gently yet firmly, two or three times upon the workbench top to

settle the surface of the compost until it is level with the base of the rim that forms the top edge of the tray

9 add more compost, and repeat the tapping, if necessary, to compensate for under-filling

10 spread out the tea towel and place the seed tray upon it

11 gently add water from the can to the compost's surface. Do so until the whole of the compost is thoroughly moistened. Do not disturb the surface of the compost with the weight of the water, as the water is added

12 note that the tea towel absorbs drainage from the

TIP 23

➔ **Lettuce is at its best when it is mature at the time of harvesting. Unlike that of most vegetables, lettuce's flavour is at its height only when the plant is fully-grown. That is because its heart is then at maximum size and density. This renders crucial the timing of the harvesting, for the stage immediately beyond full maturity is seed-head development — when lettuce becomes bitter and unpalatable. The consideration loses significance when lettuce is planted as a catch crop. Then, sustained ground employment is what matters, and, when achieved, is ample repayment for harvesting lettuce before it is fully grown, bringing slight flavour loss. In any event, whatever their flavour value, immature lettuce leaves are an asset in the kitchen.**

25

Lettuce has joined the long queue of the plants that have suffered the F1-hybridisation fate. The affected plants are mirror images of one another, the products not of seeds but of bits of themselves. That is why the gardener cannot expect to repeat such plants by harvesting their seeds. These do not reproduce true to F1 type. Only a further purchase wins a repeat of the original, bought seed.

This makes sense in the world of retail selling. Retail seed sales are increased. The greengrocer receives vegetables in uniform sizes and weights. The fruiterer receives armour-plated produce designed to withstand damage during distribution and shelf-stacker handling, and to be harvested at grower-dictated times in order to maximise production efficiency and provide extended shelf life.

Be it said, hybridisation helps to guarantee food for the masses. Notably, it has given to the world wheat, barley and oats the yields of which have been increased ten-fold or more.

Nothing, however, in the head gardener's opinion, equals home-garden produce for flavour, nutritional value and usability in the kitchen. That is so in the case of the common-or-garden, un-F1-manipulated lettuce.

slightly larger than that of the top of the seed tray

14 cover the compost-filled, watered tray with the folded newspaper

15 pass some of the John Innes seed compost through the 6mm garden sieve into a shallow container

16 leave the assembled items, undisturbed, on the workbench top for at least twenty-four hours. [**Considerations: 1** — *this long pause enables the compost to become comprehensively and evenly moistened;* **2** — *the newspaper reduces evaporation;* **3** — *being folded, the newspaper has rigidity and, hence, does not touch the surface of moistened compost;* **4** — *newspaper is cheaper, safer and easier to use than is a sheet of glass. Unlike condensation-dripping glass, it does not encourage any kind of undesirable condition of the compost's surface;* **5** — *the long pause also enables compost, seeds and water to arrive at a common ambient temperature. Overall, this promotes seed germination*]

17 remove the folded newspaper from the top of the seed tray after the twenty-four-hour pause. Discard it. [**Consideration:** *it is possible that the surface of the newspaper has become dampened by the surface of the compost. Re-used, the newspaper could help to create the conditions that provide habitat for seedling-weakening disease*]

base of the seed tray, if there is any

13 fold one of the two newspapers until its area is

18 fill the seed dispenser with the *Webb's Wonder* seeds. Do so over the uncovered tray, to avoid wastage in the event of seed spillage. Manage dispenser and foil container as is described in *CABBAGES: seedlings and plantlets*

19 post seeds from the dispenser onto the surface of the moistened compost. Position them 5cm apart in rows also spaced 5cm apart

20 dribble the powdered compost onto the trayed compost's surface through the finger tips. Do so as thinly and evenly as possible. Do so without disturbing the posted seeds. [**Consideration:** *by these means, draw as close as possible to achieving a covering of powdered John Innes the depth of which is no more than the thickness of the individual lettuce seed*]

21 label the tray, so that, later, there is no doubt about when it was seeded and what is growing in it

22 fold the second newspaper. Cover the seeded tray with it. Place the tray in a protected, darkened place. Ensure that in this place the temperature level cannot rise higher than 12°C-to-15°C (55°F-to-60°F). [**Consideration:** *when sown lettuce seeds' ambient temperature exceeds this level, germination is reduced. At the same time, the seeds that manage to germinate despite a too-high temperature level may develop into plants of reduced quality*]

23 return the surplus powdered seed compost to the compost bag

24 return the unused seeds from the dispenser to the seeds' foil container. Manage the foil container as is described in *CABBAGES: seedlings and plantlets*

25 remove the newspaper daily, and examine the tray

26 check to establish that the surface of the compost has not developed a slightly sandy appearance and does not feel slightly sandy when brushed very lightly with the finger tips. When this condition is observed, know that watering is required. Immediately apply water gently and evenly from the can through the can's fine rose. [**Consideration:** *the rule is that seeded compost must never dry out, and must be positively moist, during the germination period. Hence, it could be argued that the sandy appearance referred to above signals germination failure. In practical fact, a balance must be struck between the undesirability of saturated, seed-rotting compost (attended, perhaps, by drainings from the tray) and dried-out compost in which the seeds die of thirst. An extra consideration is that whereas lack of moisture is easily and quickly corrected, and brings relief rapidly, over-watering is not. The daily examination is the key to the whole matter*]

27 discard the daily removed newspaper. Replace it with a fresh newspaper

26

Lettuce can be cooked, a fact which is often over-looked. Steaming is the simplest way, in a basket set over a little boiling water in a saucepan. It softens in about five minutes, and can be served as if it were any other steamed, green vegetable.

Lettuce soup takes a little longer, especially when chilled (which can be delicious), but recipes for it are common.

Peas served with lettuce is different: chopped spring onions, shredded lettuce, chopped mint and a little sugar are cooked gently in a little water with a knob of butter until the jucies run. The peas are then added and simmered until softened. Then season to taste.

Cooking helps to answer the question What do we do with the weary, often scarred, end-of-season lettuce leaves? — other, that is, than committing them to the trench that awaits conversion into the next Year Area deep-trench bed.

28 keep the water can fully charged and always placed alongside the seeded tray. [***Consideration:*** *by these means, the water is at the same ambient temperature as the compost during the crucial stages of germination and early growth. Hence, germination and seedling/ plantlet development are not inhibited by sudden, traumatic, temperature changes*]

29 be alert for the first hint of green showing through the dark brown of the moist compost. Put back a fresh, folded newspaper each time

no such development is discerned

30 remove the newspaper permanently when growth is detected. Immediately place the tray in full light in a greenhouse, cold frame or conservatory, or on the sill of a window facing west, south or south-west

31 turn the tray from front to back once per day when it is on a window sill, to counter the seedlings' inclination to stretch up to the light and to lean towards it and, thus, become distorted

32 watch daily for the appearance of two baby leaves on each of the developing seedlings. When this happens, fill a second small seed tray with John Innes No 2 potting compost. Use the method described above

TIP 24

➜ **The more speedily lettuce is grown, the better is its flavour. That further explains why head gardener R J Harris favours beginning with plantlets from trays, not seed sown into the ground. It hastens the arrival at maturity. He gives this lowly plant the very best of growing conditions when producing it as a main crop. He never fails to begin with fish-blood-and-bone fertiliser applied to the first-year, single-dug bed's well-raked surface (60g to the square metre) at the start of the moon's third quarter. He also never fails to plant out at the start of the next moon's second quarter after the fertilising of the bed.**

33 place the second tray beside the seedlings' tray, so that, in due course, the two arrive at a common ambient temperature

34 water the second tray's potting-compost content, as described above

35 cover the second tray with a folded newspaper. Leave it for twenty-four hours

36 remove the newspaper after the twenty-four-hour pause. Discard it

37 make very shallow holes in the second tray's John Innes No 2 potting compost. Space the holes 5cm apart in rows 5cm apart and traced with the aid of a ruler. Use the smallest of dibbers. [**Consideration:** *a redundant, plastic-barrelled biro pen makes an ideal dibber for this purpose*]

38 transfer the seedlings from the seed tray to the John Innes No 2 potting compost in the second tray. Do so as follows, in respect of a single seedling

— hold one of the seedling's two leaves between the forefinger and the thumb. Do so gently, making no impression upon the leaf. Do not touch the seedling's stem

— tease the seedling out of its compost bed. Do so with the utmost gentleness. Use a redundant table fork (the head gardener's preferred 'tool' for this purpose) to separate the compost at the seedling stem's base and to detach the

seedling's single, hairlike root. Sacrifice adjacent seedlings in the process, if that is unavoidable

— lower the seedling's root into a waiting, dibbered hole in the second tray's potting compost

— leave as much of the seedling's stem proud of the potting compost's surface as when it grew in the seed compost

— gather the potting compost around the root. Use the table fork to do so

— bed the seedling in, using the table fork. Do so as gently as possible

39 label the filled second tray, so that, later, there is no doubt about when it was planted up and what is growing in it

40 station the second tray where the seedlings' tray has been stationed, in full light. [**Consideration:** *when placed upon a window sill, the tray must be turned front to back once per day, to prevent plantlet-stem distortion*]

TIP 25
➜ **Add the John Innes compost in which seedlings and plantlets have been raised to the surfaces of the garden's beds instead of treating it as fit only to be added to the garbage collection. Spread it as thinly as possible, in order not to jeapodise the root systems of the existing plants. Wash clean the emptied trays with Jeyes fluid, dry them and return them to store.**

27

Perfection in transplanting lettuce plantlets from tray to garden soil

— Towards the end of the day, to catch the coolest part of the day and the consequently reduced evaporation of moisture, thoroughly water the reinstated place in the bed from which a cabbage has been removed. Use a water can fitted with a medium rose.

— At the same time, gently lower the tray containing the lettuce plantlets into a depth of water. Do so until the top of its compost is just below the water's surface.

— Hold the tray there until air bubbles stop rising from the compost (*this signals that complete water penetration has taken place*).

— Remove the tray to a shaded patch of soil — not a hard surface. There, permit the surplus water to drain away (*this avoids creating the conditions that the garden's 'undesirables' may convert into a temporary residence or, at worst, a breeding place*).

— Wait for at least two hours (*this ensures that comprehensive moistening takes place and that, as a result, root systems and targeted bed area soak up as much water as they are capable of absorbing and retaining*).

— Form in the soil at the designated spot the space required to accommodate a plantlet-bearing square of the growing medium in the tray.

— Make the space slightly wider, broader and deeper than is required.

— Hold a plantlet in the tray very gently by one of its leaves. Do not hold it by its stem (*no matter how gently pressure is exerted when the stem is held, it is crushed. This causes the death of the young lettuce*).

— Cut with a narrow-bladed, sharp knife a square of the growing medium that is at the base of the plantlet's stem.

— Carefully extract the square of medium. Use the knife as a lifting tool. Place the square of medium, plus its resident plantlet, into the waiting hole in the garden soil.

— Gently firm the soil around the square without disturbing it, and without leaving space beneath it or alongside it.

— Ideally, ensure that when the square of medium is settled in, its surface is slightly below that of the surrounding soil.

— Gently and thoroughly apply water at the base of the newly-established plantlet. Use a small water can fitted with a fine rose (*at this stage, watering fuses the soil to the medium in which the plantlet has developed, enabling the plantlet's roots to begin drawing in moisture and nutrients at the earliest moment. Also, the watering causes the plantlet to be securely embedded in the soil and, hence, anchored firmly in it*).

41 be alert for the two leaves per transplanted seedling to increase to a minimum of four. Know that, at this point, the seedlings have become plantlets

42 place the plantlets in their tray on a sheltered, shaded, soft surface in the garden, to harden off.
[*Considerations: 1 — lettuce, at any stage of its development, prefers to be cool. For this reason it is often cultivated in the shadow of much taller plants; 2 — a soft surface is required so that when the parked plantlets are watered, surplus water drains away into the soft surface. Draining onto a hard surface, the water may collect and provide a breeding medium for the insects that are best kept out of the garden*]

43 cover the tray of hardening-off plantlets with a made-to-measure, protective cage built out of fine-mesh, galvanised, wire net and incorporating sufficient wire net to achieve an adequate amount of rigidity. Do so to ward off pigeon attack

44 cover the cage with a fleece blanket to place a barrier between lettuce plantlets and visiting slugs or snails. Tuck the blanket beneath the bottom edges of the cage

45 station one or two anti-slug jars close to the protected tray. Monitor these daily. Renew them with fresh jars as and when they are occupied by dead slugs. See *CABBAGES: seedlings and plantlets* for an account of the use of anti-slug jars.

[*Consideration: this is a belt-and-braces solution to a familiar problem, but it is preferable to destroyed lettuce plantlets*]

46 check the compost in the plantlets' tray daily. Wait for the very first indications of drying out, as described above, before applying water with a water can equipped with a fine rose

47 when watering, do so at the end of the day, not during the heat of the day, for the reasons already stated.
[*Considerations: 1 — water from a garden barrel is best for this purpose. Its temperature is likely to be that of the compost in which the lettuce plantlets are rooted; 2 — however, water from a mains tap may be used, for, at this stage, the plantlets have outgrown the weaknesses of their seedling stage*]

48 re-cage and re-fleece the tray immediately after each inspection and/or watering

49 note that the plantlets are ready for planting out after several days of hardening off

50 repeat the seed-to-plantlet programme throughout the growing season. At best, do so weekly; at worst, monthly.
[*Considerations: 1 — the repeated production of lettuce plantlets inevitably entails over-production. It is more important, however, to have usable plantlets always ready for transplantation, so that no available ground need remain unemployed; 2 — send to the kitchen those*

plantlets that outgrow the tray in which they live. Their small, tender, delicately-flavoured leaves are of high value for salad- and soup-making purposes. Permit them to remain in the tray to keep fresh whilst in the kitchen, for 'cut and come again' availability; 3 — when these become unusable, consign them to the trench that awaits development into a deep-trench bed in one of the Year Areas; 4 — note that the moon's quarters have no influence upon in-tray development for the practical reason that no contact exists between the trayed compost and Earth's water table]

51 be alert for lettuce-plantlet planting-out opportunities as from when cabbages begin to be taken from the cabbage section of the first-year, single-dug bed in the affected Year Area (which, within the present discusion, is the Year 1 Area). Insert a lettuce where a cabbage once stood. By these means, maintain the already-established row layout of the cabbage section. This is required, to continue to facilitate effective hoeing.

*[**Consideration:** more often than not, this order of ground utilisation entails ignoring the lunar planting-out timings that, otherwise, would be imposed by the lunar quarters. This must be accepted. It is better by far that prepared topsoil is productive without interruption]*

52 favour the youngest lettuce when planting out, whether as a catch crop or as a crop in its own right.
*[**Consideration:** the young ones adjust themselves to a change of environment more readily than do the older ones. Also, they develop into better lettuce]*

53 insert the lettuce plantlets into the ground during the evening whenever possible, not during the day.
*[**Consideration:** lettuce loves to have its full measure of moisture. This is at its most available after the warm day has dwindled into the comparatively cold end-of-day, and, as a result, evaporation has reduced. Overall, the outcome is better lettuce].*

TAKING THE YEAR 1 AREA INTO AND THROUGH THE SECOND YEAR OF ITS FOUR-YEAR PERIOD OF CONVERSION: pot marigolds

In **August or September at the end of the Year 1 Area's first year** (which is also the first year of the R J Harris-style garden-to-be), buy two or three packets of the seeds of the flower that is known as pot marigold or Calendula.

Procure these at the same time as obtaining the seeds of the broad beans, cabbages and lettuces that are to repeat in the Year 2 Area during its first year what has been achieved in the Year 1 Area during its first year.

Alternatively, procure the seeds of other first-year-specific and bed-specific vegetables chosen from *ROTATION*, for cultivation instead in the Year 2 Area during its first year.

Incorporate the newly-acquired seeds and their modified seed packets in the record-keeping system

Apply to the *POT MARIGIOLD* chapter the section/bed/Year Area-labelling, anti-bird, anti-cat, anti-slug, tread-board, bed-edge-rehabilitation, top-soil-preparation and card-index-system disciplines that are prescribed in *BROAD BEANS* and *CABBAGES* — and the recommended stones-gleaning and tools/materials-cleaning/storage practices.

Respond to the need, during the four-year garden conversion, to extend and complete the general service paths, and to apply manual weed clearance to the undeveloped Year 3 and 4 Areas.

These fundamentals are referred to only briefly throughout the remainder of '*R J Harris's Moon Gardening*'.

that is described through-out *BROAD BEANS.*
Then

1 embark upon the Year 2 Area's programme of first-year development. Emulate in all respects the activity of the first year of the Year 1 Area's four-year life span

2 dig a trench for a deep-trench bed in the outlined Year 3 Area as soon as possible after this chapter's described work is commenced. No moon-quarter involvement is entailed

3 **at the start of the second moon quarter of the soonest**

suitable month in the Spring of the second year of the garden conversion, prepare the surfaces of the Year 1 Area's first-year single-dug and deep-trench beds for seed sowing. Do so as is described in *BROAD BEANS: preparing to sow*

4 use the permanent path as much as possible in doing so, and the tread boards as little as possible, to reduce footfall upon the Year 1 Area's surface

5 ensure that the marker sticks and the garden lines that indicate the locations of the two beds remain in situ. [***Consideration:*** *work with precision in this respect. Without exact knowledge of where the two beds lie, and of the precise size of each, required sowing/ planting decisions can be made subsequently only with uncertainty*]

6 post or insert pot-marigold seeds into the surfaces of the now second-year single-dug bed and the now second-year deep-trench bed in the Year 1 Area. Note that these seeds are large enough to be posted or inserted by hand, one at a time. This is provided that no pressure is exerted upon the individual seed by the finger tips as the sowing is done

7 sow according to the instructions printed upon the seeds' packets. Do so in regimented rows, in order to facilitate methodical hoeing. [***Considerations: 1*** *— the change of crop type rests the soil from vegetable production, and, at the same time, readies it for further vegetable production during the third and fourth years of the affected Area's four-year life span;* **2** *— any*

*annual flower is suitable for this task. The pot marigold is recommended because **a)** its seeds are low-cost, very easily procured and very easy to sow, **b)** the plant reaches maturity readily, **c)** its aroma, once it is in bloom, repels many of the vegetable garden's insect pests; **d)** correctly managed, it adds brilliant, season-long colour to the vegetable garden]*

8   re-instate the Area's identifying plastic label, upon which is marked YEAR 1 AREA with a weatherproof marker. Add to this a plastic label for each bed, each marked POT MARIGOLD with a weatherproof marker

9   note that no pre-feeding of the beds' top soil is required for the pot-marigold cultivation

10   protect the prepared, sown surfaces of the Year 1 Area's two beds with anti-cat wire-net pieces until seedling stage is achieved. Then

— remove the wire-net pieces, and hope that the exposure does no incur too high a price in domestic pet interference

or

— straddle each row of germinated pot marigold with protective wire-net arches

and remove the arches once plantlet stage is reached

11   hoe the rows of pot marigold weekly throughout the Year 1 Area's second year to prevent weed-germination and to raise moisture to the soil's surface

12   remove the flower heads of the pot marigold as they decline and before they set seeds. Do so using scissors, secateurs or thumbnail and forefinger. Secure, by these means, repeat flowering until the very last moments of the Year 1 Area's second year

13   dispose of the removed flower heads off site. Do not dispose of them into the trench in the Year 3 Area. Take both measures to obviate the risk of accidental pot-marigold seed dispersal.
[***Consideration:*** *do not attempt to harvest the pot-marigold's seeds. Better, advises Mr Harris, not to run the risk of mature seeds escaping notice and sowing themselves in the beds. "Any plant in the wrong place is a*

TIP 26

➔   **Consider developing a wigwam or a rig of R J Harris's beloved sweet peas as well as the recommended pot marigold during the second year of any Year Area's four-year life span. The head gardener's deep-trench bed is the home for the aroma-laden, delightful blooms of the vines of this tall-growing plant. A massive incidental point in its favour is that it attracts the pollinators into the garden, conferring widespread benefit. Restrict the pot marigold to the single-dug bed (which is not designed to, and cannot, support sweet peas of Tresillian's magnificence). Note that this golden-headed annual is far easier to grow than is the sweet pea, and, as the season progresses, demands much less of the gardener's time and energies.**

weed, no matter how pretty it may be," comments the head gardener. "Besides," he adds, "the low price of the seeds of the pot marigold buys reduced workload, reduced back bending and reduced worry about catching the seed heads at the right time for harvesting before they explode and scatter hither and yon"]

14 **at the close of the Year 1 Area's second year**, uproot the pot-marigold plants. Time permitting, de-head them and add them to the Year 3 Area's trench. Dispose of their heads off site. Otherwise, dispose of the whole plants off site

15 spade dig the whole of the Year 1 Area's post-pot-marigold surface, which, still, is the Area's second-year surface. Achieve the ploughed-field look and surface texture that characterises the head gardener's Autumn dig. By these means, prepare the Area for its third Winter, followed by its third year of employment (see *ROTATION*)

16 **at the close of the Year 2 Area's first year**, spade dig the Area's post-broad-bean/cabbage/lettuce/deep-trench-bed-specific-vegetable

surface, still the Area's first-year surface. Achieve the ploughed-field look and surface texture that characterises the head gardener's Autumn dig — allowing for the possible presence of Winter Harvesting Cabbage. Prepare the Area, by these means, for its second Winter, followed by its second year of cultivation (pot-marigold or other chosen annual flower. See *ROTATION*)

17 note that during the third year of the garden's four-year conversion

— the first-year-specific vegetable growing and associated activity (broad beans, etc) is applied to the Year 3 Area

— the second-year-specific annual-flower growing and associated activity is applied to the Year 2 Area

— the third-year-specific vegetable growing (see *ROTATION* and later in this manual) and associated activity is applied to the Year 1 Area

and refer to the card-index system, especially during the Winter time. Note the lessons to be learned from the system's by now many notes. Apply the lessons.

ONIONS: seedlings and plantlets

Mr Harris produces his award-winning onions in two stages: as September-sown seeds developing over-Winter into plantlets in a never-fed seed bed; as Spring-transplanted plantlets encouraged to develop into mature onions in a section of one of his single-dug beds in the first year of the bed's four-year life span. The head gardener further increases his prize-winning potential by selecting *Bedfordshire Champion* (specimens of which are shown on the front cover of this

Apply to the *ONIONS* chapter the section/bed/Year Area-labelling, anti-bird, anti-cat, anti-slug, tread-board, bed-edge-rehabilitation, top-soil-preparation and card-index-system disciplines that are prescribed in *BROAD BEANS* and *CABBAGES* — as well as the recommended stones-gleaning and tools/materials-cleaning/storage practices.

Respond to the need, during the four-year garden conversion, to extend and complete the general service paths, and to apply manual weed clearance to the undeveloped Year 2, 3 and 4 Areas.

These fundamentals are referred to only briefly throughout the remainder of '*R J Harris's Moon Gardening*'.

manual) as his preferred product for culinary as well as competition purposes.

"It is a wonderful all-rounder," he comments, "with a good size of bulb, a mild flavour, and a pretty skin. It keeps well, too, so you are still using it when Winter arrives."

To emulate R J Harris's example

1 **prior to the September of the first year of the garden conversion**

— ensure that the seed bed is *in situ* and ready for use. See *BROAD BEANS: preparing to crop rotate*

— purchase one packet of the seeds of *Bedfordshire*

Champion. Quest for it whilst buying the broad-bean, cabbage and lettuce seeds. Expect to pay about £1 for approximately 250 seeds (in 2006)

2 at **the start of the moon's first quarter in the same September**, sow two rows of *Bedfordshire Champion* seeds across 50cm width the seed bed. Use the methods of seed-bed preparation, sowing and overall management, and seedling/plantlet control and anti-cat/slug-snail protection described in *CABBAGES: seedlings and plantlets*

3 modify the methods by

— inscribing the drill for the first row 30cm from one end of the seed bed

— inscribing the drill for the second row 30cm from the first drill

TIP 27
➔ **From the moment the onion seed is sown in the seed bed to the moment the fully-matured bulb is lifted for storage, no water is applied to seed, plant or soil in the walled, kitchen garden at Tresillian. The seed bed is sufficiently moist, thanks to rainfall and to Mr Harris's exploitation of the moon/water-table relationship. The bed for the planting out benefits from the combination of the moon/water-table relationship and the very thick, moisture-trapping, moisture-retaining 'sponge' of fully composted manure that the head gardener inserts beneath the bed's surface. Watering is unnecessary at Tresillian where the ground is the host medium.**

28

The *Bedforshire Champion*, the *Ailsa Craig* and the *Oakley*, the latter dating from 1800, are the head gardener's favourite onion types. He finds that they grow and store well, and have mild flavours.

The first is his award winner. He has shown it innumerable times at Cornwall's major shows, and with it has taken more prizes than he can remember.

He established a record when one of his exhibits displayed twenty-four *Bedfordshire Champions* each weighing about 2k.

"In the kitchen," he points out, "they are equally good.

"Their size in no way reduces or diminishes their flavour, nor — I am quite sure — their nutritional value."

— posting the seeds 5cm apart in the two drills, and not thinning out the seedlings. [*Considerations: 1* — coinciding with this sowing at the start of the moon's first quarter (new moon), the moon's gravitational pull upon Earth begins to increase. It continues to increase until the end of the moon's second quarter (full moon). Throughout these moon-strengthening two quarters (lasting for approximately a fortnight), Earth's water table rises in response to the moon's strengthening gravitational pull. In doing so, it exerts increasing upward presssure. A result is that the moisture content of the top soil is increasingly concentrated, making increasing moisture available for a fortnight to the sown onion seeds; *2* — the combination of increasing moisture and increasing pressure within the top soil provides the seeds of the below-the-surface developers, such as carrot — sown at the start of the first quarter — and the seeds of the above-the-surface developers, such as cabbage — sown at the start of the second quarter — with the optimum germination conditions; *3* — onion's bulb develops both above and below the surface of the ground. Hence, onion is one of the very few vegetable plants that fall between the two categories. It is cultivated as if it were a below-the-surface developer. Principally, this is because of its very great need for moisture. When this need is met to the full, a result is onion possessed of its total complement of the plumpest of rings. When the need is not met, the end-product scarcely merits the gardener's time and interest. The extra moisture, and the extra time spent absorbing the nutrients of Mr Harris's single-dug bed, both provided by the first-quarter start, help to make the difference; *4* — the differentiation between the above- and the below-the-surface developers arises partly out of the need to avoid the impractical work-load demand that would be created if it were judged that all

TIP 28
➜   The earlier the onion plantlets are inserted into the ground, the more rings they form before ring development ceases. Hence, early-planted onion plantlets tend to grow into bigger onions — given correct pre-planting preparation and management.

seed/plantlet types had to be sown/inserted at the one moon time in the given crucial month of sowing/planting in order to give them the benefit of the maximum moisture and pressure within the top soil. The extent of moisture/pressure demand is what, in the main, decides that a given plant commences its life at the beginning of the moon's period of increasing gravitational pull or half way through it]

4 note that the seed bed must be neither watered nor fed, and must not have compost of any kind applied to its surface

5 maintain a strictly weed-free seed bed by hand weeding at weekly intervals as the sown onion seeds develop into seedlings and then plantlets. [**Consideration:** in a bed as narrow as is the 50cm-wide seed bed, only a small number of maturing weeds is sufficient to rob seriously the onion seedlings — or any other seedlings — of moisture and nutrients. Unchecked, the weeds diminish the seedlings' ability to achieve their potential, with a consequently deleterious effect upon the quality of the harvested crop]

6 use the seedbed period of the onions' development to

— establish the Year 1 Area's single-dug bed. See *SINGLE-DUG BED* for an instruction

— establish and prepare the broad-bean section of the single-dug bed by **the end of the September moon's third quarter in the first year of the Year 1 Area.** See *BROAD BEANS: preparing to sow*

29

The onion ranks among the oldest and most valued of vegetables. It is supposed to have been widely distributed in pre-historic times in Western Asia. It has been so long in cultivation that its native country is unknown. What is certain is that the ancient Greeks, the Romans (who took it to Britain, it is thought) and the Egyptians grew it extensively.

It was grown in Britain at the time of the early herbalists, who knew it as a herb and valued it for its medicinal qualities. The sailors of bygone days, who had yet to discover lemons and limes, prized it as a scurvy deterrent. For centuries, ordinary men and women looked to it to help them to ameliorate the awfulness of their daily meals.

If more of it were eaten at the present time, believe many nutritionists, today's potassium lack in the human diet would not be as prevalent and as potentially damaging as it is.

— sow the broad-bean section with broad-bean seeds at **the start of the October moon's second quarter**. See *BROAD BEANS: sowing*

7 earmark for onion production the 100cm-deep, 300cm-long section that is adjacent to the broad-bean section (and is separated from it by a temporary path: see *Diagram 1*, page 14)

8 note that the commitment to onion production nullifies other cultivation in the 100cm-deep section. The section is large enough to house but one crop. As a result, the overall cabbage

production when onion is an accompanying crop is restricted to Summer and Autumn Harvesting Cabbage, cultivated in the ex-broad-bean section. In subsequent seasons, choices can be made between onion, Winter Harvesting Cabbage and Spring Harvesting Cabbage (with Summer and Autumn Harvesting Cabbage as a constant).

[**Consideration:** *this highlights the limitations imposed by the proposed dimensions of the four Year Areas. In Tresillian's extensive, walled, kitchen garden, this kind of inconvenience is unknown. Each of the head gardener's Year Areas contains several single-dug beds (as well as several deep-trench beds)*]

9 **at the start of the September moon's third quarter** (the moment that the Year 1 Area's single-dug bed is complete), dress the rough-hewn surface of the onion-section-to-be with 60g of calcified seaweed or wood ash per square metre (a total of 180g for the 100cm by 300cm Area of the onion-section-to-be)

10 turn the calcified seaweed/wood ash dressing into the surface. Use a spade to do so, not a fork, to maintain the top soil's rough-hewn surface. This surface was formed when the single-dug bed was spade created.

[**Consideration:** *acting at the start of the September moon's third quarter exploits the*

Contact R J Harris at *rjh@moongardening. fsnet.co.uk* if further explanation is required.

30

When Queen Victoria reigned, Tresillian's kitchen garden was at its production height, and its many onion types were grown from seed. To-day's onion set was then unknown.

R J Harris's aim is to return the garden to its former times and former practices, which is why his starting point for onions is the seed and the kind of bed that was used in the mid 1800s: a single-dug expanse of raised top soil based upon a layer of richly-nutritious, fully-composted farm-yard manure.

The head gardener acknowledges that the onion set considerably eases the burden upon today's sparetime gardener, and provides a guarantee of passable results.

"In no way, though, can it match the bulb that is once again the Tresillian speciality," he claims, "neither for size nor weight nor flavour nor ease of preparation in the kitchen."

---

drawing-in effect upon the top soil of the receding water table, which is permitted to fall back by the diminishing gravitation pull of the weakening moon. The drawing-in influence is upon the turned-in calcified seawood/wood ash, the fish-blood-and-bone fertiliser with which the broad-bean-section-to-be is dressed and the buried, untapped manure content of the whole of the single-dug bed]

11 leave the onion-section-to-be and the by now October-sown (and soon to be November-sown) broad-bean section to Winter's rigours.

ONIONS: planting out and managing

Equipped with flourishing onion plantlets in the seed bed and an onion section that is almost ready to receive the plantlets

1 **at the beginning of the February moon's third quarter in the first year of the Year 1 Area** (and of the garden conversion), clear away from the onion section the few weeds that may have developed since the section was created. Use a garden fork. Later, dispose of the arising weeds in accordance with the head gardener's policy on weed removal.
[***Consideration:*** *if February's weather/soil conditions place the garden out of bounds, postpone commencing onion-section preparation until — but no later than — the start of the March moon's third quarter*]

2 at the same time as de-weeding, use the garden fork to level the onion-section-to-be's 100cm by 300cm surface

3 convert the surface of the section to a fine tilth. Do so as is described in *BROAD BEANS: preparing to sow*

4 dress the surface of the onion section evenly with 115g to the square metre of fish-blood-and-bone fertiliser (345g for the size of the 100cm by 300cm onion section that is under discussion)

5 rake in the fertiliser lightly and gently

6 **at the start of the March moon's first quarter** (or April's, if soil/weather conditions necessitate this)

— peg a garden line from end to end of the 300cm length of the onion-section-to-be. Centre it within the section's 100cm width

— peg a second garden line to the right of the positioned garden line, and a third to its left. Position the three garden lines so that they are parallel to each other and 30cm apart

and note that each of the two outer garden lines is 20cm distant from one or other of the section's two sides

7 select the largest of the onion plantlets in the seed bed

8 uproot the plantlet. Do so very gently. Use a hand fork, with great care. Sacrifice as few as is possible of the selected plantlet's neighbours, as it is lifted. Lay the removed plantlet upon the bed's surface. Do not, at any time, touch its roots

9 measure, by any convenient means, the distance between the earth mark on the plantlet's stem and the end of the plantlet's roots. Make a mental note of the distance

10 replace the plantlet's roots into the hole from which they have been withdrawn. Scatter earth upon the roots, to cover them temporarily

11 excavate 19 planting-out holes 15cm apart along each of the three garden lines that are pegged onto the surface of the onion section. Use a

97

narrow trowel to do so. Position the first trowelled hole along each garden line so that it is 15cm from the end of the section. Establish, as a result of this, that the final trowelled hole is positioned 15cm from the other end of the section

12 create a total of 57 holes by these means

13 ensure that the individual planting hole is deep enough to accommodate the onion plantlet's roots without cramping or distortion

14 retrieve the temporarily replaced *Bedfordshire Champion* plantlet from the seed bed. Hold it gently by its green-leaf top growth. Do not touch its roots

15 transfer the plantlet to the onion section. Do so with all speed, so that its roots are exposed to the atmosphere for as short a time as is possible and, in consequence, suffer the least amount of dehydration

16 lower the plantlet's roots into a planting hole until the plantlet's stem's earth line is level with the surrounding earth surface

17 firm the roots in gently with the other hand, without touching them

18 lift a further 56 plantlets from the seed bed and insert them into the onion section in this way until all 57 holes have been filled. [*Consideration: for the unpracticed gardener, the planting out is best done one plantlet at a time. Mr Harris*

carefully eases a short length of a plantlets' row out of the seed bed, using a garden fork. He then separates the removed plantlets from each other by gently teasing apart their intermingled root systems. He takes care, as he does so, not to damage either the roots' systems or the plantlets' green top growth. Individually, this is 15cm-to-18cm in height]

19 hoe the onion section's surface, between the rows of plantlets, at least once per week after the planting out. [*Consideration: this prevents weed germination. It also, importantly, raises moisture to the surface. There, with weed removal, there is no competition for the augmented moisture. The developing plantlets have a very great need for the moisture, which helps them to swell and, in due course, attain their maximum size and flavour]*

20 hoe in the late afternoon or the early evening.

TIP 29
➔ **The onion is a fresh-air fiend. Locate its bed in the shade of nearby plants, trees, fences, hedges, walls or buildings — of anything that deprives it of cleansing breezes and nourishing sunlight — and it is likely to fall prey to the onion ills that result in sickly bulbs fit only for the refuse bin. As bad as cultivating in an environment of this kind is cultivating in the same place year after year. This, surprisingly, is the way even today in many vegetable gardens.**

[**Consideration:** *this is when the garden has cooled. As a result, there is reduced evaporation from the soil and, hence, increased moisture recovery for a given amount of physical effort. This is an extra step towards mature onions of the largest possible size and of optimum nutritional qualities and flavour*]

21 **at the start of the fourth moon quarter that occurs immediately prior to 21 June**, dress the surface of the onion section with 60g to the square metre of fish-blood-and-bone fertiliser

22 work in the fertiliser lightly. Use a hoe. Take the greatest possible care not to damage the developing onions' bulbs with the hoe's head, and the developing onions' green top growth with the hoe's long handle.
[**Consideration:** *21 June is the year's longest day. On or about this day, the maturing onion stops forming its rings and embarks upon thickening them. The extra feed of fish, blood and bone fertiliser, when applied at this time, provides additional nutrients just when they are most welcome and most beneficial*].

ONIONS: harvesting

From the beginning of August — still in the first year of the single-dug bed of which the onion section is a part (and of the garden-conversion project) — watch for the onions' green tops to flop to the ground. The moment that this happens, gently turn each top so that, on the ground and limp, it points to the north. Do this to increase the affected bulb's exposure to the sun and, thus, hasten and improve its ripening. Then

1 ensure that the upper part or the tip of each prone top does not touch a neighbouring bulb after it has been turned northwards. If it does, bend it to one side, so that it cannot deprive its neighbour of sunshine

2 continue the weekly weeding. Do so by hand, in view of the presence of onion tops lying prone upon the section's surface. Do so from the service path as much as possible, and

from the tread boards as little as possible

3 **at the start of the September moon's third quarter**, in respect of each onion

— carefully insert the tines of a garden fork beneath the ripened bulb

— lever the bulb up, slowly, until its roots, unbroken, are detached from the soil

— withdraw the fork

— leave the bulb in its raised position for the following two or three days

— then, lift the bulb away from the soil completely

— place the lifted bulb on the soil on its side

— marshal the attached onion top so that it cannot cover a nearby, adjusted bulb

— every other day afterwards, turn the bulb from one side

31

Once upon a time, R J Harris recalls ("long, long before my time"), the head gardeners in the private estates grew their onions in the same bed year in, year out.

"So much so," says Mr Harris, "that if you walked into one of those walled gardens of old, you could tell at a glance where the onions were produced. You looked for the surface that was considerably higher than the rest of the garden, and that would be it.

"Endless seasons of single-'spit' trenching and then stuffing with composted manure followed by a reinstatement of the top soil created a permanently and increasingly raised bed."

This was despite those gardeners of old knowing, in most cases, about the need to rotate crops as a way of countering pest, disease and nutritional deficiencies.

"It all came to a sudden halt when a new disease called white rot infested not only onions but onion beds as well," says Mr Harris. "In fact, once in the bed, it stayed there, waiting for the next planting out.

"That was when onion rotation was adopted as a general practice."

Tresillian's head gardener believes that, unknown to yesterday's seed producers and their customers, the old onion varieties were resistant to the disease.

"Increasingly," he explains, "the old types were abandoned in favour of new types — which did not have that resistance, perhaps — and so, over time and through ignorance, the resistance was lost and the disease received encouragement."

to the other, to expose different sections of it to the atmosphere and, thus, encourage it to dry

— wait for the limp, fallen top growth to wither and to become tinder dry and parchment-like in colour and texture

— remove the onion from the surface of the bed. Clean the dried earth from the onion's bulb. Gently break off the dried top growth and drop it into a receptacle, for disposal later on.

[***Considerations: 1*** *— at the start of the moon's third quarter, the water table is at its highest level. It has been approaching this point for the previous fortnight or so. In consequence, the moisture content of the top soil has been increasing and, at this juncture, is at its greatest volume. Concurrently, the upward pressure exerted by the raised water table is at its strongest;* **2** *— the combination results in the maximum take up of moisture by the ripening bulbs, bringing the onions to their juiciest and, hence, most flavoursome condition. In this state, they are at their most ready to be harvested*]

4 immediately place the harvested onions in shallow, stackable trays. Position the bulbs so that they do not touch one another. Ideally, but not essentially, use shallow trays fitted with wire-net bottoms, for the sake of the increased ventilation that the wire net admits to the trayed onions

5 stack the trays filled with well-separated, non-touching onion bulbs in a dry, airy, well-lit storage place. "Bring the new crop into use without delay,"

advises Mr Harris. "The *Bedfordshire Champion* is a very good keeper, and lasts into Winter. But it doesn't keep for ever in storage."

ONIONS: after harvesting

Replace each harvested onion with a lettuce plantlet transferred from a waiting tray of lettuce plantlets. Do so immediately, in order to exploit as much as is possible of the remainder of the current season. See *LETTUCES: seedlings and plantlets.* Expect no more than limited — but, nonetheless, welcome — results from this end-of-season planting out. Then

1 spread the dried onion tops on the unemployed surface of a bed, or on the surface of an unimportant part of the garden. Burn them. Turn the resultant ash, when it is cold, into the soil, or

2 take the material off site, instead. Ensure that, off site, it and, consequently, the pests/diseases that it almost certainly harbours, are disposed of or destroyed

3 ensure, **by the start of the September moon's third quarter** in the second year of the garden conversion, that the Year 2 Area's single-dug bed is installed. If possible, ensure, also, that the accompanying Year 2 Area's deep-trench bed is completed by the same point in the month

4 draw a close to the harvesting of lettuce half way through October

5 **at the start of the October moon's fourth quarter** in the

second year of the garden conversion, rough turn the Year 1 Area's ex-onion section's surface. Make its surface look like that of a ploughed field. Use a spade.
[*Consideration: see* CABBAGES: after harvesting, *for an explanation of the influence of the gravitational pull of the moon's fourth quarter upon working the top soil's surface with a spade*]

6 extend the rough spade turning to the surface of the ex-cabbage section, allowing for the possible presence of tardy cabbages. Ensure, in the process, that the single-dug bed's layer of animal manure and its resident broad-bean roots are not brought to the surface. Also extend the rough spade turning to the surface of the deep-trench bed

7 retain *in situ* the marker sticks that indicate where the single-dug bed and the deep-trench bed of the Year 1 Area are located.
[*Considerations: 1 — at this juncture, the deep-trench bed has been as fully employed in vegetable production as has been the single-dug bed. It has produced one or other of the first-year, deep-trench-bed-specific vegetables that are listed in* ROTATION. These are *discussed elsewhere in this manual;* **2** *— do not feed the Year 1 Area's ex-onion section at*

the close of the Area's first
year. It bears no more crops
until the following season.
Then, together with the
already dug-over remainder of
the Area, it embarks upon the
flower cultivation that marks
the second year of the
R J Harris four-year, crop-
rotation system (see TAKING
THE YEAR 1 AREA INTO AND
THROUGH THE SECOND
YEAR OF ITS FOUR-YEAR
PERIOD OF CONVERSION:
pot marigold)]

8 note that the whole of the
Year 1 Area's onion-
production programme is
repeated in the Year 2 Area if
it is decided that an onion
crop is to feature in the Year 2
Area during the first year of
its four-year life span.
Ensure, in this case, that
onion seed is sown in the seed
bed at the commencement of
the second year **at the start
of the September moon's
first quarter**

9 use Winter time to review the
onion data recorded in the
card-index system. Note the
by now many lessons to be
learned from them. Apply the
lessons.

32

'There is nothing wrong with
regimenting the sowing and
planting out of vegetables,"
argues Mr Harris. "It simplifies
management and reduces physical work load.

"What is wrong is leaving the
drawn up ranks without proper
defences."

In the walled, kitchen garden
at Tresillian the 'defences' take
the form of 'walls' of adjacent
plantings of the crops that are
well disposed towards the protected ones, and are rotated in
their company for that reason.

Thus, in the first-year single-
dug bed, the onion crop,
planted out in serried ranks,
affords protection to the nearby
carrot and parsnip crops —
each of these being in its own
third-year single-dug bed. Surrounding the whole assembly is
a single-line perimeter of pot
marigold.

"The combination bewilders
the carrot fly and the onion fly
and helps to keep the parsnip
maggot at bay," explains the
head gardener. "It also matches
my rotation system perfectly,
and looks very pretty, indeed."

DWARF FRENCH BEANS: sowing

Like the broad bean, the cabbage
and the onion, the dwarf french
bean is single-dug-bed-specific
when developed according to the
strictures of the R J Harris regime. It
is cultivated during the first year of
the single-dug bed's four-year life
span. For the purposes of this
manual, Mr Harris suggests that the
widely-available and time-honoured
Masterpiece be grown. At the same
time he acknowledges that it is but
one of a confusing myriad of
climbing, string and snap beans,
and notes that it holds out to the beginner the prospect of seemingly
endless horticultural experimentation as the seasons of vegetable
growing succeed one another.

When mature, *Masterpiece*
provides a large, bright-green, flat-
podded bean, which, de-podded, is
excellent briefly steamed. It also
freezes easily and well and has a

Apply to the *DWARF FRENCH BEANS* chapter the section/bed/Year Area-labelling, anti-bird, anti-cat, anti-slug, tread-board, bed-edge-rehabilitation, top-soil-preparation and card-index-system disciplines that are prescribed in *BROAD BEANS* and *CABBAGES*. Apply, also, the recommended stones-gleaning and tools/materials-cleaning/storage practices.

Respond to the need, during the four-year garden conversion, and as opportunity offers, to extend and complete the general service paths, and to apply manual weed clearance to the undeveloped Year 2, 3 and 4 Areas.

These fundamentals are referred to only briefly throughout the remainder of 'R J Harris's Moon Gardening'.

the Autumn-sown broad beans. This is because of the inflexible rule that the soil that has nurtured one member of a particular family is never in future required to try to support any other member of the same family. Its plant-specific nutrients have become depleted — added to which, a single season of occupancy is sufficient to create an environment into which one or other plant-specific ailment or pest can force entry and lie in ambush.

In consequence, *Masterpiece* may be planted only in the 100cm-deep, 300cm-long section of the single-dug bed that is adjacent to the broad-bean section and is separated from it by the 60cm-wide, temporary path. This section is bounded, also, by the 60cm-wide temporary path that separates the single-dug bed from the site of the deep-trench bed (see *Diagram 1*, page 14).

This must nullify plans to cultivate extra Autumn-sown broad beans. It must also modify plans to grow the head gardener's beloved onions.

For a harvest of dwarf french beans of Tresillian quality

long life in the freezer.

When young, with scarcely formed beans and chopped into small pieces, the pod can be eaten raw as a dressed side dish or as a salad ingredient.

"And," adds Mr Harris, "since the plant is less than a metre tall when mature — unlike the climbing french bean, which can go to two metres and more — you do not have to build a cane rig to support it. That adds up to one set of materials that you do not have to go shopping for, and one job less to do in the garden."

Sown in May, *Masterpiece* cannot occupy the space in the single-dug bed that has begun to be vacated by

TIP 30
➔ **Do not attempt to grow comfrey from seed. The time taken to reach mature plant stage is longer than most gardeners' needs can accommodate. Usually, one potted plantlet (bought for a song from the plants' stall of any charity event) grown on for a couple of seasons in a spare corner can be uprooted and divided into three viable sections each with a growing point. Insert these 45cm apart in a damp, sunny spot. Make sure that the growing points show above ground. Wait until they are flourishing plants and then harvest their leaves for conversion into stock ready for dilution.**

1 **during the Autumn of the first year of the garden conversion**, purchase a packet of the seeds of *Masterpiece*. Expect to pay just over £1.00 for about 150 seeds (in 2006). [***Consideration:*** *within the present general context, these seeds deliver a single harvest, which extends for about two weeks from June/July. A single plant produces about 500g of beans. Nineteen plants are proposed*]

2 note that when opportunity offers as this chapter's described work is undertaken, and at the earliest possible moment, a trench for a deep-trench bed is dug and protected with a lid in the outlined Year 2 Area

3 **at the start of the April moon's third quarter** in the first year of the garden's conversion, hoe/rake/cultivator-level for seed sowing the surface of the 100cm by 300cm dwarf-french-bean section of the first-year, single-dug bed in the Year 1 Area. Do so, in all respects, as when the surface of the broad-bean section was prepared for seed sowing (see *BROAD BEANS: preparing to sow*)

4 note the very close proximity of maturing broad-bean plants as this and subsequent work goes forward. Ensure that no impact is made accidentally upon these plants and their bed section

5 feed the top soil of the dwarf-french-bean section with 115g to the square metre of fish-blood-and-bone fertiliser. Do so, in all practical respects, as when the top soil of the broad-bean section was prepared for seed sowing. See *BROAD BEANS: preparing to sow*

6 **at the start of the May moon's second quarter**, peg a garden line on the 300cm length of the section's surface. Locate it 20cm away from the edge of the temporary path. Insert its retaining pegs where the permanent path meets the soil of the dwarf-french-bean section. Tauten it gently. [***Consideration:*** *see BROAD BEANS: sowing, for an account of the link between the moon's second quarter, the upward pressure of Earth's water table, the moisture content of the top soil, and the sowing of any seeds at this time*]

7 excavate along the 300cm length of the garden line a 30cm-wide, 5cm-deep channel. Use a garden spade. Deposit the lifted soil to the broader bed side of the channel for the whole of the channel's length. [***Consideration:*** *by these means, later, achieve relatively effortless reinstatement*]

8 remove the garden line. Insert a 30cm-long marker stick 15cm

TIP 31
➔ **Stop mice from digging up sown dwarf-french-bean seeds (and pea seeds) in two ways: 1) bathe the seeds in a small bowl of paraffin just before sowing them; 2) place short lengths of the herb catnip in the seed channel as the seeds are sown and cover them as the seeds are covered. The herb's smell attracts cats. In turn, these — or their smell — keep the mice at bay. Another explanation is that mice associate the catnip aroma with cats, and, in consequence, are repelled.**

33

The range of modern dwarf-french-bean varieties that is now available in Britain has widened considerably in step with the widening of the EC. French (not surprisingly, perhaps) and Italian varieties are being imported by the seed merchants, who continue to bring in the bean from what was its country of origin in the 1500s, the Netherlands.

Mr Harris rates the modern French varieties especially highly, noting the range of bean colours that they now make available to both sparetime and professional gardeners.

"Yellow, red, green and black," he says.

"With planned planting, one can also have marvellously contrasted blossom in the bean beds."

See *SUPPLIERS* for the head gardener's sources of supply.

into the ground at one end of one side of the channel

9 repeat at the other end, with another 30cm-long marker stick

10 repeat on the other side of the channel, with two more 30cm-long marker sticks

11 cap the tops of the four inserted, end-of-channel marker sticks, for safety's sake

12 post ten seeds 30cm apart along the nearest of the channel's two sides. Position the first seed 15cm from one end of the channel. Position the last seed 15cm from the other end of the channel

13 post nine seeds 30cm apart along the other side of the channel. Commence this other row 30cm from one end of the channel. Complete it 30cm from the other end of the channel

14 ensure that the postings of the nine are staggered in relation to the postings of the ten

15 post five seeds 10cm apart in a row commencing 15cm from one end of the channel and sited between the two rows of posted seeds. [*Consideration: this spacing ensures that transplanting the resultant plantlets later on for row-repair purposes (should*

TIP 32
➔ **The forerunner to the May sowing of dwarf french beans that is described in this chapter can be October-planted-out Spring cabbage plantlets matured until April and then finally cleared in that month in time for the April preparation that must precede the May bean-seed sowing. This good practice entails some small sacrifice in April of the last of the Spring cabbages. Also, it is possible for the first time only during the second year of the garden conversion, in the Year 2 Area. See *Panels 18* and *19*. Catch an extra month of Spring cabbages by clearing these in May and succeeding them with June-inserted dwarf-french-bean plantlets. Raise these from seed sown in April in individual small pots filled with John Innes No 2 potting compost. Protect the plantlets, as they form, in a greenhouse or a cold frame.**

34

Among the dwarf french beans being grown at Tresillian are *Jersey,* from the Channel Isles, where it has been known for centuries, *May Beans,* perhaps from Normandy and at least 200 years old, and white-podded *Navy Bean Edmund,* to which nobody and nothing lays recorded claim.

In common with almost all of the vegetables and fruits that are grown by R J Harris in the Victorian kitchen garden, the produce of these legumes is of days gone by and is unobtainable in today's supermarkets and other greengroceries.

They serve to remind everyone of the vast loss that has been made inevitable by official dictat and commercial pressures. Thanks to the HDRA's Heritage Seed Library (see *SUPPLIERS*) the loss has not been placed beyond correction.

When sanity returns, the Library's seed collections will be there to be tapped into.

that be necessary) presents no difficulty caused by too-close sowing]

16 insert a 30cm-long marker stick 15cm into the soil after the fifth posted seed, 10cm away from it. Site the marker stick in the centre of the 30cm-wide excavated channel

17 cap the top of the marker stick, for safety's sake

18 backfill the channel with the displaced soil. Use the back of a rake as a scoop, or gloved hands. Do so with the greatest possible care

19 cover the seeds with a 5cm thickness of soil. In the process, do not dislodge them from their postings

20 compress the filled-in channel's top gently and slightly with the back of a rake. Create a shallow, rain-collecting depression along the length of the double-rank row. Position the depression comfortably between the two hidden, single rows forming the double-rank row

21 ensure that the five capped marker sticks are not dislodged in the process

22 note that in exceptionally cold conditions the sowing is made in June at the start of the June moon's second quarter, not in May (or, plantlets are inserted in June). In consequence, the section is fertilised in May at the start of the May moon's third quarter, not in April

23 insert a metre-long garden cane 30cm into the earth slightly beyond one end of the double-rank row

24 insert another metre-long garden cane 30cm into the earth slightly beyond the other end of the double-rank row

25 align the insertion points of the two canes to the centre of the width of the double-rank row

TIP 33
➔ **For another and possibly less physically demanding way to sow bean seeds of any kind, see *Tips 7, 8* and *9.***

26 cap the tops of the two canes, for safety's sake

27 transfer the seeds remaining after the sowing to the kitchen store cupboard. Retain them for future use as food. Soak them for at least twenty-four hours prior to adding them to any stew- or casserole-type dish that is being assembled for oven or

hob-top preparation, or to any kind of soup

28 discard the water used for soaking. It may contain harmful toxins

29 note that these are seeds that must not be relied upon to germinate if saved and then sown during the following year.

DWARF FRENCH BEANS: managing and harvesting

A 50cm width of bed remains empty between the double-rank row of sown dwarf-french-bean seeds and the temporary path that separates the single-dug bed from the site of the deep trench bed in the Year 1 Area. At best, this width of single-dug bed could be devoted to a single row of onion plantlets inserted in March/April in advance of the sowing or planting out of the dwarf french beans (see *ONIONS*).

Equally, the space could be devoted to two rows spaced 20cm apart of 30cm-separated catch-crop lettuce, inserted as soon as plantlets become available and sustained until the end of the season (see *LETTUCES*).

It could be devoted to cabbage plantlets, these also taking over where cleared dwarf-french-bean plants stood. This is providing that Spring cabbage did not precede the dwarf french beans.

At worst, the space could be left unemployed and hoed regularly to obviate weed development.

The required decision made, move to manage the dwarf-french-bean section. To do so

1 remove the protective wire-net arches from the sown, double-rank row. Do so until the end of the season and at weekly intervals with effect from making the sowing

2 tie two lengths of gently-taughtened garden string between the end-of-row marker sticks and over the two invisible rows of seeds sown only 5cm beneath the surface of the top soil

3 hoe between the two lines and alongside them. Be guided by the lines where not to apply the hoe. Replace the protective wire-netting arches after each weekly hoeing.
[**Considerations: 1** — *hoeing prevents weed-seed germination and, thus, keeps the bed weed-free;* **2** — *in consequence, it makes nutrients available to the plants alone and reduces the slugs' and snails' food supply. It also raises extra moisture to the surface, where the developing plants' roots await it*]

4 leave the two garden lines *in situ* until seedling growth. Then remove them permanently

5 remove permanently the anti-bird guards the moment that they threaten to hamper plantlet development

6 replace non-germinating dwarf-french-bean seeds with plantlets extracted from the set

of five at one end of the double-rank row. See *BROAD BEANS: managing* for a description of head gardener R J Harris's transplantation method

7 tie six lengths of gently-taughtened garden string horizontally one above the other from one end-of-row garden cane to the other once a full complement of twenty-one plants is present in the double-rank row. Position the first length of garden string 10cm from ground level. Vertically space the lengths of garden string 10cm apart. By these simple means create support for the dwarf-french-bean plants as they develop and mature

8 secateur at ground level the surplus plantlets that are at one end of the double-rank row. Do so to avoid over-crowding. Leave their roots in the soil, for the sake of their nitrogen secretions. Dispose of the secateured material in the trench in the Year 2 Area

9 be alert for when the plantlets need to be guided onto the first rung of the ladder support. Carefully and gently introduce their tendrils to the first rung

For another Tresillian way to begin to stock the dwarf-french-bean section — and, at the same time, secure a crop which begins to harvest one month earlier — take a 160cm-long length of clean, smooth, half-round plastic roof guttering and block its two ends with 10cm-long plugs of newspaper secured in place by sticky tape. Do this on any convenient day at the beginning of April. Then

— fill the guttering between the two plugs with John Innes No 2 potting compost

— rap the base of the guttering gently yet firmly, two or three times, on the work-bench top to consolidate the compost. Add more compost and level off, if that is necessary

— moisten the compost thoroughly. Use a water can fitted with a fine rose to avoid disturbance to the com-post's surface. Cover the compost with sheets of folded newspaper to reduce evaporation

— leave the filled guttering and a packet of dwarf-french-bean seeds together on the workbench top for at least twenty-four hours, so that the compost moistens comprehensively, and seeds and compost arrive at a common ambient temperature as an aid to germination

— insert four dwarf-french-bean seeds 5cm deep in the centre of the compost's width at 30cm postings. Equidistance the set of four between the two newspaper plugs.

Produce five of these assemblies. Lodge them in a cold frame, cold green house or conservatory. Balance good ventilation against cold infiltration in accordance with the weather's performance. Be ready with sacks, fleece or redundant blankets to increase the protection of the cold frame and the small greenhouse against extreme weather conditions. Keep the compost moist all of the time as germination takes place and dwarf-french-bean plantlets develop to the stage at which each bears at least four leaves.

At the start of the May moon's second quarter, transfer the guttering assemblies to an earth surface. Water them thoroughly. Use a can fitted with a fine rose. Leave them for a few hours in a protected place to become comprehensively moistened.

Make the prescribed channel in the dwarf-french-bean section 40cm wide, 15cm from the edge of the section and as deep as the depth of the plastic gutter.

Place an empty 140cm length of the guttering at one end of the channel, against one of its sides, and another opposite to it against the other side. Pack the reinstatement earth around the two lengths of empty guttering.

Remove the empty guttering lengths, leaving two parallel, guttering-shaped and -sized moulds in the top soil. Repeat the operation, creating a pair of 280cm-long, parallel moulds where once there was an excavated channel. Carefully loosen the floor of each mould with a hand fork, to ensure adequate drainage.

Lay a plantlet-bearing, plastic guttering assembly into one end of one of the two moulds. Remove the newspaper plug that is adjacent to the end of the mould. Cut the sticky tape around the other newspaper plug. With one hand, raise the end that is still plugged a few centimetres above the floor of the mould, holding the released plug firmly with the other hand.

Carefully and gently slide the plastic guttering away from beneath the plantlet-bearing compost, holding the newspaper plug stationary. Permit the gutter-shaped length of moistened compost and its four plantlets to emerge from the unplugged end of the guttering and to settle unbroken into the formed channel. Repeat the operation, until the two moulds contain plantlets spaced 30cm apart, their postings in the two rows staggered in relation to each other. An overall result is a double-rank row of staggered dwarf-french-bean plantlets.

Gently press the surfaces of the two lengths of plantlet-bearing compost to a slightly lower level than that of the surrounding surface to create a rain-catchment area at the base of the plantlets' stems. Do so without touching and possibly damaging the plantlets' stems.

If the plantlets appear to be vulnerable to bird attack, protect them with fine-mesh wire-net arches until entanglement in the arches threatens.

Erect the prescribed stake-and-string ladder over the inserted plantlets, and be alert, subsequently, to guide the plantlets' tendrils onto the first rungs of the string ladder.

At the start of the June moon's third quarter, dress the immediate area of this May planting with a booster feed of 60g to the square metre of fish-blood-and-bone fertiliser. Subsequently, generally manage the dwarf-french-bean section, and harvest its crop, as prescribed for the seed-sown section.

36

At Tresillian, in the walled, kitchen garden, double-rank rows of dwarf-french-bean seeds are sown in June and July as well as in May to provide the longest possible season of harvest. The gardener who requires these three sowings must rethink and replan the use of the first-year single-dug bed, fundamentally restructuring the initial planting plan.

To achieve the three sowings, repeat the May sowing minus the fertiliser application at the start of the June moon's second quarter. Position the second double-rank row parallel to and 75cm from May's.

Repeat the June sowing minus the fertiliser application at the start of the July moon's second quarter. Position the third double-rank row parallel to and 75cm from June's.

Boost a June sowing with a feed of 60g to the square metre of fish-blood-and-bone fertiliser worked into the soil at the start of the July moon's third quarter. Boost a July sowing similarly, at the start of the August moon's third quarter.

10 continue to be ready, as the season develops and the plants increase in height, to guide errant tendrils onto the higher rungs

11 **at the start of the June moon's third quarter**, dress the 30cm width of the sown row with 60g to the square metre of fish-blood-and-bone fertiliser. Dress, also, the 20cm width that is between the row and the treadboard-covered temporary path. Gently work the dressing into

the soil. Use a hoe or the smallest cultivator to do so. Avoid making contact with the developing plantlets' stems

12 harvest the dwarf-french-bean pods when they are young and just short of being fully-formed. Take them every other day whether or not they are required for the kitchen. Pick from ground level up, for the reasons that are stated in *BROAD BEANS: harvesting*

13 harvest the older pods, towards the end of the harvest period, the moment that they become mature. Do not permit them to become yellow in colour, and bulbously large. At this stage, they have set seeds, and, in the main, are unfit for the kitchen

14 give away the unwanted surplus of young pods, or dispose of them off site. Do not compost them, if composting is practised. Do not place them in the bottom of the trench that awaits

TIP 34
➔ **See *RUNNER & CLIMBING FRENCH BEANS* for an instruction on producing potted bean plantlets and moving them from pot to soil. With dwarf french beans, the result can be a double rank row of plantlets inserted at the start of the second moon quarter in May (or June, if that is unavoidable), extending the Spring cabbage season by one month (see *CABBAGES*). Soil preparation and soil/plant management are as explained in this chapter.**

completion as a deep-trench bed in the Year 2 Area.
[**Consideration:** *the question Should seed-bearing vegetable matter be composted, by whatever means the responsible gardener favours? continues to be debated. R J Harris does not join in the debate, being in no doubt about the penalties likely to be paid when home-made compost is* incorporated in the top soil. "*Who wants foreign plants appearing among planned crops?*" *he asks,* "*for that is what is likely to happen when seed-bearing compost is applied. I have seen potato haulms appearing among developing marigolds, all because peelings bearing potato eyes were added to a compost bin at one time or another.*"].

DWARF FRENCH BEANS: after harvesting

Freeze the surplus of the de-podded dwarf french beans (see *BROAD BEANS: harvesting*) or donate them to friends. Also, as the plants become denuded of pods, cut their stems at ground level. Use secateurs or garden shears. Leave their roots in the ground, so that their additions of nitrogen remain where they can be of benefit. Then

1 replace each sheared stem with a catch-crop lettuce plantlet or with a Summer and Autumn Harvesting cabbage plantlet. Do so until the erstwhile double-rank row has become a double-rank row of lettuce plants, cabbage plants, or a mixture of the two. See *LETTUCES* and *CABBAGES*.
[**Consideration:** *this is not possible when Spring cabbages precede the beans*]

2 continue with the weekly weed-depressant, moisture-raising hoeing, no matter which plants the section continues to bear

3 harvest the lettuces and/or cabbages regularly, whether or not they are required by the kitchen. Donate unwanted lettuce to the waiting trench in the Year 2 Area. Include its root systems, since lettuce is an annual plant. Dispose of unwanted cabbage off site, as an extension of the sustained anti-clubroot measures

4 also progressively
— spread out to dry and then burn the dwarf-french-bean-plant vegetation on unused ground or an empty bed, turning its cold ashes into the ground's or the bed's surface

or

— destroy it off site

or

— place it in the waiting trench in the Year 2 Area

and complete the emptying of the dwarf-french-bean section by the **start of the September or October moon's third quarter** in time for the commencement of the second year of the Year 1 Area's four-year life span (which is also the second year of the garden-conversion project)

5 ensure, **by the start of the September moon's third quarter** in the second year of the garden conversion, that the Year 2 Area's single-dug bed is

installed. Ensure, also, that the accompanying Year 2 Area's deep-trench bed is completed by the same point in the month

6 **at the start of the October moon's fourth quarter** in the second year of the garden conversion, methodically rough turn the whole of the Year 1 Area's surface. Use a spade. Do so to the depth of the spade's blade. Make the surface look like that of a ploughed field. Ensure, in the process, that the single-dug bed's layer of animal manure is not brought to the surface. Ensure, also, that the resident broad-bean and dwarf-french-bean roots are not brought to the surface. If they are, return them to the depths of the soil.
[*Consideration: see* CABBAGES: after harvesting, *for an explanation of the influence of the moon's fourth quarter upon working the top soil's surface with a spade*]

7 retain *in situ* the marker sticks that indicate where the single-dug bed and the deep-trench bed of the Year 1 Area are located.
[*Consideration: at this juncture, the deep-trench bed has been as fully employed in vegetable production as has been the single-dug bed. It has produced one or other of the first-year, deep-trench-bed-specific vegetables that are listed in* ROTATION. *These are discussed later in this manual*]

8 do not feed the Year 1 Area's ex-dwarf-french-bean section at the close of the Area's first year. It bears no more crops until the following season. Then, together with the already dug-over remainder of the Area, it embarks upon the flower

cultivation that marks its second year in the R J Harris four-year, crop-rotation system

9 permit the Year 1 Area's highly broken surface to over-Winter unused and exposed to the elements in preparation for its second year's work. In R J Harris's crop rotation programme, this is the development and production of a harvest of annual flowers. See *POT MARIGOLDS*

10 note that the whole of the Year 1 Area's dwarf-french-bean production programme is repeated in the Year 2 Area if it is decided that this bean crop is to feature in the Year 2 Area during the first year of its four-year life span. Manage its cultivation during the second year in accordance with the present instruction

11 note that the catalogues of the reputable seedsmen offer information on the extensive

---

TIP 35
➜ **Remember to de-weed, manually, the Years 2, 3 and 4 Areas as the work in the Year 1 Area goes forward during the first year of the garden conversion. Aim at a monthly clearance, splitting the total task into many smaller divisions each offering an attainable goal. Seize the unoccupied moments for this essential chore. The reward after four years is a weed-free garden by cost-free, non-poisonous means, and one which is kept weed-free easily with the expenditure of little time.**

range of dwarf-french-bean types. Autumn is the time to secure them, for Winter provides the ideal moments in which to plan for what is to come and to make sowing/planting decisions. See *SUPPLIERS*

12 use Winter time to review the dwarf-french-bean data recorded in the card-index system. Note the by now many lessons to be learned from them. Apply the lessons.

PEAS: sowing

Mr Harris makes an almost continuous operation of pea production, designing it to result in harvesting which is interrupted only by the worst of Winter.

He sows seeds into the top soil at monthly intervals from March to July. He makes a final seed sowing in November, which aims at producing a very early Spring crop.

He uses a section of one of his single-dug beds in the first year of the bed's four-year life span. Inter-planted between the pea plants' rows are catch crops, which are either lettuce, spring onion or radish. His lettuce is managed as is described in *LETTUCES*.

Adopting the head gardener's methods in an adapted form — and, in the process, deliberately mis-applying one of his fundamental practices — proceed as follows

1 **during the Autumn of the first year of the garden conversion**, purchase one packet each of *Early Onward*, a first-early variety of pea, *Greenshaft*, a second-early, or mid-season, variety, and *Lincoln*, a maincrop variety. Expect to pay just over £1.00 per pack, each pack containing about 300 seeds (in 2006)

2 do not devote time to comparing the calculated returns from the pea harvest to the calculated kitchen/family/charitable needs, and then to coming to conclusions about

the size and, hence, effectiveness, of the area of the bed in which sowing takes place. Accept that, within the present context, the return from each harvest is, almost certainly, no more than just sufficient to meet the family's demands throughout the year

3 check that the three pea-seed types are dated as being suitable for sowing during the coming year. Make the check at the time of purchase

4 **at the start of the February moon's third quarter** in the first year of the garden's conversion, prepare for seed sowing the surface of the 100cm by 300cm section of the first-year, single-dug bed in the Year 1 Area. Do so, in all respects, as when the surface of the broad-bean section was prepared (see *BROAD BEANS: preparing to sow*)

5 note the very close proximity of maturing broad-bean plants as this and subsequent work goes forward. Ensure that no impact is made accidentally upon these plants and their bed section

6 dress the raked-level surface of the pea section with 115g to the square metre of fish-blood-and-bone fertiliser. Work it into the surface, gently. Use a rake

Apply to the *PEAS* chapter the section/bed/Year Area-labelling, anti-bird, anti-cat, anti-slug, tread-board, bed-edge-rehabilitation, top-soil-preparation and card-index-system disciplines that are prescribed in *BROAD BEANS* and *CABBAGES*. Apply, also, the recommended stones-gleaning and tools/materials-cleaning/storage practices.

Respond to the need, during the four-year garden conversion, and as opportunity offers, to extend and complete the general service paths, and to apply manual weed clearance to the undeveloped Year 2, 3 and 4 Areas.

These fundamentals are referred to only briefly throughout the remainder of *'R J Harris's Moon Gardening'*.

or a four-pronged cultivator. [**Consideration:** *see* BROAD BEANS: sowing *for an explanation of the link between the third and fourth quarters of the lunar cycle, Earth's water table and feeding the top soil with the fertiliser*]

7 **at the start of the March moon's second quarter**, peg a gently-taughtened garden line across the 100cm width of the 300cm-long pea section's sur-face. Locate the line 20cm away from the end of the section. [**Consideration:** BROAD BEANS: sowing *offers an account of the link between the*

moon's second quarter, the upward pressure of Earth's water table and the moisture content of the top soil]

8 excavate a 10cm-wide, 5cm-deep, 100cm-long, bed-width-long channel along the bed side of the garden line. Use the narrowest of garden hoes. Deposit the lifted soil to the bed side of the channel for the whole of the channel's length. [**Consideration:** *by these means, later, achieve relatively effortless reinstatement*]

9 remove the garden line. Insert a 30cm-long marker stick 15cm into the ground at one end of one side of the channel

10 repeat at the other end, with a 30cm-long marker stick

11 repeat on the other side of the channel, with two more 30cm-long marker sticks

12 cap the tops of the four inserted, end-of-channel marker sticks, for safety's sake

13 post thirteen *Early Onward* seeds 5cm apart along the nearest of the channel's two sides. Position the first seed 20cm from one end of the

TIP 36
➔ **For variety, sow the deliciously sweet sugar pea (also known as snap pea or mangetout). Its pods can be eaten as well, and both peas and pods are best young and raw. Grow it as described in this chapter, as an early, mid-season or main crop plant.**

> **37**
>
> The pea has been cultivated for human consumption since 10,000-to-9,000 BC. Where it began and what were its antecedents is not known. It is likely that it has been in use worldwide for most of that time — first, and for an extremely long period, in the dried form. It dries readily and easily on the plant, and then keeps almost indefinitely. It is only comparatively recently that it has been used as a fresh vegetable.
>
> In Britain, introduced — like so many of 'our' vegetables and fruits — by the Romans, it occupied a very important place in the national diet for centuries. This is not surprising: dried, it provides protein and a concentrate of essential vitamins and minerals.

channel. Position the last seed 20cm from the other end of the channel

14 post twelve seeds 5cm apart along the other side of the channel. Commence this other row 22cm-23cm from one end of the channel. Complete it 22cm-23cm from the other end of the channel

15 ensure that the postings of the twelve are staggered in relation to the postings of the thirteen

16 backfill the channel with the displaced soil. Use the back of a rake as a scoop, or gloved hands. Do either with care. Cover the seeds with a 5cm thickness of soil. In the process, do not dislodge the seeds from their postings

17 compress the sown, filled-in channel's top very gently and slightly with the back of a rake. In the process, create a shallow, rain-collecting depression along the length of the double-rank row. Position the depression comfortably between the two hidden, single rows forming the double-rank row

18 ensure that the four capped marker sticks are not dislodged in the process

19 insert a single row of five *Early Onward* seeds into the pea section's surface at a depth of 5cm and parallel to the sown double-rank row. Use a small dibber. Position the single row 20cm from the double-rank row. Space the five 10cm apart. Position the first seed 20cm from the 300cm-long side of the section.
[***Consideration:*** *this positioning ensures that the plantlets developing from the five can be reached with comfort from the tread boards. It also ensures that transplanting the resultant plantlets later on for row-repair purposes (should that be necessary) presents no difficulty caused by too-close sowing*]

20 insert a 30cm-long marker stick 15cm into the topsoil's

TIP 37
➔ **Mix two or three dwarf-french-bean seeds and/or plants into the monthly sowing/planting up of the pea section. The general management involved is the same as that of the pea. See *DWARF FRENCH BEANS: sowing.***

38

Determined to miss no opportunity to recreate Tresillian's Victorian heyday, head gardener R J Harris grows the old-fashioned asparagus pea — so called because of its slightly asparagus flavour. It is of the early 1800s, and has a pod which bears three elongated, crinkly-edged ribs. This is why it is known also as the winged pea. The whole of it is eaten when very young, for then the pod tastes as good as the pea.

The Victorians took it to their hearts, in the first place, because of its very attractive, brownish-red flower. It was grown in their flower gardens long before it found an additional home among the vegetables.

surface just before the beginning of the single, short row

21 insert a 30cm-long marker stick 15cm into the soil just beyond the end the row

22 cap the tops of the two marker sticks, for safety's sake

23 repeat the seed sowing each month, providing a total sowing programme of

— *Early Onward* for the March sowing

— *Early Onward* for the April sowing

— *Greenshaft* for the May sowing

— *Greenshaft* for the June sowing

— *Lincoln* for the July sowing

24 leave a 40cm-wide space between the monthly double-rank-row sowings. Locate the monthly single-row sowing, five seeds per month for row-repair purposes, in the centre of a 40cm-wide space and parallel to the adjacent double-rank row. [*Considerations: 1 — with the pea section thus fully stocked, one of Mr Harris's cardinal, fundamental rules is broken. This is that vegetable rows be aligned east to west, so that the top and the two sides of each row are bathed in sunlight throughout the day (see BROAD BEANS: preparing to crop rotate for a full explanation). The north-to-south alignment of the pea rows enables the sowing and management of all three of the pea types with ease. An east-to-west alignment of the rows within the proposed 100cm by 300cm dimensions of the pea section imposes inconvenience and less than comfortable gardening, as well as complexity in management; 2 — the minor*

TIP 38
➜ **Forgo the March sowing of** *Early Onward* **if the weather/soil conditions render it impossible to work in the garden. Forgo also the April sowing if Nature so dictates. In consequence, the pea section is prepared and fed with fish, blood and bone fertiliser in either March or April — whilst the total crop comprises mid-season peas sown in May and June, and maincrop peas sown in July. The moon quarters for the feeding and the sowing remain as stated.**

price paid for the broken rule is likely to be slightly later harvesting, due to the plants being in each other's shadow as the sun passes overhead. Balancing this, the lettuce catch crop (see later) benefits, being overshadowed by the pea plants. Lettuce prefers shade and shade's relative coolness. It does

not prosper in unremitting sunlight; 3 — the departure from approved practice demonstrates that rule breaking is an acceptable part of gardening provided that the gardener knows which rules are being broken and why, and what the outcome of the departure is likely to be].

PEAS: managing and harvesting

Do not fail to remove the protective, fine-mesh, wire-netting arches from the sown, double-rank rows and the single rows at weekly intervals with effect from the first sowing to facilitate the weekly hoeing of the pea section. To facilitate efficient hoeing

1 tie garden string between the pairs of end-of-double-rank-row marker sticks and end-of-single-rank-row marker sticks

2 run a hoe lightly just beneath the surface of the section's top soil between the double-rank and the single-rank sowings, and where sowings have not been made. Be guided where not to apply the hoe by the garden string tied above the rows of seeds sown only 5cm beneath the bed's surface

3 de-weed by hand the space between the sowings forming the double-rank rows

4 de-weed by hand immediately above the single-row sowings

5 de-weed by hand at the sides of each double-rank and single-rank sowing

6 leave the garden lines *in situ* until seedling growth. Then continue to leave them *in situ*

until there there is no risk of pea seedlings and plantlets being mistaken for weeds and extracted. After that, remove the garden strings and the marker sticks

7 replace the anti-bird wire-netting arches after each weekly hoeing. Continue the weekly hoeing until the end of the season

8 remove the protective arches permanently the moment that they threaten to hamper plantlet development

9 replace failed seeds within the rows with plantlets extracted from the single rows developed for row-repair purposes. See *BROAD BEANS: managing* for a

TIP 39
➔ **250cm is the length of the pea section that is taken up by the proposed five double-rank rows of *Early Onward*, *Greenshaft* and *Lincoln* plus the sowings for row-repair purposes, plus the in-between-rows of catch-crop lettuces. The unemployed 50cm width could be devoted to a bed-wide row of March-planted onion plantlets. See *ONIONS*.**

description of head gardener R J Harris's method of transplantation

10 secateur at ground level the unwanted plantlets within the single-rank rows, to make the ground available for catch-crop-lettuce purposes. Dispose of the secateured plantlets in the trench in the Year 2 Area. Leave their roots in the soil, for the sake of their nitrogen secretions. [**Consideration:** *donate the surplus pea seeds to the kitchen for use as food. See* DWARF FRENCH BEANS: sowing]

11 insert centrally-placed, single rows of three 30cm-spaced lettuce plantlets between the double-rank rows the moment that this space and lettuce plantlets become available (see *LETTUCES*). Harvest the lettuces the instant that they mature, to avoid lettuce seed setting. This is whether or not they are required by the kitchen. Replace each harvested lettuce with a lettuce plantlet, so that the ground is fully employed until the close of the season

12 maintain disciplined lettuce-row formation, so that subsequent hoeing can be carried out fully effectively and with the least amount of physical effort

13 equip each double-rank pea row with a supportive, garden-string 'ladder' once a full complement of twenty-five plantlets is present in the double-rank row. See *DWARF FRENCH BEANS:*

The head gardener uses pea plantlets to secure a four-week start in pea production. He combines their use with the first sowing of pea seeds in March or April (depending upon the prevailing weather/soil conditions).

He produces the plantlets in two ways: 1) thirteen assembled in a single row in compost in planting-out mode in a length of plastic roof guttering; 2) nine double-ranked and turf-based, in planting-out mode.

For a description of Mr Harris's plastic-guttering method see *Panel 35* in *DWARF-FRENCH BEANS: managing and harvesting.* Sow into the guttering in February. Insert the pea seeds into the compost 5cm apart and at a depth of 5cm. Transfer from the guttering to the pea section in March or April at the start of the moon's second quarter, positioning parallel single rows 10cm apart to form double-rank rows.

For his turf-based method

— at the beginning of February (no moon quarter is involved at this stage), extract from a field, or from an unimportant part of a lawn, a 30cm-square, 10cm-thick turf of grass

managing and harvesting for an instruction

14 be alert for when the plantlets, upward-reaching, need to be guided onto the garden-string ladder. Gently introduce their tendrils to the first rung

15 at **the start of the July moon's third quarter**, dress

— place the turf, upside down, upon a smooth baseboard of timber or rigid plastic sheeting. Glass is not advised, for safety reasons

— insert *Early Onward* seeds 5cm deep into the earth of the turf in two parallel, centred rows which are 10cm apart. Post the seeds 5cm from each other in the two rows

— post five seeds in one row, and four in the other. Stagger the seeds in the two rows in relation to each other.

— produce three of these sown, baseboarded turfs (or a greater number, if the bed dimensions proposed in the manual have been increased)

— lodge the sown, base-boarded turfs in a cold frame or a cold greenhouse to over-Winter. Balance good ventilation against cold infiltration in accordance with the weather's performance. In the case of the cold frame and the very small greenhouse, be ready with coverings such as sacks or fleece or redundant blankets to increase the night-time — and, if necessary, the day-time — protection. Weigh them down against the force of the wind.

Keep the turfs moist all of the time as the pea plantlets develop and reach the stage at which they bear at least four leaves

— **at the start of the March moon's second quarter,** (and/or coinciding with the first sowing of pea seeds in the Year 1 Area's pea section), transfer the sown turfs to the Area

— form a row of three joined-up, 30cm-square, 10cm deep indentations across the 100cm width of the pea section's surface parallel to the side of the section. Distance the row 10cm from the section's side. Sprinkle the resulting, surplus, top soil thinly onto bed surfaces throughout the garden

— slide the turfs from their baseboards into the indentations and press them home. Slightly depress them below the level of the surrounding ground to create a rain-catchment area at the base of the plantlets' stems. By these means, establish a double-rank row approximating in length to that of a row of sown seeds.

Manage the pea section generally, and harvest the crop, as described in this chapter.

the surface of the pea section with 60g to the square metre of fish-blood-and-bone fertiliser. Work the dressing carefully and gently into the soil. Use the narrowest of hoes. Avoid making contact with the plantlets' stems, to avoid inflicting damage.
[*Consideration: Mr Harris's practice at this point is, instead, to drench the surfaces of his pea*

beds with comfrey solution made up in the ratio of one part of comfrey stock to forty parts of water. He does so in the coolness of the end of the day, which is brought about by the lower ambient temperature. Also, his can has a medium rose, to reduce splashing onto the plants. This better practice becomes possible when comfrey plants are in the garden and available for conversion into stock, which can then be diluted]

16 begin to harvest the developing pea pods the moment that they are fully-formed and only just beginning to show bulges indicating early pea formation

17 take them, from this stage on, every other day whether or not they are required for the kitchen. Pick from ground level up, for the reasons stated in *BROAD BEANS: harvesting*

18 harvest the older pods, towards the end of the harvest period, the moment that they become mature. Do not permit them to become yellow in colour, and bulbously large. At this stage, they have set seeds, and, in the main, are of little use in the kitchen

19 give away the unwanted surplus of young pods, or dispose of them off site. Do not compost them, if composting is practised, for

40 Leave a special crop of peas to dry on the plant, suggests the head gardener, pick them, de-pod them, store them in paper bags for a few days to complete the drying and then store them in air-tight jars.

"Pre-soak them for twenty-four hours," says Mr Harris, "and then steam them as if just from the plant. Or put them, as they are, soaked or unsoaked, into stews and casseroles.

"Buy seed that is stated to be designed for this purpose," he advises. "Another way — and for a lower purchase price — is to get dry peas from the supermarket, and use them as seed. Be sure to get the unsplit kind. Split peas are damaged peas, and damaged peas cannot germinate."

fear of transfering seeds to the contents of the compost bin. Do not place them in the bottom of the trench that awaits completion as a deep-trench bed in the Year 2 Area, for the same reason.

PEAS: after harvesting

Freeze the surplus of de-podded peas (see *BROAD BEANS: harvesting* for a method description) or donate them to relatives, friends and neighbours. As the pea plants become denuded of pods, cut their stems at ground level. Use secateurs or garden shears. Leave their roots in the ground, so that their additions of nitrogen remain where they can be of benefit. Then

1 replace each cleared double-rank row with a row of 30cm-

separated, catch-crop lettuce plantlets. See *LETTUCES*

2 continue with the weekly weed-depressant, moisture-raising hoeing, no matter which plant or plants the pea section bears

3 remove the lettuces as they achieve maturity, whether or not required by the kitchen

4 donate unwanted lettuces to the waiting trench in the Year 2

Area. Include its root systems, since lettuce is an annual plant

5 progressively
— spread out to dry and then burn the redundant pea-plant vegetable matter on unused ground or an empty bed. Turn its cold ashes into the ground's or the bed's surface

or

— destroy it off site

or

— place it in the waiting trench in the Year 2 area

and complete the emptying of the pea section by the **start of the September or October moon's third quarter** to coincide with the commencement of the second year of the Year 1 Area's four-year life span (which is also the second year of the garden-conversion project)

6 ensure, **by the start of the September moon's third quarter**, that the Year 2 Area's single-dug bed is installed. Ensure also, if possible, that the accompanying Year 2 Area's deep-trench bed is completed by the same moon quarter

7 **at the start of the October moon's fourth quarter**, methodically rough turn the whole of the Year 1 Area's surface. Use a spade. Do so to the depth of the spade's blade. Make the surface look like that of a ploughed field. Ensure, in the process, that the single-dug bed's layer of animal manure is not brought to the surface. Ensure, also, that the resident broad-bean and pea

roots are not brought to the surface. If they are, return them to the depths of the soil.
[***Consideration:*** *see* CABBAGES: after harvesting, *for an explanation of the influence of the gravitational pull of the moon's fourth quarter upon working the top soil's surface with a spade*]

8 retain *in situ* the marker sticks that indicate where the single-dug bed and the deep-trench bed of the Year 1 Area are located

9 do not feed the Year 1 Area at the close of the area's first year. It bears no more crops until the following season. Then, it embarks upon the flower cultivation that marks its second year in head gardener R J Harris's four-year, crop-rotation system

10 permit the area's highly broken surface to over-Winter unused and exposed to the elements in

---

TIP 40
➜ The March- and April-sown early peas require at least twelve weeks to develop from the moment of sowing to the first harvesting. The May- and June-sown mid-season peas require fourteen to sixteen weeks, as do the July-sown maincrop peas. If March's weather/soil conditions are unsuitable for gardening, miss out the March sowing and its associated activities. Sow for the first time in April at the start of the April moon's second quarter — preceded by topsoil feeding with fish, blood and bone at the start of the previous moon's third quarter.

preparation for its second year's work

11 excavate the trench in the Year 3 Area that is to be developed into a deep-trench bed. Equip it with a lid, for safety's sake

12 at **the start of the November moon's second quarter** in the second year of the garden conversion, sow one 300cm-long double-rank row of *Lincoln* maincrop-pea seeds in the 100cm-deep by 300cm long section of the first-year, single-dug bed in the Year 2 Area. Do so as when the seeds were sown in the Year 1 Area. Site the double-rank row 20cm from, and parallel to, one of the section's two long sides, so that it has an east-to-west alignment

13 forgo the November sowing if the ground is waterlogged or frozen. Do so in line with Mr Harris's policy of avoiding horticultural problems, not trying to solve them

14 note that the dwarf pea is especially suitable for November sowing. R J Harris recommends *Little Marvel*. It is about 45cm high, thus offering the least resistance to Winter's winds

15 ensure that its supportive garden-canes-and-string rig is especially strong, in order to be able to resist Winter's driving winds and rains

16 begin to harvest the over-wintered *Little Marvel* in early Spring — in the second year of the garden conversion — the moment that it becomes available

17 empty the section of denuded pea-plant stems at the close of harvesting. Leave the stems' roots in the ground to retain and conserve their nitrogenous secretions

18 dispose of the pea-plant vegetable matter as described earlier, or deposit it in the trench for the Year 3 Area's deep-trench bed

19 note that when main-crop pea production is extended to the 100cm by 300cm section of the Year 2 Area's first-year, single-dug bed to achieve a Spring harvest, the section cannot support early, mid-season and maincrop pea cultivation. The Spring pea harvest renders the ground in which it develops unsuitable for a follow-on pea crop

20 forgo Spring-delivered *Lincoln* maincrop peas or *Little Marvel* dwarf peas in the first year of the Year 2 Area if it is decided that the early, mid-season and maincrop pea programme is to be repeated in that Area

TIP 41
➔ **The unemployed 50cm width of the pea section could be taken up by catch-crop lettuces instead of the single row of onions that is suggested earlier. The wisdom of developing onions where air movement is restricted — as it could be by maturing pea plants — is a matter for debate. Onions can be vulnerable where the breezes that disperse pests and diseases are absent.**

21 note that the catalogues of the reputable seedsmen offer useful information on the extensive range of pea types. Autumn, at the end of the first year of the garden conversion is the time to secure them, for the Winter that follows provides the ideal moments in which to plan for what is to come and to make sowing/planting decisions. See *SUPPLIERS*

22 use the Winter, also, to review the pea data recorded in the card-index system. Note the by now many lessons to be learned from them. Apply the lessons.

SINGLE-DUG BED

When newly created in the Autumn in one of the Tresillian walled, kitchen garden's four Areas, two types of bed commence a new four-year, crop-rotation programme for head gardener R J Harris. The single-dug bed is one of the two. The other is the deep-trench bed (to which there can be an alternative for those to whom digging metre-deep trenches does not come easily).

Each bed bears a different suite of compatible crops in each year of its four-year life cycle. In the Autumn of its fourth year it is exhausted and is then renewed and sets out upon a fresh four-year cycle.

Use the single-dug bed in its first year for the production of the head gardener's quality of broad beans, broccoli, cabbages, cauliflowers, dwarf french beans, kale, kohlrabi, onions, peas, savoys, spinach, swedes and turnips.

Use it in its second year, together with the deep-trench bed, for annual flowers and flowers the tubers and corms of which are lifted annually.

Use it in its third year for pot-atoes, and in its fourth year for beet-roots, carrots, celery, parsley and parsnips.

With the Year 1 Area fully out-lined prior to the commencement of the opening year of the four-year garden conversion project (see *Diag-ram 1*, page 14), and, ideally, with that Area's permanent service paths laid down (see *BROAD BEANS; pre-paring to crop rotate*), create and manage the Tresillian single-dug bed in the following way

1 re-read *BROAD BEANS: preparing to crop rotate*

2 plan a work programme that ensures the completion of the single-dug bed by no later than **the end of a chosen September's third moon quarter**.
[*Consideration: this is the optimum time for manure to be newly present in the ground. It is at this moment — with the moon-released water table fallen and still falling — that the ground is at its most receptive to the manure's nutrients and to those of any other added, organic fertiliser*]

TIP 42
➔ **The garden rake can be a dangerous tool. It has been responsible for not a few broken foreheads. When parking it against a vertical surface, ensure that its tines are not upon the ground. There, trodden upon accidentally, they can cause the long handle to leap out-wards unexpectedly and with force, to inflict a painful blow.**

41

Single-dug and deep-trench bed making, like all of the works carried out in Tresillian's walled, kitchen garden in Cornwall, closes with a return of tools and materials to their permanent homes. For head gardener R J Harris, a never-neglected element of this is the removal of earth from all aids, followed by a thorough washing and drying of all metal and timber parts. The timber and metal are then thoroughly dried and the metal parts are well oiled. The tools are then returned to their appointed places inside the kitchen garden's potting shed.

"Neatness and tidiness is all-important in good gardening," Mr Harris comments.

3 **at a selected moment in the chosen September** (dictated by the work programme), dig Trench 1 across the 300cm width of the space that has been earmarked for the Year 1 Area's single-dug bed. Use a sharpened, clean, garden spade. Trench 1 is a spade wide and a spade deep. It is positioned immediately alongside the permanent path that skirts and demarks the width of the single-trench-bed-to-be

4 place the top soil removed from Trench 1 into a wheelbarrow positioned on the permanent path and moved along the path as the digging procedes

5 separate from the top soil, as it is removed

— the uprooted annual weeds that are not in seed and their roots, and grass turfs. Place these in a receptacle for use in the trench at a later stage

— the annual weeds that are in seed and their roots, the perennial weeds and their roots and rubbish. Place these in a receptacle for removal, later, from site and disposal according to the head gardener's policy on the disposal of weeds

— the large stones and other hard, large materials that arise. Place these in a receptacle for storage, later, for specific uses in connection with other garden-development projects

6 wheel the barrow each time it is filled to the other end of the 330cm-long, designated bed area. Empty the barrow just beyond the positioned garden line (see *Diagram 1*, page 14). Do not create a single, increasingly large heap of top soil. Space out the deposited barrow loads along the length of the positioned garden line. [**Consideration:** *by these means, the discharged earth is positioned conveniently in small heaps where it can be recovered with least effort when the final trench is reinstated*]

7 brush accidentally-scattered earth from the surface of the permanent path into adjacent, newly-dug Trench 1

8 loosen the earth at the bottom of completed Trench 1 with a garden fork, to aid drainage when the bed is complete

9 distribute evenly along the bottom of Trench 1 the segregated grass turfs, turned upside down, and the

segregated annual weeds that are not in seed, plus their roots

10 fill Trench 1 with tamped-down, at-least-two-years-old animal manure. Use farmyard manure, if possible. Use horse manure if the other is not available

11 dig Trench 2. In doing so

— make it exactly like Trench 1

— position it immediately alongside manure-filled Trench 1

— conserve or dispose of the weed, grass, stones and other hard material as when digging Trench 1

— deposit the edited dug-out earth from Trench 2 on top of the farmyard manure in Trench 1. [*Consideration: do this as precisely as possible. The earth above manure-filled Trench 1 delineates one end of what is to be a single-dug bed with a raised surface*]

— loosen Trench 2's base with a garden fork, to aid drainage

— place the permissible weeds and grass in Trench 2, as before

12 fill Trench 2 with tamped-down, composted manure

13 cover the manure with the editied soil that results from digging Trench 3 immediately alongside Trench 2 and like it in all respects

14 install in this way as many manure-filled, covered trenches as are required to

almost complete the 300cm by 330cm single-dug bed

15 place the heaped soil from Trench 1 on top of the last of the manure-filled trenches, to complete the bed. The bed has a very rough, broken, spade-created surface, which is raised some 17cm above the level of the adjacent permanent path surfaces and of the surrounding ground.
[*Consideration: if possible, use R J Harris's preferred tool for earth moving when undertaking the final trench-filling operation. It is the shovel (not garden spade) with the unusually long, almost straight handle — the length of which is tailored to the gardener's height — and the pointed blade. The long handle calls for less stooping than does the handle of the spade. It also affords leverage with reduced effort. As well, its pointed blade penetrates heaped or loosened earth with less effort on the gardener's part than does the squared-off blade of the garden spade. This has largely and unjustifiably usurped the traditional shovel in the United Kingdom (although not in the U S A, to which it was taken by the founding fathers, and has never been displaced in gardeners' esteem)*]

16 note that skirting the boundary-marking garden line is a 60cm width of unprocessed ground. This is for use as a temporary path separating the single-dug bed from the site of the deep-trench-bed-to-be. See *Diagram 1*, page 14

42

'The surface of the newly-completed, single-dug bed," points out the Cornish head gardener, "is in a highly broken-up state, just as when a farmer ploughs a field.

"This is thanks to its being prepared with a spade, not a fork."

The bed, he explains, goes through Winter in that condition.

"The frost and the elements get down into its surface, break it up, moisten it, introduce air into it and, by those means, generally increase its fertility. They also kill off many of the undesirables that have been exposed by the digging.

"Those, that is, that have been missed by the robin that will have been working alongside you from the moment you struck spade or shovel into soil.".

A year after completion, and having produced its first crops, the single-dug bed is cleaned of all growth and then turned over with a spade and left in a rough condition for Winter and the birds to do their work once again.

"Note," says Mr Harris, "turned over with a spade, not a fork. And to the full length of the spade's blade. The aim, once again, is a surface with the finish of a ploughed field."

The cleaning and the spade turning are repeated at the end of each of the bed's next two years. At the end of the following year, the fourth and final year, the bed is renewed and receives its first ploughed-field finish as a part of that process.

43

If R J Harris is fortunate, the location at Tresillian of any of his two basic beds — decided by his management of his four-year, crop-rotation system — receives day-long sunshine.
If he is not, the shadow from one of the kitchen garden's four, 4m-high walls falls upon it for a part of the day.

"I take what comes and make the best of it," he comments. "After all, reduced sunshine can offer the opportunity of a slightly later crop, depending upon what kind of crop it is, of course.

"Overall, this can bring a usefully extended cropping period.

"The one location I say 'No' to, whatever the overall plan dictates, is situated immediately beneath the north-facing wall. That is an almost entirely sunless area."

17 complete the single-dug bed by **the start of the chosen September moon's fourth quarter**

18 reinstate the boundary-marking garden line, if that is necessary

19 'angle', slightly, the four edges of the bed's raised surface with the flat of the spade's or the shovel's blade. Do so as neatly and as precisely as possible

20 permit the single-dug bed to grow weeds during each of its winters. Uproot these methodically in the Spring, at the seedling/plantlet stage. Do so manually or by hoeing or by both methods

21 remove the uprooted weeds from the bed's surface, and dispose of them securely off site.
[***Consideration:*** *the reward for this painstaking effort with long-term aims is top soil in which the above-the-surface weed population steadily reduces as the seasons pass*]

22 complete the renewal of the single-dug bed by **the start of the September moon's fourth quarter** in its site's fifth year (or ninth year or thirteen year, etc) to make it ready to begin a fresh four-year, crop-rotation cycle

23 record each stage of the single-dug-bed creation in the card-index system

24 apply this instruction as the garden conversion proceeds. Record in the system the life history of each of the four new Year Areas

25 note that the ultimate, overall result is that bed creation (single-dug and deep-trench) is an annual event as four-year-old beds, exhausted, are renewed

26 note that the bed renewals take place without change of bed location.

DEEP-TRENCH BED

Use R J Harris's deep-trench bed in its first year for the production of runner beans, climbing french beans, sweet peas, marrows, courgettes and pumpkins.

Use it in its second year, together with the single-dug bed, for the production of annual flowers and flowers the tubers and corms of which are lifted annually.

Use it in its third year, again together with the single-dug bed, for potato production, and in its fourth and final year — together with the other bed — for the production of root crops such as beetroot, carrot and parsnip, and for celery and parsley.

To create the head gardener's deep-trench bed

1 decide where to dispose of, or what to do with, excavated and removed-from-site sub soil and other valueless, excavated materials

2 re-read *BROAD BEANS: preparing to crop rotate*

3 plan a programme of work which ensures the completion of the deep-trench bed at the earliest convenient moment in the Year 1 Area's first year (and in the first year of the garden-conversion programme). Ideally, make that moment **the commencement of a chosen third moon quarter**. As a result, win two advantages

— the new bed has the longest possible period, before it is used, in which to settle and to develop a slightly sunken, rain-collecting surface

— the new bed's newly-installed component materials are under the influence of the whole of a period of falling water table thanks to a weakening moon. This encourages the dissemination of their nutrients throughout the bed, readying it for the coming Spring's sowings and/or plantings out

4 **at a selected moment in the chosen month** (dictated by the work programme), spread protective sheets upon the surfaces of the sections of permanent path that skirt three sides of the outlined position of the deep-trench-bed-to-be (see *Diagram 1*, page 14)

5 ensure that the garden line delineating the fourth side of the deep-trench-to-be is correctly in position

6 loosen the top soil of the 300cm by 100cm surface of the deep-trench-to-be. Use a garden fork to the full extent of its tines

---

44

The Autumn months are notable in the Victorian walled, kitchen garden at Tresillian for the presence of men digging trenches of daunting size in readiness for deep-trench-bed formation. Each one-metre deep and one-metre-wide by any required-length-up-to-15m excavation is completed in the traditional English style, with fork and long-handled shovel, and with prodigious physical effort being called upon as well as the deployment of the rare skill that comes only from years of practice following rigorous apprenticeship training. In contrast, elsewhere in the world, hired-by-the-hour mechanical diggers stand in for men's muscle power — dealing, it must be acknowledged, with ground conditions the unfriendliness of which is not known in the United Kingdom.

The head gardener acknowledges that his choice of gardening method cannot be the choice of some weekend gardeners, and offers an alternative, less demanding design of bed. "Simply," he suggests, "make a mini deep-trench bed."

To achieve this, do as prescribed in this instruction, except

— make the trench 50cm deep, not one metre

— make the inserted layers each 9cm in thickness, not 18cm.

If the prescribed range of vegetable materials is not available

— line the bottom of the 50cm-deep trench with a 10cm thickness of waste-vegetable matter, rotted or not

— follow this with a 10cm thickness of the edited top soil

— follow this with a 20cm-thick 'sponge' made of a compacted layer of weed-killer/poison-free lawn mowings of any age from fresh to blackened. Instead, use a compacted layer of weed-killer/poison-free lawn mowings of any age from fresh to blackened and mixed with fresh leaves first shredded by a shredder or by being spread on the lawn and then run over, repeatedly, by a lawn mower.

Then fill the trench to the level of the surrounding ground with the edited top soil, and cap the filled trench with a final 20cm-thick layer of top soil to produce the required elevated bed surface.

"Expect no more than ordinary results from this half-measure deep-trench bed," the head gardener warns, "but it is far, far better than having nothing of the kind."

45

The power house of the R J Harris deep-trench bed — the element that generates its unfailingly excellent results — is the sponge that is formed by the bed's layered content of soil, vegetable-matter and animal manure. This not only provides nutrients. It also catches and retains the moisture that is directed to it from above by the bed's rain-catching, sunken surface and from below by the moisture concentration created by the upward pressure of the moon-raised water table.

This is a bed which requires no watering, even in severe drought conditions (although adding water to it harms neither it nor the plants for which it plays host).

7 lift the top soil and transfer it to the covered permanent path. Deposit it in manageable, small heaps. For reduced physical effort, do so with the kind of long-handled, pointed shovel that Mr Harris prefers for this kind of earth removal. Use a garden spade instead, if a shovel is not available. Overall, segregate this valuable medium for re-use at a later stage, so that it remains untainted by other, poorer, excavated material.
[*Consideration: top soil is darker in colour than, and clearly of different structure from, the sub soil beneath it. In most gardens, top soil is at least one spade blade's length in depth*]

8 edit the top soil as it is lifted onto the protective sheets, so that grass turfs and annual weeds not in seed, plus their roots, are separated from it. Place this waste-vegetable material in a receptacle, for use at a later stage

9 separate out the annual weeds that are in seed, with their roots, the perennial weeds and their roots, and rubbish. Remove this material from site and dispose of it securely

10 separate out the large stones and hard matter. Segregate and store this material for use in connection with other garden projects

11 loosen the revealed sub soil. Do so with a garden fork. Then use a garden shovel or spade to transfer the sub soil to a wheelbarrow. Separate out the large stones and other hard, large materials in the process. Store this material for use in connection with other garden projects. Empty the wheelbarrow each time it is full at the pre-designated storage/disposal point for sub soil and rubbish

12 continue until the trench is precisely 100cm wide, 100cm deep and 300cm long.

TIP 43
➔ The head gardener counsels: "Do not try to fight Nature when excavating the trench for the deep-trench bed. If, when the top soil has been removed, only compacted industrial deposits or sheer clay or rock is found, make do with the mini deep-trench bed. Its results are no match for the major bed's results, but it is much to be preferred to no preparation whatsoever."

46

It is worth noting that, sometimes, the head gardener places an additional bed at least two metres away from the nearest established bed should it be decided to have two or more adjacent developments of tall plants. This avoids the awkwardness that would be created otherwise by the tall plants in the one blocking out the sunlight from the plants in the other. Of course, he is fortunate in being in command of sufficient ground area for this ideal to be attainable. It is not attainable by the gardener who applies this manual's proposed Year Area dimensions without any modification.

Luckily, the awkwardness can be avoided.

The recommended east-west bed and row orientation solves the problem — and that is despite the fact that the prescribed two beds per Year Area are separated by a temporary path that is a mere 60cm wide (see *Diagram 1*, page 14).

Routinely, to underline further the many differences between R J Harris's professional world and that of most hobby gardeners, each of Tresillian's many deep-trench beds is 15m long, not the 3m prescribed in this instruction. This matches the 15m width of each of kitchen garden's four 34m-long Year Areas.

"It is also made possible," Mr Harris concedes, "by the size and skills of the labour force that is at my disposal," .

14 cover the bottom of the trench with the earmarked seedless annual weeds and any other seedless vegetation that has arisen. Position the grass turfs upside down

15 place over the added waste vegetation a 36cm thickness of the segregated top soil. [*Considerations:* **1** — *the deep-trench bed under discussion is the first to be installed in the converted garden. For that reason its trench cannot, and does not, contain a season's accumulation of acceptable (and rotted) waste vegetable matter. Were it any of the beds created subsequently in the converted garden, its trench, excavated approximately one year prior to being turned into a deep-trench bed, would*

Ensure that its sides are vertical

13 stand in the trench and loosen its base evenly with a garden fork.
[*Consideration: a hard pan at the bottom of the deep-trench bed reduces drainage and thus creates a collection point for water. Plants cannot thrive when their roots encounter such conditions. The loosening creates drainage*]

TIP 44
➔ **Creating the deep-trench bed sometimes produces a surplus of top soil. Recycle this invaluable resource into the garden, over the widest possible area of garden-bed surface. Scatter it as thinly as possible, so that — importantly to the established plants — it increases hardly at all the thickness of top soil above the established root systems.**

*contain such material to a thickness of at least 18cm. In this event, the thickness of top soil would be 18cm; **2** — when bin-composted vegetable matter at any stage of composting is available (which, for Mr Harris, it is not, in view of his opinion of the value of home-made vegetable compost), an 18cm thickness of it can be used in the bottom of the Year 1 Area trench, above the initial thickness of weed/turf material. In this event, it is followed by an 18cm thickness of the segregated top soil]*

16 follow the top soil with an 18cm thickness of old straw. Failing old straw, use fresh straw. If straw of any kind is not available, omit it. Increase slightly the thickness of each of the other materials.
*[**Consideration:** old straw is best. This is the straw that the animals have lain on, but which has not been turned into farmyard manure. Being old and once-used, it has lost the traces of the farmer's chemicals that most probably once contaminated it. The head gardener is adamant that the chemicals that the farmer uses must be kept out of the garden's soil]*

17 follow the straw with an 18cm thickness of fully-composted — ie, at least two-years-old — farmyard or horse manure

18 follow this with an 18cm thickness of the segregated top-soil

19 follow this with an 18cm thickness of fully-composted

— ie, at least two-years-old
— leaf mould

20 finish — using a garden shovel or spade — with an 18cm thickness of the segregated top soil

21 note that this creates a bed surface that is raised above the surrounding ground level by some 25cm

22 note that the surface, being shovel- or spade-created, has the appearance and texture of a ploughed field. Do nothing to change this condition

23 flatten and thus tidy the new bed's four sides with the flat of the shovel's or spade's blade

24 gather in, shake clean onto the bed's surface and fold the protective sheets. Return them to store

25 reinstate the boundary-marking garden line, if that is necessary. Note that the 60cm width of the temporary path separating the completed double-dug bed from the single-dug bed is now clearly delineated

TIP 45
➔ **R J Harris's two styles of bed are best completed in September. Circumstances dictating, October or November instead are acceptable. October, probably, is the better choice. As well as being, usually, the year's final month of gardener-friendly conditions, it is also when — in the main — the ground is empty of crops and, hence, is available to be worked upon without complications.**

26 permit the bed to over-Winter unused. Note that as the Winter months pass, the surface of the bed (whether major- or mini-style) sinks and creates a rain-collecting depression

27 permit the bed's surface to develop weeds throughout Winter. In Spring, uproot the weeds before they set seeds. Dispose of them securely off site

28 excavate the trench for a deep-trench bed in the Year 2 Area as soon as possible after completing the Year 1 Area's deep-trench bed. By these means move without delay to obviate the awkwardness created by a lack of a waste-vegetable-matter accumulator during the first year of the Year 1 Area's four-year life span. Obviate, consequently, the lack of material for the initial vegetable layer within the Year 2 Area's deep-trench bed

29 record each stage of the deep-trench-bed's creation in the card-index system

30 apply this instruction as the garden conversion proceeds. Embrace in it each of the four new Year Areas, one after the other

31 note that, as an ultimate, overall result, bed creation (single-dug and deep-trench) is an annual event as four-year-old beds, exhausted, are renewed

32 note that the renewal takes place without change of bed location

33 note that with all four deep-trench beds completed and in production, the arising waste-vegetable matter is collected not in a waiting, empty trench, for such a trench does not exist. Instead, it is collected in sacks and is held in storage until the next renewal of a deep-trench bed.

RUNNER & CLIMBING FRENCH BEANS: preparing to plant and sow

For runner- and climbing-french-bean production, head gardener R J Harris uses a section for each bean of a Tresillian deep-trench bed which is in the first year of its four-year life span. This is when the nutrients of the metre-deep, layered 'sponge' beneath its surface are untapped. It is also when the 'sponge' has maximum ability to catch and to retain the moisture that descends to it from the ground's surface and accrues to it as a result of the pressure exerted by the rise of the moon-attracted water table. The 'sponge' holds the moisture in readiness for the downward striking roots of the bean plants.

Accompanying the two kinds of bean in the first-year, deep-trench bed are marrows, courgettes, pumpkins and sweet peas. Each is in its own, adjacent section of the special bed, the 100cm width of which facilitates all stages of management without need to set foot or place hand — invariably harmfully — upon its surface.

Whilst R J Harris opts for the major deep-trench bed for climbing-bean production, it must be noted that his mini deep-trench bed is an alternative medium. Equally, it must be noted that the

Apply to the *RUNNER &
CLIMBING FRENCH BEANS*
chapter the
section/bed/Year Area-
labelling, anti-bird, anti-cat,
anti-slug, tread-board, bed-
edge-rehabilitation, top-soil-
preparation and card-index-
system disciplines that are
prescribed in *BROAD
BEANS* and *CABBAGES*.
Apply, also, the recom-
mended stones-gleaning and
tools/ materials-
cleaning/storage practices.

Respond to the need,
during the four-year garden
conversion, and as
opportunity offers, to extend
and complete the general
service paths, and to apply
manual weed clearance to
the undeveloped Year 2, 3
and 4 Areas.

These fundamentals are
referred to only briefly
throughout the remainder of
'R J Harris's Moon
Gardening'.

results of using the mini bed do not
equal those of using the maxi bed.

Taking the head gardener's
example as a guide — and, to
simplify the arising instructional
text, focusing upon the climbing
bean (for which read runner or
climbing french) — proceed as follows

1 create the head gardener's
deep-trench bed in its outlined
site in the Year 1 Area (see
Diagram 1, page 14, and *DEEP-
TRENCH BED*). Complete the
bed by **the end of the
September, October or
November moon's third**

quarter — depending upon
weather/soil conditions

2 earmark a 1m-long length of
the bed's surface at one end of
its 3m-long length for the
development of eight climbing-
bean plants growing upon a
wigwam made of eight garden
canes. The wigwam is
constructed above the 1m-
square bed section.
[***Considerations: 1*** *— the
length of the 1m-square section
is increased when a larger
number of producing plants is
required. In this event, an
elongated rig in the traditional
style is used in place of a
wigwam, with plants spaced
30cm apart along each of its
two sides. For instructional
purposes, this chapter focuses
upon the management of a
wigwam;* **2** *— having a height of
about 3m, both wigwam and rig
underscore the need at the
garden-conversion planning
stage to cater for protection from
high winds in order to reduce
the risk of a blowing-over of
what, in due course, is a
heavily-laden supportive,
garden-cane structure;* **3** *—
associated with this is the truth
that the bean's blossom is more
effective when not exposed to
the wind. This is because the
pollinators tend to avoid wind-
tossed blossom. Without
pollination, there can be no
beans;* **4** *— when cultivating a
wigwam of climbing french
beans as well as a wigwam of
runner beans, site the second
wigwam alongside the first,
leaving one third of the deep-
trench bed's surface available
for other employment*]

3 leave the newly-created, deep-
trench bed to over-Winter
undisturbed, its spade-
roughened surface fully

47

Thanks to regular seed collection during many years, an annual cropper in the walled kitchen garden at Tresillian is a runner bean the seeds of which were given to Mr Harris in the 1950s, when he was an apprentice.

It was a runner bean without a name, presented to him by the head gardener who was his tutor and mentor in horticulture.

Much later, as a qualified and senior practitioner, Mr Harris sent a sample of this runner bean's seeds to the Henry Doubleday Seed Library. This is the body that was set up with neither Government aid nor encouragement to try to maintain Britain's native stock of plants. It does so, currently, in the teeth of edicts from Brussels — where, clearly, few understand that plant diversity is essential to mankind's survival.

At the Library, the nameless seed was dubbed *John's Best*, after R J Harris.

"Probably," says the head gardener, "it was a cross between Dobie's *Yardstick* and the same firm's *Long As Your Arm*. These were two well-known varieties produced by a company which no longer exists, except in the memories of today's older gardeners."

The bean is longer than a man's forearm when ready for picking (thanks, no doubt, to the *Long As Your Arm* genes). Despite that, attests R J Harris, when harvested before maturity, it has a full flavour and is neither stringy nor tough.

exposed to the rain and to the frosts

4 at the earliest moment in the New Year, procure one packet of the seeds of *Enorma*, which contains approximately 45 seeds for about £01.70 (in 2006). This is an R J Harris favourite because of its long, slender pods, good flavour and heavy cropping potential. It freezes well and easily, and is one of a range of excellent runner-bean types

5 procure also one packet of *Blauhilde* if it is planned to grow the two types of climbing bean. The *Blauhilde* is a stringless, blue, climbing french bean. It turns green on being cooked, and freezes well. It is retailed as being especially resistant to virus diseases, and costs about £01.50 for about 40 seeds (in 2006)

6 check to ensure that the seeds are dated as being suitable for sowing during the coming few months. Make the check at the time and place of purchase

7 **in early April in the first year of the garden conversion** (and of the first year of the Year 1 Area's four-year life span; note that there is no moon-quarter involvement at this stage), loosely and completely fill an 8cm pot — or a pot of a similarly small size — with John Innes No 2 potting compost. Omit drainage stones in the base of the pot. [**Consideration:** *in so small a pot, a drainage aid is unnecessary*]

8 brush a hand across the top of the pot to level off the compost

9 tap the base of the pot, gently yet firmly, two or three times,

upon the workbench top. Settle the surface of the compost by these means, until it is level with the base of the rim that is moulded into the top of the pot

10 add more compost to compensate for under-filling. Consolidate this in the same way

11 gently and without pause, add water to the compost's surface until it threatens to overspill from the top of the pot. Use a can fitted with a fine rose. Do not disturb the surface of the compost as the water is added.
[**Consideration:** *it may be accepted that the measure of water that is added in this way is the quantity that is required for the correct moistening (i e, not over- or under-moistening) of the amount of compost that is contained in the small pot*]

12 produce twelve compost-filled, watered pots in this way.
[**Consideration:** *the number of pots prepared is decided by the size of the eventual planting out of climbing-bean plantlets and the gardener's judgement of his/her ability to raise potted plantlets successfully. Twelve is suggested as a probably sensible total for an eight-plant wigwam, and for most gardeners and kitchen gardens*]

13 group together the twelve pots upon the workbench top. Cover them with a folded newspaper. Place alongside them the bean seeds that are to be sown in them. Leave covered pots and seeds

undisturbed for at least twenty-four hours.
[**Considerations: 1** — *this enables the compost to become comprehensively moistened. It also enables compost and seeds to arrive at a common ambient temperature. This encourages seed germination;* **2** — *the newspaper reduces evaporation. It is folded to increase its rigidity and to reduce its area to one that is slightly larger than the total area of the tops of the grouped pots. Newspaper is cheaper, safer and more convenient than a sheet of glass. Unlike condensation-dripping glass, it does not encourage any kind of undesirable condition of the compost's surface*]

14 make a 3cm-deep hole in the centre of each pot's compost after the minimal twenty-four hour pause. Use an appropriately-sized dibber or improvised equivalent

15 drop a seed — runner bean or climbing french bean — into each hole. Close the compost over it

---

TIP 46
➔ **The deep-trench bed needs no watering except in the very driest of conditions — which are still rare (2006). At such times, use one part of comfrey stock to 80 parts of water once or twice per week. Apply it the safe way: in the cool conditions of the very end of the day or the early evening through a fine rose, and gently. Apply it, also, at ground level, to avoid splashing and thus scorching the stems and leaves of the affected plants.**

16 station the sown pots in a cold frame, cold greenhouse or conservatory until plantlets 7cm to 8cm high have developed

17 keep the compost in the sown pots moist all of the time. Water with a can fitted with a fine rose. Apply the water gently, to leave the compost surface undisturbed [**Consideration:** *over-watering is to be avoided. It is a greater fault than slight under-watering. Wait for the compost's surface to show faint traces of dusty dryness before applying water. Then fill until the water threatens to flow over the rim of the pot*]

18 protect the cold frame and the small cold greenhouse by night if frost threatens. Do so with fleece or redundant blankets

19 turn the pots daily if they are placed on a conservatory window sill, to correct the plantlets' tendency to develop distorted stems by leaning towards and stretching up to the light

20 **at the start of the April moon's fourth quarter**, empty the surface of the bean-section-to-be of its Winter/Spring-developed weed growth. Use a garden fork to do so. Destroy or dispose of the arising weed growth securely off site

21 prepare the section's surface for seed sowing. Do so, in all respects, as when the surface of the broad-bean section was prepared for seed sowing (see *BROAD BEANS: preparing to sow*)

22 note the very close proximity of maturing broad-bean plants as this and subsequent work goes forward. Ensure that no impact is made accidentally upon these plants and their bed section

23 dress the raked-level surface of the bean section-to-be with 115g to the square metre of fish-blood-and-bone fertiliser. Work it in lightly. Use a rake

24 maintain as far as is possible the rain-collecting depression that is a feature of the deep-trench bed. [**Consideration:** *the depression is caused by bed settlement during the Winter months. Retaining it enhances the bed's ability to remain moisture-charged in the least rainy of weather conditions*].

RUNNER & CLIMBING FRENCH BEANS: planting out and sowing

At the start of the May moon's second quarter, transfer the compost-filled pots with their developing plantlets to an earth surface. Gently water the compost. Do so as before. Then park the watered pots for a few hours in a sheltered, protected place so that their compost can become comprehensively moistened. This is essential. Well-moistened compost playing host to a plantlet's roots slides effortlessly and without breakage from the pot in which it is contained,

48

The head gardener is one of the few horticulturists who take advantage of the seldom-considered fact that the runner bean is a perennial plant.

At the end of each season, after harvesting, he cuts a selection of the beans' stems at ground level and carefully digs out the stemless roots.

From these he chooses a few of the most robust-looking, washes them clean, dries them, and stores them through the Winter in trays in a dry place. He covers them with hessian sacks to protect them from the frost.

In March, he places each in a large-enough pot filled with anything from garden soil to moss to any John Innes compost, waters it correctly, and stations it in a cold greenhouse in full light. Once shoots have developed, it goes into a cold frame to be fully developed and fully hardened off.

After this, the weather being reliably frost-free (and acting at the start of the appropriate moon's second quarter), Mr Harris inserts the sprouting roots in their undisturbed compost into a deep-trench bed at the feet of the uprights of a cane rig.

"Do this," he says, "and you pick your runner beans at least one month sooner than when starting from seed."

above the earmarked, prepared, 1m-square runner-bean section. Do so as follows, as the pot-watering process completes

— insert one cane a few centimetres into the earth at each of the four corners of the 1m by 1m section

— angle each cane inwards as it is inserted, so that the four canes' tops meet and cross each other

— fill in each of the four sides of the resultant wigwam with a single cane. The cane is equidistant from the two adjacent corner canes. Insert it into the earth as close as possible to the section's perimeter. Angle it inwards as it is inserted, so that the four canes' tops meet and cross and touch the tops of the four corner canes

— thrust the eight canes 30cm into the earth. Tie them securely at their tops with garden string. Do so, preferably, with the help of a step ladder and another person to steady the ladder as it is used

2 select the eight strongest-looking runner-bean plantlets. Earmark the unselected balance for further plantings or as presentations to friends,

making for a successful transplantation from pot to garden soil. Ensure, when parking the watered pots, that surplus water (of which there should be almost none) drains wholly onto the earth, not also onto hard standing. Then

1 erect an eight-cane wigwam of 300-cm long garden canes

TIP 47

➜ **Grow buckwheat or poached egg plant (*Limnanthes*) alongside the climbing-bean wigwam or rig. It attracts the hover fly, which feeds upon that scourge of all peas and beans, the black fly. Find space for borage and/or comfrey. It brings in the pollinators. These are then attracted to the climbing beans.**

49

The *Cherokee Trail of Tears* is one of the head gardener's favourite climbing beans. It is said to be named after the early 1800s event when the Cherokee North American Indians were required by Government order to vacate their land for reservations in other, poorer and distant territory.

Their long march became known as the Trail of Tears. Legend has it that as they journeyed, they sprinkled in their wake the bean that both formed an important part of their diet and was a central entity of their society, culture and religious beliefs.

Perhaps they looked to the day when they would return, and find awaiting them the plant that was so basic to their ability to survive.

They never did return.

The bean — purple-black, pencil-thin, about 9cm long and hailing from that mysterious time when the European was not a part of North American life — is of the variety that is known today as climbing french bean. The native North American name for it is not recorded.

the pots in which the plantlets grow

— adjust the depth of the hole so that the rim of the empty pot's top levels with the surrounding ground surface

— firm gathered-in earth around the empty pot

— remove the empty pot, with care. Leave a pot-shaped, pot-sized hollow in the surface of the climbing bean section

— loosen the earth at the base of the hollow. Use the narrowest of hand forks. [**Consideration:** *this prevents poor drainage. Poor drainage results in accumulated water, which is anathema to any developing plantlet's roots*]

— place a potted plantlet upright in the palm of one hand. Do so working as close as possible to the waiting hollow

— place the fingers of the other hand over the top of the pot. Spread the fingers, so that they pass around the stem of the plantlet. By these means avoid touching and possibly

neighbours, relatives or charity shows

3 insert one plantlet into the ground on the inside of each wigwam cane, between 5cm and 10cm away from the cane. To achieve a successful individual insertion

— trowel an approximately pot-sized, pot-shaped hole in the appropriate place

— place an empty pot in the hole that is the same size as

TIP 48

➜ **For more diverse colour at blossom time, and to help further to draw in the bees, bumble bees and other pollinators (an essential which gets scarcer and scarcer), mix the two types of climbing beans on the one wigwam or rig. The two bean types make similar demands on soil and gardener. There is a risk of untrue outcomes when sowing the seeds of this venture, for a cross between the two beans is possible. The results of such a cross are unpredictable.**

damaging what is the plant's most sensitive feature — which, when harmed, incurs death for the plantlet

— grip the top of the pot with the tips of the spread fingers. Turn the pot upside down

— support the surface of the compost, still with the fingers spread out to avoid touching the plantlet's stem, and permit the pot's contents to slide out slowly. If necessary, initiate this and encourage it to happen by first gently tapping the upturned base of the pot once or twice with a knuckle

— hold and support the pot-shaped, glistening compost root ball upside down in the palm of the hand. Place the empty pot to one side with the other hand

— using both hands, turn the compost root ball upright. Do so with the utmost gentleness and without compressing it

— immediately slip the root ball into the waiting hollow. Note that it is a perfect fit

— gently firm in the compost root ball, depressing its surface slightly below that of the surrounding ground in order to create a rain-collecting depression

4 insert a seed of either type 3cm into the soil alongside each newly-installed plantlet. Site the seed at the edge of the compost root ball. Close the soil over the seed.
[*Consideration: the reward, in the event of successful germination and the development of plantlet to mature, producing plant, is a*

50
South America can lay claim to the runner bean. This explains why it is a tender plant, like the dwarf and climbing french beans. It arrived in Britain in the mid 1500s, and was one of the many benefits to Europe of the advent of the Europeans to that hapless part of the world.

R J Harris's favourite variety may or may not hail from those days. It is *Painted Lady*, a name which began to be mentioned in the UK half way through the 1800s. This variety was also known to the Victorians as *York and Lancaster*, because of its very attractive scarlet and white blossom. Such a bean was recorded in the early 1600s and could well have been *Painted Lady*'s predecessor.

It was the runner beans' blossom that first made the legume popular. Not until later did its seed pods arrive on the meal table.

bean season that is longer than otherwise would be the case, and a wigwam or rig which doubles its productivity]

5 protect each inserted bean plantlet with fleece if frost

TIP 49
➔ **Where the local weather pattern dictates a later start to gardening in general, start off the climbing-bean plantlets in pots in early May — not in early April — and advance every other stage by one month. Much less crucially, the harvesting may or may not be delayed by the same period. This depends upon the length of the local gardening season.**

threatens. Tuck the fleece around the plantlet with care to avoid damage to the plantlet's stem. Pin down the fleece's edges to hold it *in situ* in windy conditions. Remove the fleece the moment that the weather improves. Continue to have it in readiness against the onset of night-time frost

6 remove the empty pots from site, clean them and return them to store

7 see the surplus climbing-bean seeds as additions to the kitchen's stock of dried pulses. Process them in all culinary ways as indicated in *BROAD BEANS.*

RUNNER & CLIMBING FRENCH BEANS: managing and harvesting

Be alert, daily, to guide the lengthening stems of the runner-bean or climbing-french-bean plantlets onto their accompanying garden canes. At the same time

1 keep the ground surface at the base of the wigwam turned on a weekly basis to hamper weed-seed germination and to raise extra moisture to the surface of the bed. Use a hand fork

2 note that weed growth is prevented, in the main, by the developing bean vines as they mount to the top of the wigwam and prevent light from reaching the bed surface upon which the laden wigwam stands

3 **at the start of the June moon's fourth quarter**, dress the surface of the bean section with 60g to the square metre of fish-blood-and-bone fertiliser. Turn it in lightly with a hoe, and with great care. Otherwise, use a hand fork

4 avoid touching and possibly damaging the beans' stems at ground level, as the chosen tool is applied

5 harvest the runner- or climbing french beans when they are young and not yet fully-formed. Harvest them every other day

whether or not they are required in the kitchen. Pick from ground level up.

[*Considerations*: **1** — *the bean's cropping season is six weeks or so in length. This is from when the first young pod is ready to be taken. The seeds within the pods develop rapidly. As they do so, the plant devotes most of its energies to them. This induces a general reduction in the plant's ability to bear pods. At the same time, its quickly over-maturing pods are of reducing interest to the kitchen. Harvesting aims never to permit the pea- or bean-bearing plant to bring its seeds to the stage of fulfilment;* **2** — *try using the very young beans raw and chopped into short pieces, as a salad ingredient. Equally, raw, they are*

TIP 50
➔ **If slug/snail attack removes the bean plantlet's leaves, do not uproot the bared stem and re-sow or replant. In due course, provided that all proper horticultural management measures continue to be taken, the stem produces new leaves and suffers only a check to its development. Use the anti-slug jars to deal with slug/snail attack. See *BROAD BEANS: sowing.***

51

If runner- or climbing-french-bean production is desired in stages until the season ends, instead of a once-only harvest as the product of a May wigwam, also prepare for, construct and plant up/sow a June wigwam, suggests R J Harris. Then repeat with a July wigwam, he advises, but — unlike as with the May and June wigwams — do not sow a July wigwam with seeds in addition to equipping it with plants.

In short, **for a June wigwam**

— sow seeds in pots in early May

— prepare a previously earmarked section of the deep-trench bed's surface and feed it with 115g to the square metre of fish-blood-and-bone fertiliser at the start of the May moon's fourth quarter

— build an eight-cane wigwam on the section and plant it up/sow it at the start of the June moon's second quarter

— boost feed the section's surface with 60g to the square metre of fish-blood-and-bone fertiliser at the start of the July moon's fourth quarter

and **for a July wigwam**

— sow seeds in pots in early June

— prepare a previously earmarked section of the deep-trench bed's surface and feed it with 115g to the square metre of fish-blood-and-bone fertiliser at the start of the June moon's fourth quarter

— build an eight-cane wigwam on the section and plant it up at the start of the July moon's second quarter. Do not seed sow it

— boost feed the section's surface with 60g to the square metre of fish-blood-and-bone fertiliser at the start of the August moon's fourth quarter

Note that, in the North of the U K, and where very cold conditions are experienced at the close of the season, a July wigwam probably requires anti-frost protection with all-over fleece as it bears harvestable pods in September and October.

---

excellent as an occasional 'nibble']

6 give away or freeze the unwanted surplus of harvested beans. Otherwise, dispose of them securely off site

7 leave a few beans on the vines to mature fully as the harvesting progresses, so that their seeds may be collected for

TIP 51
➔ A runner- or climbing french bean's vine always snakes up its supportive cane or string in an anti-clockwise direction. Be sure to emulate this performance when re-winding an errant stem or branch, or when introducing a plantlet to its supportive cane or string.

52

Among the climbing french beans being grown in the walled kitchen garden at Tresillian are golden-podded and -leafed *Lazy Housewife* from Spain, *Pea Bean Inca*, a creation of the Incas, and *Romanian*, from Romania.

Whilst being different from each other in habit and produced bean, they have in common seeds which, although as different from each other as are their parents, display remarkably attractive and contrasted colours.

They, and many other climbing french beans, have been released by the HDRA's Heritage Seed Library (see *SUPPLIERS*).

presumes that cross-pollination with a different bean has not taken place. If it has, the outcome is a type that is other than the type the beans of which have been saved. Only the responsible gardener can judge whether or not this matters, from either nutritional or aesthetic points of view)

11 when the wigwam is denuded of beans, cut the vines at ground level. Use secateurs or garden shears. Leave their roots in the ground, so that their nitrogen secretions remain in the soil.

RUNNER & CLIMBING FRENCH BEANS: after harvesting

With the harvest gathered in on a strictly plant/kitchen-oriented basis — runner- and/or climbing-french bean — dismantle the wig-wam and/or rig. Clean its canes and return them to store. Then either

1 — permit the vines to dry thoroughly on an unemployed bed and burn them, and then turn their cold ashes into the bed's surface, or

sowing in the following season. Mark them with ties of garden string, to avoid accidental removal. Pluck them when the pods have turned brown and have become paperlike in texture

8 complete the drying of the pods by placing them between sheets of brown paper and storing them in a dry, cool, airy place

9 de-pod the seeds. Place the seeds in a metal container. Shake the container. If the seeds rattle with a metallic sound, they are dry. If they do not, continue to dry them between sheets of brown paper and test them again

10 store the fully-dried seeds in a paper bag in a cool, dry, dark place. Do so until the next planting season. (**Consideration:** this

TIP 52
➔ **The bumble bee willingly pollinates the runner and the climbing french bean. The household bee does so reluctantly. Avoid the risk of non-pollination (bumble bees are getting scarcer and scarcer) by planting sweet peas alongside or among the runner beans. Their scent brings in the household bee, which then does not differentiate between the two kinds of blossom.**

53

Sweet corn and the climbing french bean make good companions when planted together in the same bed, advises R J Harris. The one supports the other, with the advantageous result that the bean requires no wigwam or rig.

The sweet corn is sown first of all, earlier than the bean by one month.

It is well established by the time the vines of the bean begin to quest for a climbing frame. This the sweet corn provides readily, along with the partial shade that makes the pencil-like beans a little more tender, a little more flavoursome.

"A point to watch," says the head gardener, "is that for the best results the sweet corn is grown in four-row blocks.

"This is because it is pollinated by the wind, not by insects.

"With four parallel rows sown a mere 35cm to 40cm from each other, you can be sure that pollination takes place.

"The bean is planted on the outside of the four-row block, to make sure that it does not impede the transfer of the sweet-corn pollen."

— destroy the vines off site

or

— place the vines in the trench that awaits development in the Year 2 Area into a deep-trench bed

2 at **the start of the September moon's third quarter**, give the surface of the ex-bean section its pre-Winter dig. Use a sharpened garden spade. Dig to the full length of the spade's blade. If the climbing beans'

roots are lifted by this process, turn them back into the depths of the soil

3 make this a part of the total deep-trench bed, end-of-year, pre-Winter dig. Aim for the surface finish that resembles the surface finish of a ploughed field. Complete the dig by **the start of the moon's fourth quarter**

4 permit the ex-bean-section's highly broken surface — along with the remainder of the highly broken surface of the deep-trench bed — to over-Winter unused and exposed to the elements in preparation for its second year's work. In R J Harris's crop rotation programme this is the development and production of the harvest of annual flowers

5 subject the surface of the adjacent single-dug bed in the Year 1 Area to the same treatment

6 note that the catalogues of the reputable seedsmen offer information on the extensive range of climbing-bean types. Autumn is the time to secure them, for Winter provides the ideal moments in which to plan for what is to come and to make sowing/planting decisions. See *SUPPLIERS*

7 use Winter time to review the climbing-bean data recorded in the card-index system. Note the lessons to be learned from them. Apply the lessons.

TIP 53
➔ **A large jam jar filled with water keeps surplus bean and pea pods fresh for days. Put the pods into the water stalks first.**

POTATOES: preparing to sow

R J Harris's system of moon-oriented crop rotation places potato production in the third year of the Year Area's four-year life span. Potato production — and potato production alone, for no other vegetable production is permitted during the Year Area's third year — employs the whole surface of the single-dug bed and of the deep trench bed from the very beginning of the third year to its very end. This is top soil and bed depth which have already supported first-year crops such as the Year-Area-initiating, Autumn-sown broad bean and the runner bean, and the second-year annual-flower crop. As a result, the nutrients and moisture-retentive qualities of the two beds are at the point of depletion that renders them ideal for the development of the potato.

Elsewhere, at the commencement of the Year 1 Area's third year, the Year 2 Area's first year is complete, and the flower crop of its second year is in preparation. At the same time, in the Year 3 Area, the single-dug bed and the deep-trench bed are being installed and readied for their first-year employment. Also, in the Year 4 Area, the trench for a first-year deep-trench bed is being, if not installed, then certainly viewed as amounting to a task which is to be undertaken very soon.

The head gardener's potato-production method could not be less complicated. Parallel rows of healthy, flourishing plants awaiting harvesting begin as excavated, parallel trenches in each of which seeds are posted and then covered with the excavate in stages as above-the-surface growth develops in order to support the below-the-surface clusters of swelling tubers. Simple preventive steps are taken to keep the top growth free from the potentially destructive blight and the pests that are potato-specific, as well as to quell the germination of certain weeds.

To secure R J Harris's scope and quality of potato crop

1 at **the start of the September or October moon's fourth quarter** at the commencement of the Year 1 Area's third year, remove the garden lines that establish the locations and shapes of the Area's two beds, and that indicate the sitings of the two temporary paths (see *Diagram 1*, page 14)

2 leave *in situ* the garden canes to which the garden lines were tied. Drive each deeper into the soil, if that is required, in order to secure their sitings. [***Consideration:*** *knowledge of the locations of the two beds must not be lost. They will have to be revisited for bed-renewal purposes when the four-year-old Year 1 Area dies, is rejuvenated with fresh beds and*

TIP 54

➜ **At the start of the Year 1 Area's third year, in the Autumn and when the siting of the potato-bed-to-be's trenches has been determined, hunt for soot from a coal fire and apply it to that part of the bed that is to be used to grow the maincrop — but not early — potatoes. Apply the soot at the start of the October moon's fourth quarter. Turn it in well with a sharpened spade, at the same time preserving the ploughed-field texture of the top soil's surface. Leave it to over-Winter. The coal-fire soot deters the black keel slug, which is a potato pest.**

Apply to the *POTATOES* chapter the section/bed/Year Area-labelling, anti-bird, anti-cat, anti-slug, tread-board, bed-edge-rehabilitation, top-soil-preparation and card-index-system disciplines that are prescribed in *BROAD BEANS* and *CABBAGES*. Apply, also, the recommended stones-gleaning and tools/materials-cleaning/storage practices. See *BROAD BEANS: preparing to sow*

Respond to the need, during the four-year garden conversion, to extend and complete the general service paths, and to apply manual weed clearance to the undeveloped Year 4 Area.

These fundamentals are referred to only briefly throughout the remainder of 'R J Harris's Moon Gardening'.

newly-dug, deep-trench-bed trench. This, just excavated and lidded for safety's sake, awaits the permissible waste vegetable matter of the third year of the four-year, overall garden conversion programme before being completed in the fourth year as the Year 4 Area's first-year, deep-trench bed]

5 subject the entire surface of the Year 1 Area to its end-of-season, pre-Winter, fertility-enhancing dig. Use a sharpened garden spade. Do not use a garden fork. Dig as deep as the full length of the spade's blade. Achieve a surface finish that is similar to that of a ploughed field. [***Consideration:*** *this meets the R J Harris requirement that at the end of year one, year two and year three of his four-year crop-rotation programme, the beds' surfaces are opened as much as possible (hence the deep digging with a garden spade) to await Winter's worst. The surface is penetrated by Winter's rain, frost and air, which increase the top soil's*

immediately embarks upon the first of its four years as the Year 5 Area]

3 clear the entire surface of the Year 1 Area of the flower-crop and weed growth that may have survived from the second-year season just ended. Use a garden fork and a rake. Work from the Area's permanent and temporary paths

4 dispose of the cleared material off site. [***Consideration:*** *this material's inevitable seed content renders it unfit for the Year 4 Area's*

TIP 55

➔ **Seek out the seed tubers that are sold by weight. Choose the smaller seeds from the bin when selecting a required number — each about the size of an egg — and, thus, reduce the price of the purchase. The bigger seed, if it must be bought, can be cut into two or four pieces lengthwise just prior to planting. First, it must be fully chitted (sprouted). Each piece must bear two or three sprouts. This underlines the advantage of buying where the seeds are displayed loose, in open trays, and of not buying prepacked, net bags.**

54

The potato, R J Harris is convinced, is the most valuable of the vegetable garden's products.

"It rates alongside the apple," he comments. "Probably, too, the pair of them are the most taken for granted.

"Through the years, many a family has been reared on not much other than the common spud, grown just outside the back door. They have done well on it, and have given to society some notable men and women."

Mr Harris's own sowings can be seen as a tribute to this heritage. He produces all three types: the first-early; the second-early; the maincrop. He chooses from among the scores of available varieties some of the oldest. Among these is the waxy potato (known to all potato-salad makers and lovers), which, in today's green-grocery displays, is a rarity.

"The *Duke of York* is one of the old ones," he says. "It appeared in 1891. It was the result of crossing the even older *Early Primrose* and *King Kidney* — neither now any longer seen. It is an oval-long tuber, with yellow skin and pale yellow flesh and a very fine flavour.

"The oddest is the *Pink Fir Apple*.

"All we know about it is that it was first shown in the catalogues at the end of the 1800s.

"It is a long, oval tuber with yellow, waxy flesh. It keeps its new flavour for a very long time."

This variety, the head gardener points out, holds comparatively less water, so it fries well.

fertility and go some way towards solving the pest problem]

6 be alert as from January of the Year 1 Area's third year for the first display by the retail seedsmen in open, marked crates of their newly-arrived first-early, second-early and maincrop seed potatoes. Alternatively, consult the newly-arrived seedsmen's catalogues

7 buy or place orders for selected varieties of the three types of seed potato the moment that they become available. [***Consideration:*** *competition for seed potatoes can sharpen as January becomes February, and as the potato enthusiasts descend upon the specialist suppliers (of which many remain, in 2006) to diminish with extraordinary speed the stocks of the favourite varieties and types. Only the earliest of visits to the retail outlets ensures having the widest range of seeds from which to select]*

8 choose the varieties declared by displayed printed or hand-written statements to be

— of reputable origin

— free from virus diseases. [***Consideration:*** *this is guaranteed by a certificate*

TIP 56

➔ **Potato varieties differ in moisture content. Choose according to what happens to the harvested tuber once it gets into the kitchen. Eg, if frying is a culinary practice, sow a variety that has a high dry content. It splutters less in the frying pan.**

number, which the purchaser is advised to note]

— blight resistant. *[**Consideration:** this quality, plus the blight-preventive spraying at a later stage that the head gardener strongly recommends, offers as reliable a guarantee as is achievable against the onset of the crop-spoiling potato blight]*

— of a stated moisture content, so that comparisons can be made

9 do not buy where such declarations are not displayed or obtainable

10 note that the individual potato trench aligns south to north across the 490cm length of the whole of the Year 1 Area (see *Diagram 1,* page 14). As a result, it offers accommodation for 15 seed potatoes posted 30cm apart

11 note that the 300cm width of the whole of the Year 1 Area provides space for four parallel, 25cm-wide trenches spaced 60cm apart. Hence, buy at least 4 x 15 = 60 seeds made up of 22 first-early potatoes, 23 second-early potatoes and 15 maincrop potatoes

12 add at least half a dozen of each type to cater for unexpected eventualities

13 house each of the three types in its own tray. Do so as soon as they are purchased

14 position the seeds in their trays so that they support each other in an upright position

15 note that the ends of the seeds that show eyes must be uppermost. *[**Consideration:** the eyes are at the broadest end of the seed. They take the form of indents, or dimples]*

16 label the trays, so that there can be no doubt about which kind of seed is in each

17 locate the filled trays in a protected, unheated, frost-free location

18 ensure that each tray receives full daylight — but not direct sunlight. Do not stack the trays

19 examine the trays daily. Remove and dispose of any seed that shows signs of rotting. Otherwise, leave the trays undisturbed as each seed produces from its eyes dark-green or purplish sprouts. *[**Consideration:** this process occupies one month to six weeks. It enables the growing process to begin well before the garden shakes itself free of Winter's grip and is ready to begin to work. It gives the gardener a lead growing time of up to sixteen weeks. It also permits the gardener to wait for non-frosty growing conditions without risking deterioration of the seeds. The process also, R J Harris believes, results in crops that are superior to those obtained by the planting of unsprouted seed tubers]*

20 at **the start of the March moon's fourth quarter** in the third year, clear the Year 1 Area of the early, still-developing weeds that are

struggling to establish a
footing. Use a garden fork

21 dispose of the removed
weeds securely off site

22 prepare the Year 1 Area's
surface for feeding as when
the Area's broad-bean
section was prepared. See
*BROAD BEANS: preparing to
sow*. Note that there are two
differences

— a fine tilth is not a
requirement. Aim,
instead, to achieve a
coarsely-broken-down
Area surface

— an overall level surface is
required, or one that is as
close to being level overall
as it is possible to
achieve. This entails
raking soil from the
elevated surface of the
single-dug bed to the
depressed surface of the
deep-trench bed and over
the two intervening,
temporary paths.

Achieving a level surface
overall is required to
facilitate trench digging

23 ensure that the garden
canes indicating the
locations and sizes of the
two bed types remain firmly
in situ

24 still at **the start of the
March moon's fourth
quarter**, dress the levelled
surface of the potato-bed-to-
be evenly with 115g to the
square metre of fish-blood-
and-bone fertiliser. Work it
in lightly. Use a rake. Better,
use the R J Harris-
preferred, three-tined
cultivator.
[**Consideration:** *for
perfection in surface
preparation for potato
sowing, the three-tined
cultivator is the best tool. It
provides an ideally coarse
tilth, especially when it is
made to penetrate the
surface as deeply as its three
tines permit*].

POTATOES: sowing

At the beginning of the April
moon's first quarter (or May's,
if the weather/soil conditions so
insist), peg a garden line across the
490cm length of the third-year, Year
1 Area's surface at a distance of
25cm from, and parallel to, one of
the Area's two 490cm-long permanent paths. See *Diagram 1*, page 14.

The choice of the first moon
quarter emphasises that the potato
seed is especially a moisture lover,
as are the majority of the below-the-
surface developers. For this reason,
the additional week or so of exposure to the increasingly-moisture-
charged, increasingly-pressurised
top soil is crucial — both conditions

being thanks to a water table which
begins to rise from its lowest level as
the dead March moon begins to
develop into the April moon, and as
the awakening moon begins to exert
an increasing gravitational pull
upon planet Earth and its water
table.

To continue the sowing

1 peg
— a second garden line 60cm
from the first and parallel to
it

— a third garden line 25cm
from the second and parallel
to it

— a fourth garden line 60cm from the third and parallel to it

— a fifth garden line 25cm from the fourth and parallel to it

— a sixth garden line 60cm from the fifth and parallel to it

2 cover with a sheet of protective material the length of the surface of the permanent path that is adjacent and parallel to the sixth garden line

3 excavate a 25cm-wide, spade-deep, Area-long (490cm) trench between the first garden line and the uncovered permanent path that is adjacent to it

4 deposit the arising top soil between the first garden line and the second garden line, upon the Area's surface and at the edge of the forming trench. Shape a neatly-fashioned ridge which is no more than 20cm wide at its base and leaves blank a 40cm width of the 60cm width that separates the first garden line from the second.
[**Consideration:** *the positioning of the ridge, and its maximum width at its base, relates to the use of Mexican Marigolds as a barrier between the developing potatoes and potato diseases and pests, and weed development. See* MEXICAN MARIGOLDS: seedlings and plantlets *immediately after this chapter*]

5 excavate in the same way between the second and third garden lines, the fourth and fifth garden lines, and the sixth garden line and the adjacent, covered permanent path. By these means create four

parallel trenches which are 60cm or so apart, and three of which are accompanied by a precisely-positioned, 20cm-wide-at-its-base, intervening ridge of excavated soil. Employ the whole of the Year 1 Area's surface in this way

6 place the ridge of soil accompanying the fourth trench upon the sheet of protective material that protects the surface of the permanent path. Precise positioning and size in respect of this fourth ridge are not significant

7 remove the garden lines and their affixing pegs. Clean them and return them to store

8 insert a 30cm-long marker stick 15cm into the soil of the

TIP 57
➔ **Note the difference between the so-called waxy potato and the so-called floury potato. Those who love the former (this reporter is one of them) loathe the latter. Those who cannot abide the former, dote upon the comparative blandness and texture of the latter. The waxy potato is without match for potato-salad and other salad-making purposes — a claim that is out of the floury potato's reach. The waxy potato refuses to break down when boiled or steamed, unlike its less fortunate cousin, which boils/steams to slush all too readily. The floury kind is for roasting and baking; the waxy kind is above that kind of culinary processing. The wise gardener has all of this in mind when deciding which kind of seed tuber to buy.**

55

New potatoes for Christmas Day is an R J Harris favourite. His 'recipe' is as follows: 1) in September's first week, place drainage stones in a 25cm pot; 2) cover them with a 6cm-thick layer of compacted John Innes No 2 potting compost; 3) sit a sprouted tuber on top of the compost; 4) fill with the John Innes No 2, leaving room for watering; 5) keep constantly, correctly moist — ie, always slightly under watered, which is far better than over-watered; 6) place the pot in a cold frame, unheated greenhouse or conservatory and keep it protected from the frost; 7) ignore the moon's phases, this being crop production minus garden-soil connection.

Arran Pilot, Duke of York and *Sharp's Express* are Mr Harris's favourites for this treatment.

60cm space between the first and second potato trench. Equidistance it between the two trenches. Position it, also, 10cm from the formed ridge of soil and one metre from the nearest permanent path

9 repeat with another marker stick at the other ends of the two trenches

10 insert two more 30cm-long marker sticks in the same way in respect of the third and fourth trenches.
[*Considerations:* **1** — *the marker sticks indicate where Mexican Marigold is to be planted as a barrier between the developing tubers and pest, disease and weed. See* MEXICAN MARIGOLDS:

seedlings and plantlets *immediately after this chapter;* **2** — *note that when the decision is made not to add Mexican Marigolds to the potato bed, the four marker sticks are not inserted*]

11 still at **the beginning of the April moon's first quarter**, line the bottom of the first trench with a 7cm thickness of fully-composted leaf mould (ie, leaf mould which is at least two years old) .
[*Considerations:* **1** — *the potato seed develops best in soil possessing a very low pH (see* pH*). Placing leaf mould in the trench prior to potato seed sowing reduces the prevailing pH better than by any other means;* **2** — *a bonus of this method is that the leaf mould endows the crop with skins which are clean and minus unsightly scab*]

12 line the bottom of the trench with comfrey leaves instead if fully-composted leaf mould is not available.
[*Considerations:* **1** — *use wilted comfrey leaves. This is comfrey the stems of which are cut at surface level and then left upon the ground for several hours before being employed. Wilted and, hence, limp, it settles unprotestingly into the bottom of the trench;* **2** — *comfrey does not reduce the prevailing pH. Like leafmould, however, it traps and retains moisture where the developing, moisture-craving young potatoes await it*]

13 return a 2cm thickness of the excavated top soil to the trench. Take it from the ridge of soil that is parked alongside the edge of the trench. Place it evenly on top of the installed vegetable matter. Firm the added soil gently with the back of a rake

14 prepare the second and the third trench in the same way. Do so immediately

15 note that the fourth trench remains empty, accompanied by the ridge of excavated top soil that rests upon the protective covering upon the permanent path's surface

16 ensure that the inserted marker sticks are not disturbed as excavate is moved

17 place fifteen sprouted, first-early seed potatoes on top of the added soil in the first trench, sprouts uppermost. Space them 30cm apart, commencing about 15cm from one end of the trench. Position them firmly. Take care not to damage the sprouts as this is done

18 place seven first-early seed potatoes on top of the added soil in the second trench, sprouts uppermost. Space them 30cm apart, commencing about 15cm from one end of the trench. Position them firmly. Take care not to damage the sprouts as this is done

19 place eight second-early seed potatoes on top of the added soil in the second trench, sprouts uppermost. Space them 30cm apart, commencing 30cm from the final first-early seed tuber. Position them firmly. Take care not to damage the sprouts as this is done

56
Exactly where in the world the potato came from has been discussed hotly, and with no little disagreement, since horticultural records first named it.

Page 49 of Webbs's 1888 *Spring Catalogue* sustained what, clearly, was a long-running debate by stating that there was no doubt that it was an American plant cultivated by the Peruvians or Chilians long before the advent to the New World of the Europeans.

It reached Ireland in about 1586, taken there by Thomas Heriot, one of Sir Walter Raleigh's companions. He was on his way back from Virginia.

Whether it was a sweet potato or the potato that is familiar in Western kitchens today Webbs's catalogue did not question, although it added that the tuber was believed to have been sent to Europe before 1586, and by the Spaniards.

A picture of the plant appeared in Britain in 1597. It illustrated a specimen known to have been sent from Virginia.

There is, today, agreement that the potato is one of the few plants that can be said to have helped to mould the shape of western history, and to have helped considerably to bring us to where we are at the present time.

20 place fifteen second-early seed potatoes on top of the added soil in the third trench, sprouts uppermost. Space them 30cm apart, commencing about 15cm from one end of the trench. Position them firmly. Take care not to damage the sprouts as this is done

21 rake a 5cm-to-7cm thickness of earth over the positioned seeds. Fully cover them, so that no part of any seed is visible. Leave the balance of the excavated soil where it is, at the three trenches' edges

22 replace the four marker sticks by inserted Mexican Marigold plantlets. See

MEXICAN MARIGOLDS: seedlings and plantlets

23 at **the beginning of the May moon's first quarter**, one month later, repeat the complete sowing programme in respect of the fourth trench and the maincrop seed tubers. Complete the sowing of the seed tubers by the end of May at the latest.

POTATOES: managing

The south-to-north (or north-to-south) alignment of the four trenches ensures that no fully-developed potato top, springing from the ground at the points dictated by the prescribed dimensions, is able to block out sunlight from its immediate neighbours. It is the 60cm width of the separation between the trenches that accounts for this apparent breaking of the head gardener's golden rule that rows of annual or permanent plants — floral, vegetable, soft fruit or hard fruit — be aligned east-to-west or west-to-east.

As green shoots appear through the soil in the sown, incompletely-filled trenches, cover them with further soil raked in from the excavate parked at the edges of the trenches. Do so with the utmost care. Ensure that, in the process, the four inserted Mexican Marigold plants are not disturbed (see *MEXICAN MARIGOLDS: seedlings and plantlets*). Then go on to

1 remove the fresh weed growth at the same time. Dispose of it off site.
[**Consideration:** *note that as the potato top growth gets higher and thicker, the weeds are smothered and find it less and less easy to germinate and to develop*]

2 continue to earth up as the sown tubers continue to produce green shoots. Eventually, the four trenches become filled and most of the surplus soil is reinstated.
[**Consideration:** *earthing up in this way ensures that no young potatoes are developed close to the surface of the soil and, thus, exposed to sun and air. Permitted to be so exposed, they become green and, hence, unfit for human consumption*]

3 be alert to protect especially the newly-emergent shoots of the first-early seed tubers when frost threatens. Ensure that these shoots never appear above the gradually increased thickness of the soil taken from

TIP 58
➔ **When heavy, humid, thundery weather coincides with developing potato tops, expect the onset of potato blight. Once arrived, this disease cannot be combated, and brings an end to the crop. Prevention is the only course, by correctly-managed, regular spraying with Bordeaux mixture bought from any garden centre or ironmonger.**

the trenches' edges for as long as the threat is present. [**Consideration:** *no harm is done by thus anticipating the sustained earthing up that is an essential part of potato production. The prevailing aim is to have protection in place before the arrival of Winter's frost*]

4 continue to earth up as more shoots appear, using a rake to draw up earth from both sides of each line of top growth. [**Consideration:** *the result is ridges where once there were trenches. The top growth emerges from the top and, eventually, the sides of the ridges. The troughs created by the eathing up direct rain water to where the developing young potatoes await it*]

5 note that neatness is of paramount importance at this stage, and that, from now on, it is to be pursued constantly. It results in totally weed-free, arrow-straight, parallel ridges of evenly, coarsely structured earth, each of the same height and of an equal, even width at its base

6 avert the onset of potato blight by spraying Bordeaux mixture on the potato foliage at seven- or ten-day intervals as from

early June. Use a proprietory Bordeaux mixture bought at a garden centre or hardware store. Follow its maker's instructions precisely. Apply it with a manually pumped-up pressure sprayer. Spray, especially, the undersides of the potatoes' foliage. Spray in the cool of the end of day. No moon quarter is involved. [**Considerations: 1** — *the cool of the end of the day is when the least number of the beneficial insects is present;* **2** *it is also when plants are at their coolest and, hence, most able to receive a cold spray without suffering growth check*]

7 continue the Bordeaux spraying of the living tops for as long as these are massed above the potato ridges, and are bright green in colour

8 stop the Bordeaux spraying when the green of all of the potato tops has changed to yellow. [**Considerations: 1** — *the change of colour signals that the potato tops have done their job and that they are at the end of their life. It also indicates that developed tubers are underground, waiting to be lifted;* **2** — *the first-early sowing yellows first, then the second-early, then the maincrop*].

POTATOES: harvesting

Twenty weeks after sowing the first-early seed tubers, excavate carefully at one end of the first of the four rows in the potato bed of the third-year, Year 1 Area to reveal one or two of the underground first-early developments. Do so to find out whether or not this first crop is ready for use. Replace the removed

TIP 59
➜ It is essential that nearby, outdoor tomatoes be included in the blight-preventive spraying of the potato tops (including those in next door's garden, if that can be negotiated). Potatoes and tomatoes are of the same family, botanically. Either can attract the disease and/or transmit it to the other.

57

Over the years, R J Harris's choice of seed tubers for cultivation has narrowed to

First earlies
Arran Comet, a 1927 waxy type
Arron Pilot, a 1930 floury type
Duke of York, an 1891 floury type
Epicure, an 1897 floury type
Homeguard, a 1942 floury type
Red Duke of York, an 1891 floury type
Sharpes Express, a 1901 floury type
Ulster Chieftain, a floury type of unknown vintage

Second earlies
Belle de Fontenay, a waxy type of unknown date
Catriona, a 1920 floury type
Edzell Blue, a pre-1900 floury type

Maincrop
Dunbar Standard, a 1936 floury type
Golden Wonder, a 1906 floury type
Kerrs Pink, a 1917 waxy type
King Edward, a 1902 floury type
Majestic, a 1911 floury type
Pink Fir Apple, a pre-1900 waxy type.

earth immediately if no further action is taken. Remember that potatoes exposed to the daylight eventually turn green, and that greened potatoes are not for human consumption. Then

1 investigate the first-earlies once per day

2 begin to lift them when selected unearthed specimens win the kitchen's approval. Then take

on a daily basis, as required, for consumption. Otherwise, leave the new tubers where they are, with the excavated earth replaced to prevent daylight from reaching them. [**Consideration:** *consumed daily, the first-earlies are exhausted before there is need to consider storing them, and before they are at risk from the potato-loving pests*]

3 repeat with the second-early crop. Make the first inspection twenty-two weeks after sowing

4 watch — at the same time — for the tops of the second-earlies to change in colour from green to yellow and to droop as they begin to die. Take this as an incontrovertible signal that the second-earlies' crop is ready to be used

5 lift the mature second-earlies as they are required by the kitchen. Leave the unrequired tubers in the ground until they are demanded by the kitchen

6 check the maincrop tubers for suitability when they reach their twenty-sixth to twenty-eighth week in the soil

7 lift the maincrop when the plants' tops have died completely and have collapsed to the ground, and when end-of-row inspection reveals that the tubers await harvesting

8 choose **the first fine day of the moon's fourth quarter** to commence and to complete the maincrop harvest (or ignore the dictates of the moon and the state of the weather if this combination cannot be attained).
[**Considerations: 1** — *the aim is lifted maincrop tubers that*

are free from damp or wet mud, although, possibly, coated with dry earth. In this condition, they keep longer when stored. They are more likely to be unmuddied during the moon's fourth quarter than at any other time, due to the reduced moisture content of the top soil; 2 — a related aim is lifted tubers containing the least amount of moisture. This, too, increases storage time, for the less the volume of retained moisture the longer before the onset of rot. This general horticultural truth affects all of the garden's horticultural populations; 3 — the water table is the controlling agent. For the duration of the moon's fourth quarter it is at its lowest level, released by the satellite planet's fourth-quarter-reduced gravitational pull upon Earth. Hence, it exerts the least upward pressure upon the top soil, causing a reduction in the concentration of the moisture content of the top soil and of everything rooted in it; 4 — the reduced upward pressure further encourages comparative dryness within the harvested tubers by placing them under reduced compulsion to absorb moisture from the top soil]

9   lift the tubers with a carefully-applied garden fork

10   isolate any tuber that is speared by the fork, and earmark it for immediate use by the kitchen. Do not attempt to store it

11   remove by hand any earth that clings to the lifted tubers. Do so immediately and gently. Do not use any

kind of implement. In the process, do not bruise or scrape the skin of the lifted tuber

12   withhold any diseased products and keep them separate from the perfect specimens. Dispose of them securely off site

13   place the harvested, cleaned, perfect tubers in stout (ideally, double-walled), dry, paper sacks or in timber boxes. Do not use plastic sacks or plastic trays or plastic containers for storage purposes.
[**Consideration:** *these — especially the plastic sacks — may transmit condensate to the stored products, with little possibility of the consequent moisture venting to the external atmosphere*]

14   do not add any other materials to the sacked/boxed harvest

15   seal the paper sacks or place a close-fitting lid on the timber boxes

16   store the filled sacks/boxes in a dark, cool, frost-free, dry, accessible place.
[**Consideration:** *the paramount need, at this stage, is for darkness as quickly as possible (to avert greening) and frost-free dryness (to help to prevent rotting). This is why, contrary to some gardeners' practice, the head gardener does not expose his lifted tubers on the earth's surface for a period to dry. For him, dryness is not a consideration. It does not have to be. He harvests on a fine, dry day during the moon's fourth quarter*].

POTATOES: after harvesting

Remove the dead potato tops from the third-year, Year 1 Area's surface the moment that all of the tubers have been gathered in for kitchen use or storage. Dispose of the tops off site. Do not attempt to compost them. Do not add them to the trench that waits completion as a deep-trench bed in the Year 4 Area. The risk is too great that they harbour pest and/or disease. Then

1 at **the start of the October moon's third quarter** in the now fourth year, subject the entire Year 1 Area to its pre-Winter, fertility-enhancing, deep dig. Use a sharpened garden spade. Dig to the full length of the spade's blade. If overlooked tubers are brought to the surface, come to conclusions about their state and then send them to the kitchen or dispose of them off site

2 aim for the top-soil surface finish that resembles the surface finish of a ploughed field. Complete the dig by **the start of the moon's fourth quarter**

3 permit the fourth-year, Year 1 Area's highly broken surface to over-Winter unused and

exposed to the elements in preparation for its fourth and final year's work. In the head gardener's crop rotation programme this is the production of root crops

4 note that the catalogues of the reputable seedsmen offer information on the extensive ranges of carrots, parsnips and similar below-the-surface developers. Autumn is the time to secure them, for Winter provides the ideal moments in which to plan for what is to come and to make sowing/planting decisions. See *SUPPLIERS*

5 use Winter time to review the potato data recorded in the card-index system. Note the lessons to be learned from them. Apply the lessons in the next Year Area to be committed to potatoes. Within the present context, this is the Year 2 Area, in its coming third-year. Note that, in that year, the Year 3 Area is committed to flower production

6 examine the stored tubers regularly as Winter progresses. Extract and destroy any that show signs of deterioration.

MEXICAN MARIGOLDS: seedlings and plantlets

The roots of the unusual, semi-hardy annual that is known as Mexican Marigold protect the developing potato tubers from eelworm, the black keel slug, mice and moles, and the potato bed from couch grass, bind weed and ground elder for the length of the vegetable-growing season. They do so for a

radius around the parent plant's stem of approximately two metres. The overall advantage, the Cornish head gardener believes, is far better achieved by applying this environment-protective, extremely low-cost, fauna-compatible and non-invasive plant than by what can be bought at the garden centre and

Apply to the *MEXICAN MARIGOLDS* chapter the anti-bird, anti-cat, anti-slug, and card-index-system disciplines that are prescribed in *BROAD BEANS* and *CABBAGES*.

Respond to the need, during the four-year garden conversion, and as opportunity offers, to extend and complete the general service paths, and to apply manual weed clearance to the undeveloped Year 4 Area.

These fundamentals are referred to only briefly throughout the remainder of 'R J Harris's Moon Gardening'.

sprayed on.

The Mexican Marigold is a flowering plant which attains a height of 2m to 3m. It is a thing of little beauty. Its plantlets are produced in an heated greenhouse and cold frame, or in an heatable spare room equipped with a suitable window. Inserted strategically into the potato bed's soil, it reaches its life's end when Winter's frost strikes.

The spare-room production method is described in the second half of this chapter section.

To use the heated-greenhouse method — which is R J Harris's, made possible for him by the presence in the walled, kitchen garden at Tresillian in Cornwall of an heated greenhouse and several cold frames — proceed as follows (no lunar quarter being involved)

1 adjust the greenhouse's heating system's temperature level to18°C-20°C (65°F-68°F). Do so on any day in early February in the third year of the four-year garden-conversion project. Do so during each successive Year Area's third year, to begin to be ready to cater for the cultivation of potatoes

2 assemble in the greenhouse as it heats, in full daylight and upon a workbench top

— a packet of Mexican Marigold seeds. These are most easily available, in this writer's experience, from Suffolk Herbs (see *SUPPLIERS*)
— two seed trays
— John Innes seed compost
— John Innes No 1 potting compost
— a container to hold sieved compost
— a 6mm garden sieve
— a redundant teatowel
— several newspapers

and add to the assembly a water container that is

— deep enough and large enough in area at the top to permit the lowering into it of the base of a compost-filled seed tray

— filled sensibly short of its top with cold water

3 fill one seed tray with the John Innes seed compost. Do so to within 10mm-to-12mm of its top. Level the compost's surface

4 consolidate the compost by tapping the base of the tray gently once or twice upon the workbench top

5 add compost to raise the level of the compost to within 10mm-to-12mm of the tray's top, if that is necessary

6 consolidate the added John Innes seed compost

157

7 lower the base of the filled tray into the container of water until the tray's top is just above water level

8 note that moisture enters the tray through the drainage holes in its base. Note that this effects a moistening of the compost without the disturbance to the compost's surface that would be caused by the use of a water can, no matter how fine the can's rose

9 wait for a count of ten. Lift the tray out. Permit the surplus water to drain back into the water container

10 repeat the moistening several times. Pause after each lowering and raising to allow the surplus water to drain back into the water container

11 note that, in stages, the colour of the compost's surface changes from an even light brown to an even dark brown. Know, when this colour is arrived at, that the compost is fully moistened without being over-moistened

12 place the wet tray on the redundant teatowel on the workbench top, so that the final, minor drainings are aborbed by the towel

13 fold a newspaper so that it is slightly larger in area than the area of the top of the compost-filled tray, and so that it possesses increased rigidity

14 cover the tray with the folded newspaper, to reduce evaporation as the compost in the tray waits to be seeded.

[**Consideration:** *this is cheaper, safer and more convenient than covering with a sheet of glass. Unlike condensation-dripping glass, the newspaper does not encourage any kind of undesirable condition of the compost's surface*]

15 pass some of the seed compost through the 6mm garden sieve to remove lumps and hard material. Place the sieved, powdered compost in a container situated conveniently on the workbench top

16 return the unsieved seed compost to the compost bag

17 leave the covered tray and the other items on the workbench top, undisturbed, for at least twenty-four hours to ensure that the moistened compost, the seeds and the powdered compost arrive at the greenhouse's ambient temperature of 18°C-20°C (65°F-68°F).
[**Consideration:** *overall, this creates the optimum conditions for seed germination*]

18 remove the newspaper from the compost-filled tray after the twenty-four-hour pause. Discard it, so that it cannot be re-used for tray-covering purposes.
[**Consideration:** *being no longer a dry newspaper, it could encourage the creation of undesirable surface conditions if used to cover another compost-filled tray*]

19 open the packet of Mexican Marigold seeds. Do so over the tray.
[**Consideration:** *this ensures*

58

'The seed that is germinated and brought on through seedling stage to plantlet stage in a greenhouse or a conservatory or a spare bedroom in trays, pots or containers does not benefit by being sown or taken care of according to any phase of the moon," points out R J Harris.

"That is because it is not in the soil, and so cannot be influenced by Earth's water table.

"As a plantlet in the ground, developing above the water table, it does benefit from the moon's quarters at times such as planting-out and soil-feeding.

"This applies as much to the *Mexican Marigold* as to any other plant."

that accidentally-spilled seeds drop onto the compost and, hence, are not wasted]

20 transfer some of the seeds to a seed dispenser of the kind that enables controlled sowing without contact between seeds and fingers. Do so whilst still working over the tray, Fill the dispenser without touching the seeds with the fingers

21 post the seeds onto the surface of the moistened seed compost. Do so in 20mm-separated rows. Space the seeds 20mm apart in the rows.
[**Consideration:** *the result is that, after germination, the Mexican Marigold seedlings are markedly widely separated from each other and, thus, removable with ease for transplantation purposes*]

22 dribble the powdered compost onto the seeds through the finger tips as thinly as possible

23 achieve a compost covering the depth of which is no more than twice the thickness of the individual seed.
[**Consideration:** *this is standard practice when sowing seeds, whether into compost or garden soil*]

24 return the surplus powdered compost to the compost bag. Return unused seed from the dispenser to the seed packet

25 label the tray, so that, later, there is no doubt about what is sown in it, and when the seeds were sown

26 re-cover the tray with a fresh, folded newspaper. Leave the covered tray on the workbench top

27 check the tray at least twice daily. Ensure that

— the compost in the tray remains moist. Note that the appearance of slight sandiness on the compost's surface indicates that watering is required. When watering, use the dipping method that was used at the outset, not a water can. Take care not to over-water

— a fresh newspaper is used each time the watered tray is re-covered, and that the previous newspaper is discarded

28 note the moment that there is a hint of green growth

59

When making holes in the No 1 John Innes potting compost to receive the transplanted Mexican Marigold seedlings, Mr Harris uses one of his kit of several home-made, carved, ashwood dibbers. This is an extension of his policy of spending as little as possible — nothing, ideally — upon the tools of his craft. It is also an illustration of his preference for employing the natural materials. Another is the poles with which he replaces the long, straight handles of his treasured shovels. Invariably, these come from the nearest hedgerow.

"We never spend money on such as that," he comments.

"Of course," he observes, "you can buy a professional's dibber at a very low price at most garden centres.

"It is made of plastic, usually. It has a wide base at one end to make the holes for the large seedlings and a narrow base at the other end for accommodating the small seedlings.

"It is a neat little job and well worth seeking out if DIY wooden dibbers like mine can't be improvised."

that the greenhouse continues to be heated at 18°C-20°C (65°F-68°F)

31 watch for the appearance of two 'baby' leaves on each seedling

32 watch for either of the two 'baby' leaves to become large enough to be gripped — with utmost gentleness — between forefinger and thumb

33 fill the other seed tray with John Innes No 1 potting compost. Moisten the compost. Do so as when preparing the first tray

34 cover the newly-filled tray with a folded newspaper, as before. Set it aside

35 return to the seedling tray, and water it using the dipping method

36 station dip-watered seedlings and newspaper-covered tray upon the workbench top for at least twenty-four hours, so that their compost can become moistened evenly throughout

37 remove the folded newspaper from its tray after the twenty-four-hour wait

38 excavate 24 square holes in four rows of six in the now fully-moistened John Innes No 1 potting compost. Make each hole 4mm-to-5mm square and 4mm-to-5mm deep. Use a suitably-sized dibber to do so. Space the holes from each other so that the whole of the surface of the compost is employed

showing through the dark brown of the moist seed compost. When this is seen, know that germination has taken place and that seedlings are developing

29 remove the newspaper covering instantly and permanently. Discard the newspaper

30 post the uncovered tray permanently in full light on the workbench top. Ensure

39 ease one seedling at a time — rooted in a 4mm-to-5mm-square 'nest' of moist seed compost — out of the seedling tray. Hold it by nothing other than one of its 'baby' leaves. Use a small, sharp knife to cut out — and to help to lift out — the square of host compost. If necessary, sacrifice one or two adjacent neighbours in the process

40 take care not to touch and, hence, run the risk of crushing the seedling's stem

41 transfer the square of compost and its contained seedling to one of the prepared holes in the potting-compost-filled tray

42 firm in the square of compost and its seedling. Use the knife as a firming-in tool

43 continue to transplant in this way until all of the waiting holes in the potting compost are filled

44 label the planted-up tray, indicating what has been transplanted and when

45 remove the now-unemployed seedling tray from the heated greenhouse

46 dispose of the surplus of seedlings in the trench that waits development into a deep-trench bed in the Year 4 Area. Include their roots and the minute quantity of their host compost

47 wash and dry the seedling tray and return it to store. Remove the other aids for cleaning and/or storage

48 station the tray of young *Mexican Marigold* plantlets in full light upon the workbench top to grow on in the heated greenhouse. Maintain the temperature at the 18°C-20°C (65°F-68°F) level. Do so until each plantlet bears at least four leaves

49 move the four-leafed plantlets in their tray to a cold frame. Do so only when the weather has improved

50 open the cold frame's top fully during the day

51 close it fully at about 1600 hours each day. Cover it with several layers of sacking, fleece or redundant blankets to shut out the night-time cold

52 monitor the tray's compost for moisture each day. Water whenever necessary. Use the dipping method. [**Consideration**: *mains water may be used, first placed in a container having a suitably-sized top. Water in a fully-filled, external water butt may be used, if this is possible. In this case, the tray is lowered into the water via the butt's open top. Water temperature level is not of significance at this relatively advanced stage of plantlet development*]

53 leave the plantlets in the cold frame for about one month, so that they become almost fully hardened off

54 remove them from the cold frame. Expose them day and night to the elements in a sheltered spot in the garden. Do so for two or three days, so that they become fully hardened off and ready to be inserted into the potato bed.

When neither heatable greenhouse nor cold frame is available, produce *Mexican Marigold* seedlings and then develop them into plantlets in an heatable spare room in the house. Applying this method, proceed in late February (no moon-quarter is involved at this stage) as follows

55 take over a spare room in the house, or a garden room, which is not required for any other purpose for the coming month or six weeks

56 note that a room that possesses

— a west-facing window is the ideal

— a south-facing window is acceptable, provided that the window has a light curtain drawn over it permanently

— a south-west-facing window is acceptable, provided that the window has a light curtain drawn over it permanently

57 note that the room not to be used is the one with a window facing directly or partially east or directly or partially north

58 note that in the chosen room, single-, double- or triple-glazing makes no difference to the room's effectiveness

59 note that in the chosen room, also

— the window possesses a sill that is wide and

60

'Of course," the head gardener reminds, "the moment hardening off is considered for the Mexican Marigold plantlets, strict allowance must be made for weather conditions.

"The half-hardy flowering plant — which this is — is a tender creature, designed by Nature for climates other than ours.

"If the British weather is throwing its worst at the garden, the hardening-off stage must be delayed until conditions get better.

"It does not matter if the plantlets grow on a little in their tray or trays as a result of this — so long, of course, as those being reared with the help of a spare room's window sill are turned on the sill twice per day to counter stem distortion and legginess."

strong enough to support a seedling/plantlet tray

— there is a stout table, with a protected or cleanable top, for use as a work bench

60 close the room's window fully and keep it closed during all of the propagation period, to obviate draughts

61 close the room's door at all times other then when entering or leaving the room. Lock the door with a removable key, so that entry by unauthorised persons is prevented

62 turn on the room's central-heating radiator/s or bring in a portable heater

63 raise the room's temperature to a measured (use a room thermometer) 18°C-20°C (65°F-68°F) by night and by day, and keep it at that level for all of the time that seedlings and plantlets are being developed

64 assemble on the work table's top

— a packet of Mexican Marigold seeds. These are most easily available, in this writer's experience, from Suffolk Herbs (see *SUPPLIERS*)
— two seed trays
— John Innes seed compost
— John Innes No 1 potting compost
— a container to hold sieved compost

65 add to the assembly

— a 6mm garden sieve
— an unwanted teatowel
— several newspapers

66 add, also, to the assembly, a water container that is

— deep enough and large enough in area at the top to permit the lowering into it of the base of a compost-filled seed tray

— filled sensibly short of its top with cold water

67 fill one seed tray with the John Innes seed compost. Do so to within 10mm-to-12mm of its top. Level the compost's surface

68 consolidate the compost by tapping the base of the filled tray gently once or twice upon the work table's top

69 add compost to raise the level of the compost to

within 10mm-to-12mm of the tray's top, if that is necessary

70 consolidate the added John Innes seed compost

71 lower the base of the filled tray into the container of water until the tray's top is just above water level

72 note that moisture enters the tray through the drainage holes in its base. Note that this effects a moistening of the compost without the disturbance to the compost's surface that would be caused by the use of a water can, no matter how fine the can's rose

73 wait for a count of ten. Lift the tray out. Permit the surplus water to drain back into the water container

74 repeat the moistening several times. Pause after each lowering and raising to allow the surplus water to drain back into the water container

75 note that, in stages, the colour of the compost's

TIP 60
➜ **"You transplant only when the host medium and the target medium have been fully moisted — never, never when one is dry, or both are dry,"** advises the Cornish head gardener. **"Try ignoring that rule, and you can count on it that your seedlings and your plantlets will either never recover from the operation and fade away, or suffer a check that takes them a long time to get over."**

surface changes from an even light brown to an even dark brown. Know, when this colour is arrived at, that the compost is fully moistened without being over-moistened

76 place the wet tray on the redundant teatowel on the work table's top, so that the final, minor drainings are aborbed by the towel

77 fold a newspaper so that it is slightly larger in area than the area of the top of the compost-filled tray, and so that it possesses increased rigidity

78 cover the tray with the folded newspaper, to reduce evaporation as the compost in the tray waits to be seeded.
[***Consideration:*** *this is cheaper, safer and more convenient than covering with a sheet of glass. Unlike condensation-dripping glass, the newspaper does not encourage any kind of undesirable condition of the compost's surface*]

79 pass some of the seed compost through the 6mm garden sieve to remove lumps and hard material. Place the sieved, powdered compost in a container situated conveniently on the work table's top

80 return the unsieved seed compost to the compost bag

81 leave the covered tray and the other items undisturbed for at least twenty-four hours to ensure that the moistened compost, the

seeds and the powdered compost arrive at the spare room's ambient temperature of 18°C-20°C (65°F-68°F).
[***Consideration:*** *overall, this creates the optimum conditions for seed germination*]

82 remove the newspaper from the compost-filled tray after the twenty-four-hour pause. Discard it, so that it cannot be re-used for tray-covering purposes.
[***Consideration:*** *being no longer a dry newspaper, it could encourage the creation of undesirable surface conditions if used to cover another compost-filled tray*]

83 open the packet of *Mexican Marigold* seeds. Do so over the tray.
[***Consideration:*** *this ensures that accidentally-spilled seeds drop onto the compost and, hence, are not wasted*]

84 transfer some of the seeds to a seed dispenser of the kind that enables controlled sowing without contact between seeds and fingers. Do so whilst still working over the tray. Fill the dispenser without touching the seeds with the fingers

85 post the seeds onto the surface of the moistened seed compost. Do so in 20mm-separated rows. Space the seeds 20mm apart in the rows.
[***Consideration:*** *the result is that, after germination, the* Mexican Marigold *seedlings are markedly widely separated from each other and, thus, removable with ease for transplantation purposes*]

86 dribble the powdered compost onto the seeds through the finger tips as thinly as possible

87 achieve a compost covering the depth of which is no more than twice the thickness of the individual seed.
[**Consideration:** *this is standard practice when sowing seeds, whether into compost or garden soil*]

88 return the surplus powdered compost to the compost bag. Return unused seed from the dispenser to the seed packet

89 label the tray, so that, later, there is no doubt about what is sown in it, and when the seeds were sown

90 re-cover the tray with a fresh, folded newspaper. Leave the covered tray on the work table's top

91 check the tray at least twice daily. Ensure

— that the compost in the tray remains moist. Note that the appearance of slight sandiness on the compost's surface indicates that watering is required. When watering, use the dipping method that was used at the outset, not a water can. Take care not to over-water

— that a fresh newspaper is used each time the watered tray is re-covered, and the previous newspaper is discarded

92 note the moment that there is a hint of green growth

showing through the dark brown of the moist seed compost. Know, then, that germination has taken place

93 remove the newspaper covering instantly and permanently. Discard the newspaper

94 move the uncovered seed tray to the window-sill and station it there throughout the day. Ensure that the room continues to be heated at 18°C-20°C (65°F-68°F)

95 turn the tray through 180° twice per day to compensate for the risk that the developing seedlings become distorted and 'leggy' as they stretch up towards the window to find the light

96 return the uncovered seed tray by night to the work table's top, well away from the window-sill

97 watch for the appearance of two 'baby' leaves on each seedling

98 watch for either of the two 'baby' leaves to become large enough to be gripped — with the utmost gentleness — between forefinger and thumb

99 fill and moisten the other seed tray with John Innes No 1 potting compost. Do so as when preparing the first tray

100 cover the newly-filled tray with a folded newspaper

101 water the seedlings in their tray at the same time. Use the dipping method to do so

102 station dip-watered seedlings and newspaper-covered tray upon the work table's top in the heated spare room for at least twenty-four hours, so that their compost can become moistened evenly throughout

103 remove the newspaper from its tray after the twenty-four-hour wait

104 excavate 24 square holes in four rows of six in the now fully-moistened John Innes No 1 potting compost. Make each hole 4mm-to-5mm square and 4mm-to-5mm deep. Use a suitably-sized dibber to do so. Space the holes from each other so that the whole of the surface of the compost is employed

105 ease one seedling at a time — rooted in a 4mm-to-5mm-square 'nest' of moist seed compost — out of the seedling tray. Hold it by nothing other than one of its 'baby' leaves. Use a small, sharp knife to cut out — and to help to lift out — the square of host compost. If necessary, sacrifice one or two adjacent neighbours in the process

106 take care not to touch and, hence, run the risk of crushing the seedling's stem

107 transfer the square of compost and its contained

seedling to one of the prepared holes in the potting-compost-filled tray

108 firm in the square of compost and its retained seedling. Use the knife as a firming-in tool

109 continue to transplant in this way until all of the waiting holes in the potting compost are filled

110 label the planted-up tray, indicating what has been transplanted and when

111 remove the now-unemployed seedling tray from the heated spare room

112 dispose of the surplus of seedlings in the trench that waits development into a deep-trench bed in the Year 4 Area. Include their roots and the minute quantity of their host compost

113 wash and dry the seedling tray and return it to store

114 remove the other aids for cleaning and/or storage

115 lodge the tray of plantlets upon the window sill in the spare room by day, and upon the work table by night

116 turn the tray through 180° on the window sill twice per day. Maintain the correct watering of the compost

117 be alert for each of the plantlets to bear at least four fully-formed leaves.

When this stage is reached, turn off the heating permanently. Permit the room to cool

118 either

— move the plantlets in their tray to a protected, sunny location in the garden during the day if the weather has by this time improved. During the night, return them to the unheated room and position them away from the window-sill

or

— wait until the weather has improved (mid-April at the earliest), if that is necessary. Retain the plantlets in the unheated room during this time. Locate them on the window-sill by day and away from it by night. Maintain the anti-'legginess' regime

and maintain the garden-by-day/room-by-night procedure for several days

once this procedure has been embarked upon

119 ensure that the tray's No 1 John Innes compost is never permitted to dry out during this hardening-off period

120 moisten the compost, as required, by means of the repeated dipping and counting method

121 station the plantlets permanently in the garden once hardening-off has been achieved, as they await removal to their permanent home in the potato bed between the potato trenches (see the next chapter section). [***Consideration:*** *warm enough weather and soil conditions is the aim at this stage, bearing in mind that the* Mexican Marigold, *being a half-hardy annual flowering plant, does not have sufficient time in which to reach maturity if planted after July*].

MEXICAN MARIGOLDS: planting out and managing

Insert the trayed, hardened-off, *Mexican Marigold* plantlets in the potato bed the moment that the weather/soil conditions make this possible. Importantly, bear in mind that the *Mexican Marigold*, not being a native of the British Isles, does not have sufficient time in which to reach maturity if planted after July.

Doing as the head gardener does

1 in **April (or later**, if Winter lingers on), at **the start of the moon's second quarter**, water the compost in the tray containing the above-the-

surface-developing *Mexican Marigold* plantlets. Do so adjacent to the potato bed. Do so by the dipping method, employing either mains or butt water. Do so thoroughly. Do so on soil, not onto a hard surface.

[***Consideration:*** *by these means, avoid creating standing water and, hence, possible habitat for disease and pest*]

2 note that the watering is best done in the mid-to-late afternoon, to make it likely that

61

The head gardener's supplier of Mexican Marigold seeds, Suffolk Herbs (see *SUPPLIERS*), reports that, for centuries, South American Indians have been drying the plant's leaves in order to flavour soups and meat dishes with them. Surplus oven heat does an effective job of drying this material, and so the possibility is offered of some interesting culinary experiments.

Fortunately, Britain's gardeners do not, like the Indians, have to rely upon the plant for mosquito control as well as for protecting the potato crop from eelworm — although current predictions (in 2006) by the climatologists' suggest that the day will come when the mosquito and its malaria-conveying properties will be as familiar in Britain as it is in the tropical regions of this now rapidly-changing planet.

same time (see *POTATOES*). Do so thoroughly, saturating the earth's surface in the immediate neighbourhood of each marker stick

4 wait for at least two hours for tray and planting-out sites to become comprehensively moistened

5 transfer plantlets from tray to marker-stick positions as when promoting the seedlings to the plantlets' tray in heated greenhouse or spare room

6 clean and return the marker sticks to store

7 post the tray of surplus plantlets close to the potato bed. Do so until it is clear that the inserted plantlets have transferred successfully

8 make repairs instantly if the transferred plantlets have not

the planting out of the *Mexican Marigolds* takes place in the relative coolness of the very late afternoon or early evening. [*Consideration: thus, the plantlets enter their new environment when there is the least evaporation of moisture and, hence, the garden soil is at its most moist (noting, also, the significance, in terms of watering, of the start of the second lunar quarter). It is also when the plant begins its new life with the immediate advantage of the coming night-time hours of maximum moisture and lack of moisture-evaporating, day-time warmth*]

3 water the four marker-stick-indicated planting-out sites within the potato bed at the

TIP 61
➔ **Some gardeners are more confident when transferring potted plantlets than they are when transferring trayed plantlets to permanent positions in the garden. If this way is preferred, move on the *Mexican Marigold* seedlings not to plantlet trays but to 70mm-to-80mm pots — one per pot — filled with twenty-hour-moistened John Innes No 1 potting compost. Manage the pots in all respects as if they were trays. This applies whether the propagation takes place in a heated greenhouse or heated spare room. See *RUNNER & CLIMBING FRENCH BEANS: planting out and sowing* for an instruction on growing in, and transplanting from, pots.**

9   dispose of the surplus plantlets and their host compost in the Year 4 Area trench

10   note that as the *Mexican Marigolds* develop to their maximum height of two or three metres, they do not require to be staked

11   cut the plants at ground level after frost has destroyed them

12   remove their roots from the ground. Cut the roots into small pieces.
[**Consideration:** *left in the ground to rot, the roots — which are very large — are likely to impede the pre-Winter dig of the affected Year Area*]

13   transfer root pieces and cut-down stems to the trench in the Year 4 Area that awaits completion into that Year Area's deep-trench bed. Do so even when the stems' heads contain seeds.
[**Consideration:** *being of a*

62

R J Harris, speaking in the walled, kitchen garden at Tresillian one late November: "Here we are, nearly December, and our *Mexican Marigolds* are still trying to flower. They now exceed four metres in height, and with the night-time frost that we have just had I came out this morning expecting to see them black and shrivelled.

"Not a bit of it. There they were, standing proud in the Winter sunshine and looking lovely.

"A couple of people came round the garden with me yesterday and they said, 'Well, what is that?' and I told them, and they said they had never seen or heard of anything like it."

---

half-hardy plant, the seeds will not germinate if they survive in the completed deep-trench bed. By the same token, the pieces of root have no future and value other than that of rotted vegetable matter].

CARROTS: preparing to sow

The carrot (like the beetroot and the parsnip and the other below-the-surface developers) is a guest in the Year 1 Area in that Year Area's fourth and final year of production. Afterwards, the Year 1 Area becomes the Year 5 Area, doing so in the broad-bean-laden early months of the Year 5 Area's first year (and of the garden's first year of being fully-converted to the R J Harris way of vegetable production).

Annually, the head gardener produces the early carrot and the maincrop carrot in five monthly, pot-marigold-protected sowings (despite which, for the reasons stated later, this instruction discusses a four-monthly sowing schedule, not five-monthly). He does so in either or both of his single-dug bed and deep-trench bed.

He devotes the whole of a growing season to the two carrot types, exploiting top soil which has borne crops during each of the three previous years, and which, in consequence, has undergone four major, fertility-enhancing loosenings and aerations with spade and fork. At the same time, the top soil's animal-manure content is more than three

Apply to the *CARROTS* chapter the section/bed/Year Area-labelling, anti-bird, anti-cat, anti-slug, tread-board, bed-edge-rehabilitation, top-soil-preparation and card-index-system disciplines that are prescribed in *BROAD BEANS* and *CABBAGES*.

Apply, also, the recommended stones-gleaning and tools/materials-cleaning/storage practices. See *BROAD BEANS: preparing to sow*

Respond to the need, during the four-year garden conversion, to extend and complete the general service paths, and to apply manual weed clearance to the about-to-be-developed Year 4 Area.

These fundamentals are referred to only briefly throughout the remainder of *'R J Harris's Moon Gardening'*.

years old and, because of that, almost fully dissipated.

The combination thus created of well-worked top soil and dissipated animal-manure content renders the fourth-year Year Area ideal for the growing of the loosened-earth-loving carrot and its below-the-surface compatriots. These also abhor animal manure which retains the full strength of its unemployed nutrients — and, especially, when it is added to the soil, most unwisely in the case of the root crops, just prior to seed sowing.

To seek to win results similar to those of the head gardener in the walled, kitchen garden at Tresillian

1 at the earliest moment in the fourth year of the Year 1 Area, acquire the seeds of

— the selected variety of early carrots. Mr Harris suggests *Amsterdam Forcing*

— the selected variety of maincrop carrots. Mr Harris suggests *Autumn King*

— any variety of spring onion

— *Orange King* or *Scotch Prize* pot marigold, the packets of which are marked, usually, *Calendula*. If these two types are not available, procure the seeds of any old-fashioned, pot marigold

2 at **the start of the February moon's fourth quarter** in the fourth year, fork over the spade-created surface of the whole of the Year 1 Area. Create a levelled, fork-broken surface

3 gather together and remove any weed growth that arises out of the forking over. Dispose of the weeds securely off site

4 note that elsewhere in the garden at this time the Year 2 Area is preparing to receive seed potatoes, the Year 3 Area is preparing to receive flower seed, and the newly-established Year 4 Area has received its Autumn-sown broad bean seeds

5 ensure that the bed-marking, capped (for safety's sake) garden canes remain firmly *in situ* in the Year 1 Area to indicate the locations of the original single-dug bed and of the original deep-trench bed

6 dress the surface of the Year 1 Area with a thickness of fully-composted leaf mould. Ideally,

63

The carrot has been known in Britain since the 1500s. It arrived from Afghanistan via Europe. Viewed by many as an annual plant, it is, strictly speaking, biennial. It belongs to the very many vegetables and flowers that begin as seeds in a given Spring and set seeds in the following Spring.

The greengrocers of before the 1600s would not recognise to-day's roots. For them, the humble carrot was coloured purple, white or yellow. It was those master horticulturists, the Dutch, who recognised and seized the marketing opportunity presented by the colour that we know today. They were guided to it by the clog-shod gardener who espied and conserved an offspring of the purple root that had changed its complexion to deep orange.

The purples, the whites and the yellows have disappeared from the shops, and only where gardeners sow the seeds of these ancient roots is the secret of the coloured carrots preserved. These are the gardeners who know about Tuckers of Newton Abbot, one of Mr Harris's seed suppliers. See *SUPPLIERS*.

but not essentially, first pass the leafmould through a shredder to make it easier to incorporate into the soil

7 turn in the leafmould as far as a garden fork's tines sink into the top soil. Work as much as possible from the permanent path that bounds the Year Area's four sides

8 reduce footfall upon the bed to as close to nil as it is possible

to get. Where this aim is unachievable, use tread boards positioned strategically and trodden upon as few times as possible. Otherwise, accept footfall, and subsequently restore the affected surface with rake or hoe used to the full length of its handle and plied from the permanent path

9 omit the leaf mould if it is not available. With leaf mould, the resultant crop is a superior one. Also, within the context of this general instruction, the quality of the soil is enhanced

10 convert the surface of the soil to a fine tilth for seed sowing. Do so as is described in *BROAD BEANS; preparing to sow*

11 dress the Year 1 Area's surface with 115g to the square metre of fish-blood-and-bone fertiliser. Lightly rake it in. Maintain the levelness of the surface at the same time

12 at **the start of the March moon's first quarter** — choosing, if possible, the morning of what promises to be a fine, dry day — peg a garden line across the 300cm width of the Year 1 Area. Position the line 60cm away from and parallel to the

TIP 62
➜ **Decide at the outset whether to grow short or long carrots. Sow the seeds of the former in shallow soil or any free-standing container, and the seeds of the latter in deep soil.**

64

The carrot fly and the parsnip fly are foes to be taken seriously. In the face of successful onslaughts by the grubs of these pests, many a gardener gives up trying to produce these two extremely valuable root crops.

Sending as many different signals as possible at the one time is the key to confusing and thus deterring the questing flies.

In addition to acting upon this section's suggestions, alternate carrot and parsnip rows either in the one bed or in the one monthly sowing. Their soil/nutritional/management needs are almost identical. See *PARSNIPS*.

nearest adjacent permanent path

13 inscribe a 180cm-long, 12mm-deep drill along the garden line. Do so with the edge of a hoe or with a suitable stick. Commence and end the drill 60cm from the adjacent, opposite two sides of the permanent perimeter path.
[**Consideration:** *inscribing a drill which is 12mm deep is not easy. Simplify the task by*

noting that the aim, for best results, is too shallow a drill rather than too deep a drill]

14 leave the drill open and unsown from morning until late afternoon.
[**Considerations: 1** — *the carrot seed gets its best start in comparatively warm soil. A drill opened in the morning and exposed to the sun and the air throughout the day becomes relatively warmed, helping to achieve the desired warm start;* **2** — *Mr Harris does not recommend the not uncommon practice of dribbling freshly-boiled water from a kettle into the drill as a short-cut way to achieve warmth and, thus, to hasten sowing. The soil's structure within the drill is spoiled by the extremely hot water, he believes. He is certain, too, that the creatures of the soil do not include hot baths among the high points of their daily lives. Equally, "In any event," he comments, "why go to that kind of trouble, which includes carrying an extremely hot receptacle from kitchen to garden, when patience and a few hours of time do the job so much more safely, efficiently, cheaply and considerately?"*].

CARROTS: sowing and managing

Ideally, just before sowing the carrot seed, spray the now almost day-old drill with a mint or thyme solution to help to deter the carrot fly, the carrot's principal and crop-spoiling enemy. Make the solution by boiling a handful of chopped mint or thyme in a litre of water. Filter the resultant liquid when it has cooled, to remove the herb particles. Spray as a fine and penetrative mist with a pump-up pressure spray.

If time presses, or if a pressure spray is not available, do not filter the solution. Fill a cup with it and gently discharge it along the length of the drill. Keep back as much as possible of the herb particles. If a few of these escape into the drill, no harm is done.

Omit this pre-sowing treatment if neither herb is available. Then, still at **the start of the March moon's first quarter**

1 mark each end of the 180cm-long drill with a 30cm-long marker stick inserted 15cm into the soil. Site each of the two sticks 15cm from its end of the drill

2 sow early carrot seeds into the drill in the late afternoon. Do so with a dispenser obtained from a garden centre. Fill it from the seed packet without touching the seeds with the fingers.
[**Consideration:** *fine seeds sown by hand are at risk of being crushed by the fingers. Crushed seeds are unlikely to germinate*]

3 post the sown seeds 5mm away from each other in the drill.
[**Considerations:** *the spaced posting is essential. Almost invariably, it renders subsequent seedling thinning unnecessary. This helps, because the extraction of carrot seedlings from the earth as the row is thinned creates a far-reaching aroma which draws in the carrot fly*]

4 reinstate the sown drill with earth brushed carefully by hand and/or by the back of a rake from the surrounding bed surface

5 cover the row with a carefully-placed, loose layer of very small, bushy twigs.
[**Considerations: 1** — *the top growth of this early sowing is vulnerable to the early season's uncertain weather conditions. The twigs provide protection;* **2** — *the twigs are removable when they are no longer*

necessary without damage being inflicted upon the young seedlings' top growth; **3** — *do not lay fleece on top of the reinstated drill, in lieu of twigs. Entangled within it by their developing tops, the seedlings are likely to be pulled out of the earth as the fleece is lifted prior to removal*]

6 at **the start of the March moon's second quarter**, box in the sown row with four pegged-down garden lines. Site three of the lines 10cm away from the three adjacent sides of the permanent path

7 site the fourth line 50cm from, and parallel to, the sown row

8 ensure that the lines form a right-angled box

TIP 63
➔ **R J Harris recommends an ancient carrot-seed-sowing trick. Instead of brushing earth from the bed's surface into the sown drill, fill the drill carefully by hand with a sieved mixture of one part of wood ash to four parts of earth by volume. Use a 6mm garden sieve. The ash improves the quality of the crop. Return the gravel in the sieve to the Year Area, scattered as thinly as possible. Where sections of the affected drill cannot be reached by hand without imposing a foot upon the bed's surface, apply the earth-ash mixture as far as the stretched-out arm reaches, and then reinstate the unreachable section with earth from the bed, using the back of a carefully-applied rake. More-than-good-enough results can be obtained without the wood ash, so omit the material if is not available.**

9 note that
— the formed, garden-lines box is 100cm wide and 280cm long

— the sown row is precisely centred within the box

10 excavate a 12mm-deep drill along the inner side of each of the four garden lines. Do so with the edge of a hoe or with a suitable stick. Work from the permanent paths

11 station pairs of pot-marigold seeds in the drill at 15cm intervals. Use the finger tips to do so, with care. Touch these very large seeds as little as possible in order to reduce the risk of inhibiting germination

12 brush earth from the bed's surface into the four drills containing the pot-marigold seeds. Tamp the brushed-in earth slightly and gently with the back of a rake. [*Considerations:* **1** — *the pot marigolds are very vigorous in germination and in growth. For this reason, the thinnest of sowings is required;* **2** — *the aroma of the marigolds helps to confuse and, thus, deter the carrot fly as it quests for territory in which to lay its eggs;* **3** — *ensure that the 50cm spacing between the nearest carrots and pot marigolds is observed. This makes it unlikely that the fully-grown pot marigolds deprive the carrots of sunlight. Also, if the pot marigolds flop, they are unlikely to impinge upon and, as a result, possibly damage, the carrots' tops*]

13 repeat the March carrot/pot-marigold/bushy-twig

assembly in its entirety at **the start of the April moon's first quarter** (for the carrot seed) and at **the start of the April moon's second quarter** (for the pot marigiold seed). Use early carrot seeds. Site the 100cm-wide, 280cm-long assembly 10cm from the March assembly, so that a 10cm gap separates the two rows that now form an intervening double-rank row of sown pot-marigold seeds

14 repeat the
— April assembly's sowing in May. Do so at **the start of the May moon's first quarter and second quarter**. Use maincrop carrot seeds. Do not use the bushy twigs. The protection is not necessary during the Summer months

— May assembly's sowing in June. Do so at **the start of the June moon's first quarter and second**

TIP 64

➔ **Resist the temptation to omit the double-rank rows of pot marigold between the monthly carrot developments, and to use single rows instead. The greater strength of the aroma of the two closely-spaced rows is a required weapon within the anti-carrot-fly armoury. Note that where more space than this manual acknowledges is available, more than one row of carrot seeds may be sown each month within the box of protective pot marigolds. Multiple rows are sited 30mm apart, with the 50cm gap between pot marigolds and nearest carrots being maintained.**

65

The head gardener counsels: "In the colder parts of the country, it pays to pre-warm the whole area where the carrot seeds are to be sown. Do this as from the end of February."

Cloches can be used. Once the ground preparation has been completed, line them up over where the drills are to be inscribed. Leave them in situ until the start of the March moon's first quarter. Then form the drills and sow.

"This is if soil and weather conditions permit," comments R J Harris.

Bad conditions may enforce a wait until March/April or even April/May.

"If a March sowing *is* achieved, leave the cloches on as the young plants grow. In this case, protective twigs over the drill are not necessary.

"Remove the cloches the moment warmer conditions arrive."

Cheaper (and safer, perhaps) than cloches incorporating glass panes is heavy-gauge, clear plastic sheeting. Place a generous strip of this over each drill site. Use improvised, hooped wire supports to keep it from touching the earth's surface. This obviates condensation and, consequently, undesirable humidity between it and the earth's surface. Tuck the edges of the plastic strip into the soil to prevent wind lift.

Place the material over its hoops after sowing, until top growth insists that it be removed.

is not necessary during the Summer months

15 ensure that each of the four 180cm-long rows is centralised within its box of sown pot-marigold seeds

16 at **the start of each moon's second quarter**, from the earliest moment of sowing, scrape four indentations in the surface of the ground between each pair of sown pot-marigold and carrot drills. Centre the indentations within the bed's width and between the sown pot-marigold/carrot rows. [***Consideration:*** *site with precision, to facilitate subsequent hoeing. Imprecision makes it well nigh impossible, later, to hoe without the risk of inflicting*

TIP 65
➔ **The head gardener makes five monthly sowings of the carrot seeds, not four, as specified in this chapter section. His fifth sowing, in July, is of the maincrop seeds. It is omitted from the present instruction due to lack of space within the prescribed Year Area. To accommodate it, the Year Area would have to be longer than the prescribed 490cm. Where this instruction's proposed single-dug-bed length can be increased, the fifth sowing should be made. Note must be taken beforehand of, and allowance made for, the impact upon the other dimensions by this modification — and of the likelihood that an additional 60cm-wide, temporary path must be provided across the 300cm width of the single-dug bed.**

quarter. Use maincrop carrot seeds. Do not use the bushy twigs. The protection

66

The old-fashioned pot mari-gold (known as *Calendula*) furnishes more than protection against the carrot fly and a decorative, dark-eyed, deep-orange flower standing some 45cm high.

The petals of this hardy and extremely gardener-friendly plant decorate green salads beautifully (scatter them over — they are edible) and add a subtle orange-yellow tint to the oven-baked rice pudding.

The Elizabethan gardeners were very fond of it. So were the surgeons of their day. They used poltices of it to help to heal wounds.

The farmers' wives of the time coloured their cheeses with it.

damage to developing young plants with the head of the hoe]

17 post a cluster of four or five spring onion seeds in each of the indentations via a seed dispenser. Cover the posted seeds with a dusting of soil first passed through a 6mm garden sieve.
[**Consideration:** *the resultant intermixed plant development helps further to confuse the carrot fly as it seeks egg-laying opportunities*]

18 remove the bushy twigs when the germination of the carrot seeds has taken place, and when, revealing this, there is visible growth above ground

19 examine the carrot bed daily as the roots' green, feathery tops begin to form. Extract every other young carrot as the season progresses, to

achieve, eventually, a spacing of plantlets of 5cm

20 thin in this way only if the initial posting of the carrot seeds does not result in the ideal 5cm spacing

21 remove the carrot thinnings, if any, from site instantly, whether to the kitchen or to a secure disposal point.
[**Consideration:** *the aroma created by the pulling of the young carrots — if that has to be done — is powerful, and attracts the carrot fly. So does the aroma of the thinnings when they are left lying upon the ground*]

22 note that perfection in thinning is no thinning at all — hence the need for disciplined seed posting — and, as a consequence, no disturbance to soil and plantlets. Note that if there are extracted young carrots, some of them may be finger-thick and welcome in the kitchen

23 maintain hoeing throughout the season to prevent weed development and to raise residual moisture to where the developing roots await it

24 join the end-of-row marker sticks of the maincrop-carrot

TIP 66
➔ **Sow chives instead of pot marigolds as an anti-carrot-fly barrier, in the same defensive positions in relation to the drills of carrot seeds and at the second moon quarter. Hoe regularly, as advocated by R J Harris, to prevent the chives from re-seeding, as well as to raise moisture.**

rows with garden line at the earliest moment. Be guided by the lines where not to apply the hoe. Be guided in the same way by the lines indicating where the pot-marigold seeds are sown

25 note that as the quite long carrot season takes the Year 1 Area to its closing days in September and October, opportunities must be found to service the Year 2 Area, now coming to the end of its potato-laden third year, the flower-furnished Year 3 Area, now coming to the end of its second year, and the Year 4 Area, now coming to the end of its broad-bean/cabbage-producing first year.

CARROTS: harvesting

Do not, at any stage, harvest the spring onions. Leave them *in situ* for as long as the carrots are *in situ* and at risk, to retain the benefit of their anti-carrot-fly aroma. Also, as the fourth year of the garden-conversion project draws to a close, bringing complete conversion to head gardener Harris's way of gardening, harvest and consume the carrots before they reach full maturity. Thus, fully clear and consume the early-carrot crop as soon as possible. The timing ensures roots of the best texture, and that storage is not a requirement.

Frequent test checks to ascertain root development are well worth the time spent making them. The merest earth removal at the base of the green top growth, followed by an inspection and earth replacement, suffices. Equally, the earliest removal of roots from the bed reduces the scope and consequence of successful carrot-fly attack.

Whilst observing this general practice

1 loosen the soil before harvesting the carrots. Use a garden fork to the full length of its tines. This secures unbroken specimens and reduces carrot aroma

2 extract the maincrop carrots for consumption as they approach maturity. Consume them when they are young rather than when they are fully grown

3 at **the start of the September moon's fourth quarter**, complete the harvesting by lifting all of the crop. Do so without root breakage. Use a garden fork to the fullest depth that its tines permit. [*Considerations:* **1** — *this moon quarter is when the below-the-surface developers (tubers as well as roots) contain the least amount of moisture and, hence, are at their driest. This ensures the longest possible storage period;* **2** — *the reduced moisture is caused by the moon-released, falling water*

TIP 67
➔ **450cm of the Year Area's overall prescribed length of 490cm is occupied by the four assemblies of carrots and pot marigolds. Fill the blank 40cm-wide by 300cm long strip with a single row of catch-crop lettuces as soon as lettuce plantlets become available. Take the lettuces the moment that they are mature, whether or not required by the kitchen. Replace them regularly. See** *LETTUCES.*

67

Monthly, from September to January, acting outside of the crop-rotation system, correctly fill three 25cm pots with John Innes No 2 potting compost. Moisten the compost correctly. Scatter the seeds of an early short carrot very thinly onto its surface. Use a seed dispenser.

Early Shorthorn is one of the head gardener's favourites for this purpose.

Cover the seeds with a dusting of the compost, obtained by passing some of the compost through a 6mm-mesh sieve. Then lodge the pots in a cold frame, a cold greenhouse or a conservatory. Protect the cold frame and the very small greenhouse against frost by day and/or by night. Keep the compost moist.

Make a monthly chore of this and harvest finger-thick roots in time for and as from Christmas. Use them scrubbed clean and unscraped.

table. *This falls during the moon's third and fourth quarters, reducing its pressure upon the top soil, and the moisture content of the top soil and everything growing in it]*

4 clean the lifted roots by lightly brushing the dried earth from them with a hand. Do not use a tool for this purpose, to preserve each root's outer skin. Do not wash the roots

5 check that the carrots show no tiny holes indicating the presence internally of carrot-fly grubs. Check that there are no external traces of tunnelling by the grubs in the form of grooves in the outer skin

6 withhold those that show either of these signs. Do not consign them to the kitchen in the hope that the head chef may be able to rescue usable sections. Remove the whole of each grub-ridden root and its green top from site and destroy it

7 de-leaf the retained, lifted carrots by cutting off or twisting off their tops. In each case, leave 5cm or so of the top growth attached to the parent root.
[***Consideration:*** *at this time of the year — September/October — the carrot fly is no longer present to be attracted by the aroma of the lifting of the carrots and of the detaching of the green tops]*

8 consign the removed tops to the garden-refuse plastic sacks that wait in store for the renewal in September or October of the Year 1 Area's (now Year 5 Area's) deep-trench bed.
[***Considerations:*** *1 — the first step in the renewal is the digging of the required 1m x 1m x 3m trench. It is into the bottom of this that goes the ensacked waste vegetable matter, including the carrot debris;* **2** *—*

TIP 68
➜ **Leaving mature carrots in the ground with the intention of lifting them as Autumn ends and Winter progresses is bad practice. Once September comes to a close, the feathery, green carrot tops deteriorate rapidly and the roots beneath them cease to increase in size. The roots then split and are attacked by the hungry creatures of the soil and the garden. After that comes messy, in-soil deterioration.**

the entrenched carrot tops are buried beneath the depth of other matter that marks the completed deep-trench bed. This is prior to the re-appearance of the pest in the following late Spring. As a result, its aroma is undetectable even by that creature's hyper-sensitive olfactory organs]

9 note that whilst the standard practice is to compost the carrots' redundant vegetation in the garden compost bin, the head gardener does not do so. He believes that the material almost certainly harbours pests. Also, it may carry the

beginnings of disease — and not only disease related to the carrot. These conditions may not be destroyed by the conventional composting process. Safer, he is convinced, to dispose of the material as suggested above

10 remove from the bed what is left of the pot marigolds and spring onions. Ensack these for the trench in what is to be the Year 5 Area, and is still the Year 1 Area

11 send the fork-damaged carrots to the kitchen for use or for secure disposal.

CARROTS: after harvesting

Pack the perfect, carefully de-earthed, still dirty carrots for storage in layers in timber boxes. Place a thickness of dry peat or dry sand between the layers. Note that it does not matter if the roots touch one another within the layers. Then

1 lodge the filled boxes in a cold, dry, frost-free, easily-accessible place

2 expect the carrots to store throughout the Winter of the Year 5 Area (and of the first year of the fully-converted garden), and into the following Spring until March or April. Begin to consume them without delay, to reduce the risk of loss due to deterioration

3 **by the start of the September or the October moon's third quarter** immediately after the carrot harvesting, fork over the emptied carrot bed. This remains, for the moment, the whole of the Year 1/Year 5 Area. Leave it thus for a day or

two, so that the birds may have an opportunity to investigate its insect life

4 **by the end of the September or October moon's third quarter**, install in the defunct carrot bed (now defunct Year 1 Area) a fresh, single-dug bed and a fresh deep-trench bed. Be guided by the inserted garden-cane marker sticks where these beds were installed during this Year Area's first year, four years previously. The

> **TIP 69**
> ➔ **Lose no time between carefully lifting the carrot crop and storing it between layers of material such as bone-dry sand or bone-dry peat in closed, stout, wooden boxes. The aim is to give the roots no opportunity to suffer moisture evaporation and, hence, reduced flavour. For the best keepability, store dirty (but not earth-encrusted) roots.**

installation returns the Year Area to its first-year look and layout (*see Diagram 1*, page 14). It also readies the now-Year 5 Area for the first year of its new, four-year rotation cycle in accordance with the requirements of the R J Harris crop-rotation programme

5 turn the surfaces of the two new beds with a sharpened spade. Ensure that they acquire the ploughed-field appearance that has typified the advent of each of the garden's four Winters during its four-year conversion project

6 note that the catalogues of the reputable seedsmen offer information on the extensive ranges of broad-beans, cabbages and other first-year vegetables, now required by the Year 5 Area. Autumn is the time to study them, for Winter provides the ideal moments in which to plan for what is to come and to make sowing/planting decisions.

7 use Winter time to review the data recorded in the card-index system. Within the context of the present chapter they stem from four complete years of vegetable production in head gardener style. They present the high points and the low points in each of the four years.

68

If the wire-net way of protecting a bed's surface from visiting cats (see *BROAD BEANS: managing*) becomes too laborious, advises the head gardener, try small jars half filled with ammonia and inserted into the soil at 250cm intervals throughout the garden. The result is garden-wide protection, but the wire net still has a role to play where small, specific, highly important areas are at risk.

The cats detect the ammonia's smell over quite long distances, mistake it for that of their own kind, and, in the head gardener's words, "sheer off".

"Buy the ammonia from a chemist's shop," says Mr Harris.

The method is a sanitised version of the old, old practice, which entailed taking liquid from the bucket of the end-of-garden privy and scattering it around the vegetable beds. That, too, was not to feline liking.

Note the lessons to be learned from them. Apply the lessons in all four of the now fully operational, crop-rotational Year Areas. These are the brand-new Year 5 Area (previously the Year 1 Area), the Year 2 Area, the Year 3 Area and the Year 4 Area.

PARSNIPS: preparing to sow

Like the beetroot, the carrot and the other below-the-surface-developing roots, the parsnip is grown annually during the fourth and final year of a given Year Area's four-year life span. Within the context of the present discussion, it is the Year 1 Area that is affected,

the whole of the space that is made up of the prescribed single-dug bed added to the prescribed deep-trench bed being filled with parsnips or a combination of parsnips and carrots. The two products make very similar demands upon the soil, and upon the responsible gardener.

Apply to the *PARSNIPS* chapter the section/bed/Year Area-labelling, anti-bird, anti-cat, anti-slug, tread-board, bed-edge-rehabilitation, top-soil-preparation and card-index-system disciplines that are prescribed in *BROAD BEANS* and *CABBAGES*.
Apply, also, the recommended stones-gleaning and tools/materials-cleaning/storage practices. See *BROAD BEANS: preparing to sow*

Respond to the need, during the four-year garden conversion, to extend and complete the general service paths, and to apply manual weed clearance to the about-to-be-developed Year 4 Area.

These fundamentals are referred to only briefly throughout the remainder of 'R J Harris's Moon Gardening'.

In the walled, kitchen garden at Tresillian, under Mr Harris's management, a feature of the carrot/parsnip development is the very close proximity to it of the onion bed. This is desirable, for the smell of the growing onions joins that of the growing pot marigolds, spring onions and chives to persuade the carrot fly and the parsnip fly to veer away to more salubrious territory in which to investigate egg-laying opportunities.

The feature stems from, and underlines a hidden advantage of, the R J Harris ordering of the employment of the four crop-rotation areas. It ensures that,

physically, the onion and root developments are side by side and, although occupying each its own Year Area, are close neighbours.

See *ROTATION* for a detailed examination of the head gardener's system of crop rotation.

In common with all of the root crops, the parsnip finds its ideal habitat in soil which is in its fourth year of being prepared soil containing almost-fully-dissipated, four-year-old animal manure, and which has borne unrelated crops during each of its previous three years.

For splendour, R J Harris's parsnips almost equal the onions (see *ONIONS*) with which the head gardener wins awards year after year. To achieve his results

1 at the earliest moment in the fourth year of the Year 1 Area, acquire the seeds of

— the selected variety of parsnip. Mr Harris suggests *Imperial Crown.* This, being a long parsnip, benefits especially from the Year 1 Area's fourth-year, deep, much-loosened top soil

— any variety of spring onion

— any variety of chive

— *Orange King* or *Scotch Prize* pot marigold, the packets of which are marked, usually, *Calendula.* If these two types are not available, procure the seeds of any old-fashioned pot marigold

2 at **the start of the February moon's fourth quarter** in the fourth year, fork over the spade-created surface of the whole of the Year 1 Area. Create a levelled, fork-broken surface

3 gather together and remove any weed growth that arises out of

the forking over. Dispose of this material securely off site

4 note that elsewhere in the garden at this time the Year 2 Area is preparing to receive seed potatoes, the Year 3 Area is preparing to receive flower seed, and the newly-established Year 4 Area has received its Autumn-sown broad bean seeds

5 ensure that the bed-marking, capped (for safety's sake) garden canes remain firmly *in situ* in the Year 1 Area. They indicate the locations of the original single-dug bed and of the original deep-trench bed

6 dress the surface of the Year 1 Area with a generous thickness of fully-composted leaf mould. Ideally, but not essentially, first pass the leafmould through a shredder to make it easier to incorporate into the soil

7 turn in the leafmould as far as a garden fork's tines sink into the top soil. Work as much as possible from the permanent path that bounds the Year Area's four sides

8 reduce footfall upon the surface of the bed's top soil to as close to nil as it is possible to get. Where this aim is unachievable, use tread boards positioned strategically and trodden upon as few times as possible. Otherwise, accept footfall, and subsequently restore the affected surface with rake or hoe used to the full length of its handle and plied from the nearest surface of permanent path

9 omit the leaf mould if it is not available. With leaf mould, the resultant crop is a superior one. Also, within the context of this general instruction, the quality of the soil is enhanced

10 convert the surface of the soil to a fine tilth for seed sowing. Do so as described in *BROAD BEANS; preparing to sow*

11 still at **the start of the February moon's fourth quarter** in the fourth year, dress the Year 1 Area's surface with 115g to the square metre of fish-blood-and-bone fertiliser. Lightly rake it in. Maintain the levelness of the surface

12 at **the start of the March moon's first quarter** — choosing, if possible, the morning of what promises to be a fine, dry day — peg a garden line across the 300cm width of the Year 1 Area. Position the line 60cm away from and parallel to the nearest adjacent permanent path

TIP 70
➔ **The parsnip (and the carrot and the beetroot) hates heavy, wet, clayey, cold soil and poor drainage — although it does its best in even these inhospitable conditions. Soil of this quality is not to be found in the R J Harris-style vegetable garden, but not all gardens are governed by Mr Harris's beneficial diktat. Lighten such soil by first digging in a dressing of finely-sifted coal ash or permissibly-harvested peat or fully-composted leaf mould (the latter, in any event, featuring among his recommendations for preparing the parsnip bed).**

13 inscribe a 180cm-long, 12mm-deep drill along the garden line. Do so with the edge of a hoe or with a suitable stick. Commence and end the drill 60cm from the adjacent, opposite two sides of the permanent perimeter path.
[**Consideration:** *inscribing a drill which is 12mm deep is not easy, sometimes. Simplify the task by noting that the aim, for best results and with non-tall-growing plants, is too shallow a drill rather than too deep a drill*]

14 leave the drill unsown from morning until late afternoon.
[**Considerations: 1** — *the parsnip seed gets its best start in comparatively warm soil. A drill opened in the morning and exposed to the sun and the air throughout the day becomes relatively warmed, helping to achieve the desired warm start;* **2** — *Mr Harris does not recommend the not uncommon practice of dribbling boiling water from a kettle into the drill as a short-cut way to achieve warmth and, thus, to hasten sowing. The soil's structure within the drill is spoiled by the extremely hot water, he believes. He is certain, too, that the creatures of the soil do not include hot baths among the high points of their daily lives. Equally, "In any event," he comments, "why go to that kind of trouble, which includes carrying an extremely hot receptacle from kitchen to garden, when patience and a few hours of time do the job so much more safely, efficiently, cheaply and considerately?"*].

PARSNIPS: sowing

Ideally, just before sowing the parsnip seed, spray the now almost day-old drill with a mint or thyme solution to help to deter the parsnip fly, the parsnip's principal and crop-spoiling enemy. Make the solution by boiling a handful of chopped mint or thyme in a litre of water. Filter the resultant liquid when it has cooled, to remove the herb particles. Spray as a fine and penetrative mist with a pump-up pressure spray.

If there is insufficient time in which to do this, or if a pressure spray is not available, do not filter the solution. Fill a cup with it and gently discharge it along the length of the drill. Keep back as much as possible of the herb particles. If a few of these escape into the drill, no harm is done.

Omit this pre-sowing treatment if neither herb is available. Then, still at **the start of the March moon's first quarter** in the fourth year of the Year 1 Area

1 mark each end of the 180cm-long drill with a 30cm-long marker stick inserted 15cm into the soil. Site each of the two sticks 15cm from its end of the drill

2 sow parsnip seeds into the drill in the late afternoon. Do so in groups of three, the three being positioned close to one another. Station the groups 15cm apart

3 post the groups of these very large seeds with the tips of the fingers. Touch them as little as possible, to reduce the risk of inflicting damage and, thus, diminishing their ability to germinate.
[**Considerations: 1** — *seeds,*

69

The parsnip — one of the most accommodating, patient and understanding of crops — is that rare vegetable, a native of the British Isles, which did not attain its present form until the gardeners of that long period known as the Middle Ages took it in hand.

The results can be seen at their most impressive on the display benches of today's horticultural shows up and down the country. There, groups of three or four matched 120cm-long-plus specimens retaining full flavour are not unusual. They are grown by enthusiasts, most of whom are prepared to undertake the preparation of the necessary deep parsnip bed at least two years before showing.

These are growers many of whom contrive special growth conditions and techniques involving lengths of drainage pipe, special composts and endless, tender, loving care.

*small and large, that are sown by hand, are in risk of being crushed by the fingers and, in consequence, rendered unlikely to germinate; **2** — the spaced posting of the seeds' groups is essential. It reduces subsequent seedling thinning considerably. This helps, because the extraction of parsnip seedlings from the earth, as the row is thinned, creates a far-reaching aroma. It is this that draws in the parsnip fly]*

4 reinstate the sown drill with earth brushed carefully by hand and/or by the back of a rake from the surrounding bed surface

5 cover the reinstated, sown, parsnip row with a carefully-placed, loose layer of very small, bushy twigs.
[***Considerations: 1*** *— the top growth of this early sowing is vulnerable to the early season's uncertain weather conditions. The twigs provide protection;* **2** *— sufficient care being exercised, the twigs are removable when they are no longer necessary without damage being inflicted upon the young seedlings' top growth;* **3** *— do not lay fleece on top of the reinstated drill, in lieu of twigs. Entangled within it by their developing tops, the seedlings are likely to be pulled out of the earth as the fleece is lifted prior to removal]*

6 at **the start of the March moon's second quarter**, box in the sown row with four pegged-down garden lines. Site three of the lines 10cm away from the three adjacent sides of the permanent path

7 site the fourth line 50cm from, and parallel to, the sown row

8 ensure that the lines form a right-angled box

9 note that
— the formed, garden-lines box is 100cm wide and 280cm long
— the sown row is precisely centred within the box

TIP 71
➔ See *Tip 63* for a description of the head gardener's wood-ash method when reinstating sown carrot drills. It is equally effective when applied to the sowing of parsnip seeds.

10 excavate a 12mm-deep drill along the inner side of each of the four garden lines. Do so with the edge of a hoe or with a suitable stick. Work from the permanent paths

11 station pairs of pot-marigold seeds in the drill at 15cm intervals. Use the finger tips to do so, with care. Touch these very large seeds as little as possible in order to reduce the risk of inhibiting germination

12 brush earth from the bed's surface into the four drills containing the pot-marigold seeds. Tamp the brushed-in earth slightly and gently with the back of a rake.
[*Considerations:* **1** — *the pot marigolds are very vigorous in germination and in growth. For this reason, the thinnest of sowings is required;* **2** — *the aroma of the marigolds helps to confuse and, thus, deter the parsnip fly as it quests for territory in which to lay its eggs;* **3** — *ensure that the 50cm spacing between parsnip and pot-marigold seeds is observed. This makes it unlikely that the fully-grown pot marigolds deprive the parsnips of sunlight. Also, if the pot marigolds flop, they are unlikely to impinge upon and, as a result, possibly damage, the parsnips' tops*]

13 repeat the March parsnip/pot-marigold/bushy-twig assembly in its entirety at **the start of the April moon's first quarter** (for the parsnip seed) and at **the start of the April moon's second quarter** (for the pot marigiold seed). Site the 100cm-wide, 280cm-long

assembly 10cm from the March assembly, so that a 10cm gap separates the two rows that now form an intervening double-rank row of sown pot-marigold seeds

14 repeat the

— April assembly's sowing in May. Do so at **the start of the May moon's first quarter** (for the parsnip seed) and **second quarter** (for the pot-marigold seed). Do not use the bushy twigs. The protection is not necessary during the early Summer months

— May assembly's sowing in June. Do so at **the start of the June moon's first**

TIP 72
➔ **Mr Harris's favourite drill-inscribing 'tool' is the marked-up end of a rake handle. It carries easily-discernible marks at 12cm, 24cm, 36cm and 48cm intervals from the handle's tip. This approximately half-inch (in imperial measure) spacing, representing the possible depths of the drills that he prefers, underscores his general practice of deep as opposed to shallow sowing when sowing tall-growing plants into the top soil. This, he argues, ensures extra root length and, hence, reduced likelihood of plants being blown over by strong winds. He cites the example of the early-sown pea, in this connection. His sowing of the shorter plants into the soil or into compost in containers or pots follows his other rule. This is that this type of sown seed must lie no more than twice its own thickness beneath the surface of the growing medium.**

quarter (for the parsnip seed) and **second quarter** (for the pot-marigold seed). Do not use the bushy twigs. The protection is not necessary during the Summer months

15 ensure that each of the four 180cm-long rows is centralised within its box of sown pot-marigold seeds

16 at **the start of each moon's second quarter**, from the earliest moment of sowing, scrape four indentations in the surface of the ground between each pair of sown pot-marigold and parsnip drills. Centre the indentations within the bed's 300cm width and between the sown pot-marigold and

parsnip rows.
[*Consideration: site with precision, to facilitate subsequent hoeing. Imprecision makes it well nigh impossible, later, to hoe without the risk of inflicting damage to developing young plants with the head of the hoe*]

17 post a cluster of four or five spring onion seeds or chive seeds, or a mix of the two, in each of the indentations via a seed dispenser. Cover the posted seeds with a dusting of soil first passed through a 6mm garden sieve.
[*Consideration: the resultant intermixed plant development helps further to confuse the parsnip fly as it seeks egg-laying opportunities*].

PARSNIPS: managing

Remove the bushy twigs when the germination of the parsnip seeds has taken place, when there is visible growth above ground. Then

1 remove the two weakest-looking of the three young parsnips at each posting in the rows. Do so carefully, so as not to disturb the strongest-looking plantlet. Arrive at, eventually, a 15cm spacing of the plantlets

2 immediately place the thinnings in a plastic bag and close the top of the bag firmly after each addition is made. Do not permit any thinning to rest upon the ground's surface, even momentarily. Thin in this way with minimal disturbance to soil and plantlets

3 tie the plastic bag securely the moment that the thinning is

complete. Immediately dispose of it securely off site. By these means diminish the impact of, and remove, a parsnip-fly attractant.

TIP 73
➔ **If a February initiation of parsnip development is not possible because of adverse weather/soil conditions, postpone activity until March or April. Nothing is lost. Be sure to observe in the month of commencement the start of the fourth moon quarter for the preliminary feeding, and — in the following month — the start of the first moon quarter for sowing the parsnips. Follow this, at the start of the second moon quarter, with the sowing of the protective marigolds and spring onions.**

70

The most unlikely of culinary partnerships is that of the parsnip and the banana. That their flavours complement each other is accounted for by the presence in both of potassium. That the partnership is hardly ever exploited in the kitchens of the West is due to the strict segregation by chefs of edible plants into fruit and vegetable. The parsnip, without doubt is vegetable, whilst the banana, indubitably, is fruit. Crossing over is forbidden.

The cooks of the tropical parts of the world have known better for centuries, and evidence of this is India's banana and parsnip curry.

Peel and slice parsnips and gently boil them in water with sultanas for ten minutes.

Gently soften chopped onion and green pepper in oil. Add curry powder, ground ginger and sugar, and cook further.

Combine the parsnip water, lemon zest, lemon juice and peanut butter to make a thick sauce. Mix in the prepared parsnip and sultanas, and heat gently but thoroughly. Add uncooked sliced banana, and serve with cooked whole-grain brown rice. Chopped pine-apple (tinned is sutiable), sliced oranges mixed with chopped onion and lemon juice, and dry-fried peanuts make fine side dishes.

Patty Fisher records this gem in her 1969 *Vegetarian Cookery*, published by Hamlyn under the ISBN 0 600 03436 6 and still in print in 1985.

[*Consideration:* the aroma created by the pulling of the young parsnips — which cannot be avoided — is powerful, and attracts the parsnip fly. So does the aroma of the thinnings when they are left upon the ground]

4 join the end-of-row marker sticks of the third and fourth sowings with garden line at the earliest moment. Place the line at ground-surface level

5 maintain hoeing throughout the season to prevent weed development and to raise residual moisture to where the developing roots await it. Be guided by the lines over the sown rows where not to apply the hoe. Be guided in the same way and with the same result by the lines indicating where the pot-marigold seeds are sown

6 remove the garden lines once germination has produced row-indicating positions, and for that reason are no longer required

7 note that as the quite long parsnip season takes the Year 1 Area to its closing days in September and October, opportunities must be found to service the Year 2 Area, now

TIP 74
➜ "Buy the *Guernsey Half Stump* if you can find it when shopping for parsnip seed," advises R J Harris. "It is one of the old-fashioned ones. It grows to about 30cm long, and has a fantastic sweet flavour." Other varieties to win the head gardener's recommendation are *The Student, Hollow Crown* and — his favourite for show purposes — *Tender & True.* "Expect lengths of between 45cm and 60cm with this one," he says.

coming to the end of its potato-laden third year, the flower-furnished Year 3 Area, now coming to the end of its second year, and the Year 4 Area, now coming to the end of its broad-bean/cabbage-producing first year.

PARSNIPS: harvesting

Do not, at any stage, harvest the spring onions and the chives. Leave them *in situ* for as long as the parsnips are *in situ* and at risk, to retain the benefit of their anti-parsnip-fly aroma. Also, as the fourth year of the garden-conversion project draws to a close, bringing complete conversion to head gardener R J Harris's way of gardening, progressively harvest and consume the parsnips as they reach usable size.

Frequent test checks as from the end of August to ascertain root development are well worth the time spent making them. The merest earth removal at the base of the green top growth, followed by an inspection and earth replacement, suffices. Equally, the earliest removal of usable roots from the bed reduces the scope and consequence of successful parsnip-fly attack.

Note that a March sowing can, in ideal conditions, result in roots which are usable in late August/very early September.

Whilst observing this general practice

1 loosen the soil well before harvesting the parsnips. Use a garden fork to the full length of its tines. This secures unbroken specimens and reduces parsnip aroma

2 at **the start of the September moon's fourth quarter**, lift all of the remaining parsnips. Do so without root breakage, as far as possible. Use a garden fork to the fullest depth that its tines permit.

[***Considerations: 1*** *— this moon quarter is when the below-the-surface developers (tubers as well as roots) contain the least amount of moisture and, hence, are at their driest. This ensures the longest possible storage period;* ***2*** *— it is also when the top soil is at its least moist, creating the driest conditions for root extraction. The result is least-mud-clad, lifted roots;* ***3*** *— the reduced moisture content is caused by the moon-released, falling water table. This falls during the moon's third and fourth quarters, reducing its pressure upon the top soil, and, in consequence, the moisture content of the top soil and everything growing in it*]

3 lift the roots at the end of the day, when the sun is at its lowest ebb or the ambient temperature is at is lowest level.
[***Consideration:*** *the exposed parsnips are best not subjected to the heat of the sun or to the day's highest ambient temperature level. If they are, they become limp and unlikely to store successfully*]

4 clean the lifted roots by lightly brushing the dried earth from them with a hand. Do not use a tool for this purpose, to preserve each root's outer skin. Do not wash the roots

5 check that the parsnips show no tiny holes indicating the

presence internally of parsnip-fly grubs. Check that there are no external traces of tunnelling by the grubs in the form of grooves in the outer skin

6 withhold those that show either of these signs. Do not consign them to the kitchen in the hope that the head chef may be able to rescue usable sections. Remove the whole of each grub-ridden root and its green top from site and destroy it

7 de-leaf the retained, lifted parsnips by cutting off or twisting off their tops. In each case, permit 5cm or so of the top growth to remain attached to the parent root. [**Consideration:** *at this time of the year, the parsnip fly is no longer present to be attracted by the aroma of the lifting of the parsnips and of the detaching of the green tops*]

8 consign the removed tops to the garden-refuse sacks that wait in store for the renewal (albeit at a delayed moment) of the Year 1 Area's (now Year 5 Area's) deep-trench bed. [**Considerations: 1** — *the first step in the renewal is the digging of the required 1m x 1m x 3m trench. It is into the bottom of this that goes the ensacked waste vegetable matter collected during the fourth year of the garden-conversion project and including the parsnip debris;* **2** — *the entrenched parsnip tops are buried beneath the depth of other matter that marks the completed deep-trench bed. This is prior to the re-appearance of the pest in the following late Spring. As a result, the parsnips' tops aroma is undetectable even by that creature's hyper-sensitive olfactory organs*]

9 note that whilst the standard practice is to compost the parsnips' redundant vegetation in a garden compost bin, the head gardener does not do so. He believes that the material almost certainly harbours pests. Also, it may carry the beginnings of disease — and not only disease related to the parsnip. These conditions may not be destroyed by the conventional composting process. Safer, he is convinced, to dispose of the material as suggested above

10 uproot and remove from the bed what is left of the marigold and spring onion/chive developments. Place these in the trench in

---

TIP 75

➔ **Frost does no harm to the parsnip. Indeed, many gardeners believe that it enhances the root's flavour and natural sweetness. For this reason (and noting that the parsnip is resistant to in-soil pest attack), it is often left in the soil through Winter until March, when it is removed before it can set seed and attempt to continue its life cycle. Unhappily, the practice disrupts the crop-rotation system, for the all-important single-dug and deep-trench beds cannot be installed where parsnips continue in residence from November onwards. As a compromise, to obtain the benefit of the frost-improved flavour, the July parsnip row can be positioned where it creates no big obstacle to the continuation of the crop-rotation system. This requires planning at the earliest stages.**

the erstwhile Year 1, now Year 5, Area. Send the fork-damaged parsnips to the kitchen for use or secure disposal.

PARSNIPS: after harvesting

For storage, pack the perfect, carefully de-earthed, still dirty parsnips in layers in timber boxes. Place a thickness of dry peat or dry sand between the layers. Note that it does not matter if the roots touch one another within the layers. Then

1 lodge the filled boxes in a cold, dry, frost-free, easily-accessible place.
[*Consideration: of these conditions, that of ease of accessibility is the most significant, probably. Many a stored product has lain unused and, eventually, unusable, solely because extricating its container has become too energy- and time-consuming a task. Rules must be laid down and never broken. A helpful one is that nothing may be placed upon the top of the storage container, or in front if it, impeding or blocking access*]

2 expect the parsnips to store throughout the Winter of the Year 5 Area (and of the first year of the fully-converted garden), and into the following Spring until March or April. Begin to consume them without delay, to reduce the risk of loss due to deterioration

3 commit the sand or peat from the emptied storage container to other, non-storage tasks. Do not re-use it as an aid to storage. It is likely to be less than dry

4 fork over the emptied parsnip bed immediately after harvesting. This remains, for the moment, the whole of the Year 1/Year 5 Area. Leave it thus for a day or two, so that the birds may have an opportunity to investigate its insect life

5 **by the end of the October moon's third quarter,** install in the defunct parsnip bed (which covers the whole of the Year Area's surface) a new, single-dug bed and a new deep-trench bed. Be guided by the inserted garden-cane marker sticks where these beds were installed during this Year Area's first year, four years previously. The installation returns the Year Area to its first-year look and layout (*see Diagram 1*, page 14), and promotes the erstwhile Year 1 Area to what is now the Year 5 Area. It also readies the Year 5 Area for the first year of its four-year rotation cycle in accordance with the requirements of the R J Harris crop-rotation programme.
[*Consideration: the alternative is to commence installing the new beds during unfriendly November at the start of the November moon's third quarter. At this time, the weather/ ground conditions are likely to be unfavourable*]

6 turn the surfaces of the two new beds with a sharpened

TIP 76
➜ **Re-read the panels and tips of *CARROTS* for information about pests and storage which applies equally to the parsnip.**

spade. Ensure that they acquire the ploughed-field appearance that has typified the advent of each of the garden's four Winters during its four-year conversion project, and will do so for all of the time that the converted garden continues as an R J Harris-style vegetable producer

7 note that the catalogues of the reputable seedsmen offer information on the extensive ranges of broad beans, cabbages and other first-year vegetables, now required by the Year 5 Area. They offer, also, information about the third- and fourth-year vegetables, now required by the Year 2, Year 3 and Year 4 Areas. Autumn is the time to study them, for Winter provides the ideal moments in which to plan for what is to come and to make sowing/planting decisions.

8 use Winter time to review the data recorded in the card-index system. Within the context of the present chapter they stem from four complete years of vegetable production in the head gardener's style. They report the high and the low points in each of the four of the Year Areas. Note the lessons to be learned from them. Apply the lessons in all four of the now fully operational Year Areas. These are the Year 5 Area, previously the Year 1 Area, the Year 2 Area, the Year 3 Area and the Year 4 Area.

BEETROOTS: preparing to sow

The head gardener grows beetroot throughout the vegetable-production season, at Tresillian, in its own section of one of his single-dug beds or one of his deep-trench beds during the fourth and final year of the two beds' four-year life span. They are in rows spaced 30cm-to-45cm from each other, each containing plants spaced 15cm-to-20cm apart. Mr Harris aims at three monthly sowings, commencing at the start of the May moon's first quarter.

At this point, the beds have borne year-specific crops during each of the previous three years. In consequence, the top soil has received major, pre-Winter loosenings and, hence, fertility-enhancing aerations with spade and fork at least three times. Additionally, the soil's manure content has been employed three times and, as a result, is almost fully dissipated. The combination renders it ideal for the growing of root crops.

Accompanying the beetroot in the Tresillian vegetable beds are this manual's highlighted carrot and parsnip, each in its own adjacent section of the employed bed or beds, and each grown in some considerable volume.

This combination and level of volume are not attainable within the context of this manual's general instruction, so, accepting the limitation, to achieve the results with beetroots that are achieved in Tresillian's walled, kitchen garden

1 at the earliest moment at the commencement of the fourth year of the Year 1 Area, acquire the seeds of the selected variety of beetroot. Mr Harris recommends *Libero*. It provides the ball shape and the deep red colour that everyone expects in the beetroot, and is perfectly suited for the final sowing in

Apply to the *BEETROOTS* chapter the section/bed/Year Area-labelling, anti-bird, anti-cat, anti-slug, tread-board, bed-edge-rehabilitation, top-soil-preparation and card-index-system disciplines that are prescribed in *BROAD BEANS* and *CABBAGES*. Apply, also, the recommended stones-gleaning and tools/materials-cleaning/storage practices. See *BROAD BEANS: preparing to sow*

Respond to the need, during the four-year garden conversion, to extend and complete the general service paths, and to apply manual weed clearance to the about-to-be-developed Year 4 Area.

These fundamentals are referred to only briefly throughout the remainder of 'R J Harris's Moon Gardening'.

July. It is well worth its slightly elevated price of around 80p for a packet of 150 seeds (in 2006/7)

2 at **the start of the April moon's fourth quarter** in the Year 1 Area's fourth year, fork over the spade-turned surface of the whole of the Year 1 Area. [***Consideration:*** *this is the post-potato surface resulting from the third year of the Year 1 Area. It was created immediately the potato crop had been lifted, and, beneficially, has over-wintered for the fourth time*]

3 gather together and remove from the surface any weed growth that arises out of the forking over. Dispose of this material securely off site

4 ensure that the bed-marking, capped (for safety's sake) garden canes remain firmly *in situ* in the Year 1 Area. They indicate the locations of the original single-dug and deep-trench beds

5 minimise severely footfall upon the surface of the Year Area's top soil. Where this is not possible, use tread boards positioned strategically and trodden upon as few times as possible. Otherwise, accept footfall, and subsequently restore the affected surface with rake or hoe used to the full length of its handle and

TIP 77
➔　**Sand taken from the wind-blown dunes of the Cornish beaches is one of Mr Harris's aids to beetroot cultivation. He spreads 500g of it to the square metre just after the pre-Winter dig of the fourth-year beetroot-bed-to-be with a sharpened spade. He leaves it on the roughly-broken surface throughout Winter, and then incorporates it as the surface is made ready at the start of the April moon's fourth quarter for seed-sowing at the start of the May moon's first quarter. The sand's very slight salt content converts the top soil into a very unfriendly habitat for the slugs. Also, the soil's drainage is improved (the beetroot loves well-drained as well as warm soil) — and the addition "does marvels for the colour of the beetroot", to use the head gardener's own words.**

plied from the nearest permanent path

6 convert the surface of the soil to a fine tilth for seed sowing. Do so as described in *BROAD BEANS; preparing to sow*

7 note that elsewhere in the garden at this time the Year 2 Area is preparing to receive seed potatoes, and the Year 3 Area flower seed. Note, also, that the newly-established Year 4 Area has received Autumn-sown broad-bean seeds in its single-dug bed

8 still **at the start of the April moon's fourth quarter**, dress the surface of the rake-levelled beetroot-bed-to-be with 115g to the square metre of fish-blood-and-bone fertiliser. Lightly rake

it into the surface. Restore the levelness of the surface at the same time

9 at **the start of the May moon's first quarter** — choosing, if possible, the morning of what promises to be a fine, dry day — peg a garden line across the 300cm width of the Year 1 Area. Position the line 30cm from and parallel to the nearest permanent path

10 inscribe a 270cm-long, 25mm-deep drill along the garden line. Do so with the edge of a hoe or with a suitable stick. Commence and end the drill 15cm from each of the two opposite sides of the permanent perimeter path.

BEETROOTS: sowing

Leave the newly-inscribed drill open and unsown from morning until late afternoon. Like the carrot seed and the parsnip seed, the beetroot seed gets its best start in comparatively warm soil. A drill opened in the morning and exposed to the sun and the air throughout the day becomes relatively warmed, helping to achieve the desired warm start. Also as with the carrot and the parsnip, and for the same reasons (see *CARROTS: preparing to sow* and *PARSNIPS: preparing to sow*), Mr Harris does not recommend the application of boiling water to the open drill in order to achieve instantly a localised increase in soil temperature.

Then, still at **the start of the May moon's first quarter** in the fourth year of the Year 1 Area

1 station single beetroot seeds 30mm apart in the drill. Do so

with a seed dispenser, not by hand. Station the first seed at the commencement of the drill, and the final seed at the other end of the drill.
[**Consideration:** *even the very large seeds of the beetroot are in risk of being crushed by the fingers when sown by hand. Crushed seeds are unlikely to germinate*]

2 reinstate the sown drill with earth brushed carefully from the surrounding bed surface by hand and/or by the back of a rake

3 cover the reinstated, seeded row with a carefully-placed, loose layer of very small, bushy twigs.
[**Considerations: 1** — *this is done not to warm the soil, as in the case of the carrot's and the*

parsnip's initial sowings. May's weather and soil conditions render that unnecessary. The twigs create a protective barrier to ward off the birds, which are attracted to the very visible, vivid red of the beetroot seedlings as they appear above ground. They cannot resist the temptation to tug at the seedlings, and, hence, pull them from the soil; **2** — sufficient care being exercised, the twigs are removable when they are no longer necessary without damage being inflicted upon the young seedlings' top growth; **3** — do not lay fleece on top of the reinstated drill, in lieu of twigs, as a possibly protective barrier. Entangled within the fleece by their developing tops, the seedlings are likely to be uprooted from the earth as the fleece is lifted prior to removal. Fleece supported and raised from the surface of the earth by improvised wire hoops reduces the risk of this only a very little]

4 position a second sown drill 30cm from and parallel to the first, if a doubling of beetroots per month is required. Repeat the general sowing method

5 at **the start of the June moon's first quarter**, repeat the May beetroot sowing in its entirety

6 at **the start of the July moon's first quarter**, repeat the June beetroot sowing in its entirety.

71

'Useful' is the word that head gardener R J Harris applies to the beetroot. Certainly, that has been the common view in Britain since the 1600s, when its cultivation was mentioned in written records for the first time. It was an immigrant, arriving from southern Europe, where it had been grown for centuries. As with so much of today's vegetable produce, it was around when the ancient Greeks were doing and writing about their gardening.

Its 17th-century migration deprived it of one advantage: it was no longer able to remain in the ground and — like the parsnip — to be lifted for the kitchen through Winter, as when in its native habitat. The cold and the damp of the British Winter proved to be too much for it.

Like its fellows the carrot, the parsnip and the turnip, it is, truly, a biennial plant.

"It makes a fleshy root from a seed during its first year, in which it stores all of the necessary food to enable it to produce a strong, flowering stem and an abundant crop of seeds during the following year," explains Mr Harris.

"This," he points out, "is how the seed merchants are able to keep on supplying. They grow it from seed to death, harvesting the seeds at the end of its second season.

"We gardeners catch it at its fleshy root stage in its first season, and get the benefit of all that goodness accumulated for another purpose."

Also like its compatriots, the beetroot stores well through Winter provided that the storage conditions are right for it.

Almost every variety available in Britain has been grown in the kitchen garden at Tresillian during the head gardener's term of office "and not one of them has been other than very, very useful, indeed," he comments.

72

For exhibition-quality beet-roots, advises Mr Harris, sow seed into the unmanured soil in the base of a cold frame in March at the start of the moon's first quarter. First of all, feed the soil with a very light dusting of fish-blood-and-bone fertiliser. Do this at the start of the fourth quarter of the February moon.

With the seeds sown, ventilate the frame regularly by day.

Close it by night whilst cold conditions obtain.

By these means, achieve a protected, earlier start, a longer growing season and, in conse-quence, globes of a size that merits competitive showing.

BEETROOTS: managing

When, as the season progresses, germination of the beetroot seeds takes place and there is visible growth above ground, take care to maintain the protective, bushy, anti-bird twigs over the row or rows until the seedlings are at least about 5cm high. Then, remove the twigs. After that

1 examine the beetroot section daily as the roots' red tops begin to appear and then develop, and as the plantlets begin to swell, each at its base, and the affected row begins to become crowded

2 extract every other plantlet, to begin to reduce the congestion. Do so with minimal disturbance to the soil and to the plantlets

3 continue thinning until a final spacing of 15cm between the

maturing plants has been achieved

4 remove the extractions to the plastic sacks in which waste vegetable matter is held until the creation of the deep-trench bed in the soon-to-be Year 5 Area (the present Year 1 Area, soon to be renewed)

5 donate the extracted young beetroots to the kitchen for salad-making purposes as they become finger thick

6 maintain hoeing throughout the season to prevent weed development and to raise residual moisture to where the developing roots await it

7 note that as the quite long beetroot season progresses (or carrot plus beetroot season, or parsnip plus beetroot season, if, as a part of pre-preparation planning, it is decided to cultivate two selected roots in the available space instead of one) opportunities must be found to service the other Year Areas. During this time, the Year 2 Area approaches the end of its potato-laden third year, the flower-furnished Year 3 Area the end of its second year, and the Year 4 Area the end of its broad-bean/cabbage-producing first year.

TIP 78
→ **Ideally, thin the beetroot seedlings in dull, damp weather conditions as the season progresses. If that is not possible, thin in the evening, when the heat of the sun has reduced. This is a root which dislikes disturbance under the full heat of daytime sunshine. When it is so disturbed, it is a root of diminished quality.**

BEETROOTS: harvesting

As the fourth year of the garden-conversion project draws to a close, bringing complete conversion to head gardener R J Harris's way of gardening, progressively harvest and consume the beetroots as they become just short of full maturity, and just short of equalling a tennis ball in size. By these means ensure roots of the best flavour and texture.

Frequent test checks made from the end of July to ascertain root development are well worth the time spent making them. The merest earth removal at the base of the by-now red/green top growth, followed by an in-spection and earth replacement, suffice.

Note that the initial beetroot sowing in May can, in ideal conditions, result in roots which are usable in late August or very early September. To harvest

1 insert a garden fork to the full length of its tines to loosen the soil well before removing the two or three beetroots that usually equal the kitchen's current demand. This helps to secure unbroken, unbruised specimens. This is of importance, bearing in mind the fragility of the newly-removed plant and, especially, its unique colour and shape

2 lift the whole of the beetroot crop by no later than **the start of the September moon's fourth quarter**. Do so, as far as is possible, without root bruising or breakage.
[*Consideration: this moon quarter is when roots and tubers contain the least amount of moisture and, hence, are at their driest. This increases the length of their life during storage. The reduced moisture is caused by the falling water table. This falls during the moon's third and fourth quarters, reducing the pressure upon the top soil and, hence, the moisture content of the top soil and of all that is in it*]

3 clean the roots by lightly brushing the earth from them with one hand. In doing so, take care not to break their skins. The beetroot's quality declines more than that of any other root when its outer surface is damaged. Subsequently, do not wash the lifted globes.

4 twist off the tops of the beetroots immediately after lifting. Do not cut them off. In each case, leave some 5cm of the top growth attached to the parent root.
[*Consideration: twisting off, not cutting off, eliminates bleeding and consequent loss of sap from the beetroot. Bleeding results in loss of colour and flavour*]

TIP 79
➔ **Remember to replace each harvested beetroot (and carrot, parsnip, and turnip) with a lettuce plantlet. Treating the invaluable lettuce in this way, as a catch crop, demands that a tray of suitable lettuce plantlets always be available. This requires pre-planning (see LETTUCES). Remember, also, to harvest the lettuce the moment it is ready to be taken. Very quickly after that, it prepares to bear seed and becomes unusable in any way in the kitchen. Note that lettuce is for light steaming as well as for inclusion in salads.**

73

The head gardener advises: when a developing beetroot receives a sudden check to its growth, it panics and sets seed in the year of sowing instead of waiting, as it should, until the following year.

When it does this, it becomes useless as an edible root.

Too early sowing, or cultivating the seedlings in cold or draughty conditions, can produce the same result.

A May sowing helps to avert this. So does regular hoeing of the beetroot bed, to raise moisture to the depth at which the roots quest for it.

"Do not counter possible drought by watering," counsels Mr Harris.

"Trust, instead, to the hoeing and to the correct observation of the moon quarters when preparing, feeding and sowing.

"And have faith in the design and construction of the bed in which the seeds have been sown, be it single-dug or deep-trench."

5 use the removed tops as an addition to the ensacked waste material that awaits the installation of the rejuvenated Year 1 Area's deep-trench bed.

[*Consideration: the standard practice is to compost this kind of redundant vegetation. The head gardener does not do so. He believes that the material almost certainly harbours pest. Also, it may carry the beginnings of disease — and not only disease related to the beetroot. These conditions may not be destroyed by the composting process. Better and safer, he is certain, to burn it, or to bury it and all that it may harbour, beneath the deep-trench bed's dense filling*]

6 use the removed tops, instead, as leaves which, after very thorough washing, become an addition to the kitchen's salad ingredients.

[*Consideration: this emulates the growing perception (in 2006) that almost all root tops are edible in salad form, some in a minor rather than a major capacity. The practice extends the age-old use of turnip and brussel-sprout tops, both once commonly on sale in the now defunct neighbourhood greengroceries, both now banished by current supermarket policies, field management at farming levels and, in fairness, the ignorance and timidity of the vast majority that forms the country's non-gardening public*].

BEETROOTS: after harvesting

As soon as possible after harvesting the beetroots, isolate the damaged specimens, if any, and send them to the kitchen so that their usable parts may be rescued and then served as side dishes acknowledged to be sub-standard. Otherwise, dispose of them securely off site. Then

1 pack the perfect beetroots — still hand cleaned, still unwashed — for storage in layers in timber boxes. Place a thickness of dry peat or dry sand between the layers. Note that it does not matter if the roots touch each other within the layers

2 lodge the filled boxes in a cold, dry, frost-free, easily-accessible place.
[**Consideration:** *of these conditions, that of ease of access is the most significant, probably. Many a stored product has lain unused and, eventually, unusable, solely because extricating its container has become too energy- and time-consuming a task. Rules must be laid down and must never be broken. A helpful one is that nothing may be placed upon the top of the storage container, or in front if it or at its sides, impeding or blocking access*]

3 expect the beetroots to store well throughout the Winter of the Year 5 Area (and of the first year of the fully-converted garden), and into the following Spring until March or April. Begin to consume the roots without delay, to reduce the risk of loss due to deterioration

4 commit the sand or peat from the emptied storage container to other, non-storage tasks.

74

Converting the beetroot from a dirt-covered globe topped by the remains of its green top growth, and just lifted from a four-year-old Year Area, into a dish guaranteed to tempt all sitting at the table is a simple matter — but time, patience and care are required.

For an average serving, take four roots. Scrub them clean under a running tap — with consideration, so that the skins remain unbroken. Break the skins, and the gorgeous hue that is a part of the beetroot's glory is lost during the cooking process.

Place the roots in a saucepan and fill it with cold water until the roots are just covered.

Transfer the roots to a saucer or a plate, place them to one side, put a lid upon the saucepan and bring the water to the boil.

Use a slotted spoon carefully to lower the roots, one at a time, into the boiling water. In doing so, preserve the unbroken skins. Cover the pan and bring the water back to a gentle boil.

Maintain the boil for one hour.

Retrieve a root with the slotted spoon, place it upon a saucer or a plate, wait a few moments for it to cool slightly, then very gently and carefully (for the root is hot) pinch the skin without breaking it.

If the skin detaches easily, the root is cooked. If it does not, return the root to the pan and continue .the boiling. Repeat the test at half-hour intervals (no more than a further two such tests are required, usually) until the tested root gives up its skin without protest, and a knife gently inserted into its centre declares that the root is tender.

Remove the cooked roots from the boiling water, drain them in a colander, wait for them to cool totally, skin them, slice them using a knife and a fork to maintain unstained fingers, and serve the slices as a salad accompaniment (see *Tip 80*).

Warnings: do not use as a salad ingredient unless a plum-red salad is required; do not test during the boiling with an inserted skewer. The skewer breaks the skin, and, probably, rich, red boiling water containing anaemic-looking roots is the unhelpful result.

Do not re-use it as an aid to storage. It is likely to be less than dry

5 fork over the emptied, exhausted bed that has produced beetroots immediately after harvesting. This remains, for the moment, the whole of the now-redundant Year 1 Area. Leave it thus for a day or two, so that the birds may have an opportunity to investigate its insect life

6 **by the end of the October moon's third quarter**, install in what is now the Year 5 Area a new, single-dug bed and a new deep-trench bed. Be guided by the inserted garden-cane marker sticks where these beds were installed during the Year Area's first year, four years previously. The installation returns the Year Area to its first-year look and layout (*see Diagram 1*, page 14, *SINGLE-DUG BED* and *DEEP-TRENCH BED*). It also readies the Year 5 Area for the first year of its four-year rotation cycle in accordance with the requirements of the R J Harris crop-rotation programme. [*Consideration: the alternative is to commence installing the new beds during unfriendly November at the start of the November moon's third quarter. At this time, the weather/ ground conditions are likely to be unfavourable*]

7 leave the surfaces of the two new beds roughly turned with a sharpened spade. Ensure that they acquire the ploughed-field appearance that has typified the advent of each of the garden's four Winters during its four-year conversion project, and will do so for all of the time that the converted garden

continues as an R J Harris-style vegetable producer

8 note that the catalogues of the reputable seedsmen offer information on the extensive ranges of broad beans, cabbages and other first-year vegetables, required by the Year 5 Area during its first year of production. They offer, also, information about the fourth- and third-year vegetables, now required by the Year 2 and Year 3 Areas. Autumn is the time to study them, for Winter provides the ideal moments in which to plan for what is to come and to make sowing/planting decisions.

9 use Winter time to review the data recorded in the card-index system. Within the context of the present chapter they stem from four completed years of vegetable production according

---

TIP 80
➔ **Skinned, cooked and sliced or cubed beetroot is excellent served as a hot accompaniment to any prepared meat dish, the head gardener points out. Steam it for five minutes, he directs, then serve it as it is or mashed or creamed (like creamed potato). Bee Nilson in her 1972 *The Penguin Cookery Book* (now, alas, out of print) suggests making a roux sauce in the customary way with 3 tablespoons of malt or other vinegar made up to half a pint with water. When the roux is prepared, she adds to it one tablespoon of sugar, and salt and pepper seasoning. She then adds 1lb (500 grammes) of pre-cooked, cold, cubed beetroot, cooks the combination gently for five minutes, and serves it piping hot.**

to the head gardener. They report the high and the low points in each of the four years and Year Areas. Note the lessons to be learned from them. Apply the lessons in all four of the now fully operational Year Areas. These are the Year 5 Area, previously the Year 1 Area, the Year 2 Area, the Year 3 Area and the Year 4 Area.

TURNIPS: preparing to sow

The turnip is that rare member of the vegetable population, the provider of a substantial addition to the kitchen's repertoire that can serve as both a main crop and a catch crop. Indeed, as the latter, with correct pre-planning and forward-looking bed management, it need take up not a square millimetre of unemployed garden space. This is remarkable, considering the sheer volume of food that it can be made to supply, and considering the range of its culinary applications.

All of this, of course, is in respect of the item that is taken from the vegetable garden just short of arriving at full maturity and instantly prepared for the table — whether cooked, as a casserole ingredient or a steamed or baked dish in its own right, or raw and grated, as an addition to a green salad.

This cannot be claimed for the farm-produced, storage-weary, gas-ridden, shrink-wrapped, months-old ball of substitute for woodcarver's timber that is proffered by the supermarket's fruit and veg display.

Surprisingly, to the unitiated, the turnip is a member of the cabbage family. This accounts, secretly, for the high regard in which its green top growth has been held for centuries. Alas, today, this excellent addition to the cabbage suite is unknown to those who do not grow the turnip, for it is seen by few farmers and supermarket buyers as being sufficiently value-adding.

As a brassica, the turnip is one of Mr Harris's first-year products, requiring accommodation in the Year Area that is in the first year of its four-year life span. Within the context of the present discussion, that is the Year 1 Area.

Acquire the seeds of the selected turnip varieties at the earliest moment prior to the commencement of the first year of the Year 1 Area. Mr Harris's favourites are *Early White Stone*, white-skinned and white-fleshed, *Green Top Stone*, also known as *Manchester Market* and first cultivated in Britain in 1857, and *Snowball*, which was introduced to British gardeners in 1826: "a very fast-growing, lovely turnip," comments Mr Harris, "best eaten very young, can be grated and eaten raw in green salads and either roasted whole or sliced and steamed."

His other favourites are *Aberdeen*, "a good all-rounder", and the comparatively enormous 15cm-diameter, 15cm-long *Green Top Yellow* of 1852, which is for winter harvesting and, Mr Harris notes, very good green tops.

To prepare to sow, and to convert the sowings into a fast-growing maincrop (for the rapidly-grown turnip is the sweeter and the better-flavoured for being hurried from seedling to harvested vegetable)

1 at **the start of the April moon's fourth quarter** in the Year 1 Area's first year, fork over the spade-turned surface of the 100cm-deep remainder of the single-dug bed that is adjacent to the maturing broad-bean development. It is

Apply to the *TURNIPS* chapter the section/bed/Year Area-labelling, anti-bird, anti-cat, anti-slug, tread-board, bed-edge-rehabilitation, top-soil-preparation and card-index-system disciplines that are prescribed in *BROAD BEANS* and *CABBAGES*. Apply, also, the recommended stones-gleaning and tools/materials-cleaning/storage practices. See *BROAD BEANS: preparing to sow*

Respond to the need, during the four-year garden conversion, to extend and complete the general service paths, and to apply manual weed clearance to the to-be-developed Year, 2, 3 and 4 Areas.

These fundamentals are referred to only briefly throughout the remainder of 'R J Harris's Moon Gardening'.

separated from the broad beans by a 60cm-wide, temporary, trodden path (see *Diagram 1*, page 14 and *BROAD BEANS: preparing to sow*).
[**Consideration:** *at this time, this 100cm-deep and 300cm-long remainder of the first-year single-dug bed has borne no crops other than Nature's addition of young weeds*]

2 gather together and remove from the turnip-section-to-be's surface any weed growth that arises out of the forking over. Dispose of this material securely off site

3 ensure that the bed-marking, capped (for safety's sake) garden canes remain firmly *in situ* in the Year 1 Area. They continue to indicate the locations and sizes of the single-dug bed and the deep-trench bed

4 minimise severely footfall upon the surface of the Year 1 Area's top soil. Work solely from the two temporary, trodden paths and the permanent paths

5 convert the surface of the turnip-section-to-be to a fine tilth for seed sowing. Do so as is described in *BROAD BEANS: preparing to sow*

6 note that elsewhere in the garden at this time the outlined Year 2, Year 3 and Year 4 Areas are undeveloped, and that the incomplete permanent path encloses only the Year 1 Area

7 still **at the start of the April moon's fourth quarter**, dress the surface of the rake-levelled turnip-bed-to-be with 60g to the square metre of fish-blood-and-bone fertiliser. Lightly rake it into the surface.Level the surface at the same time

---

TIP 81
➔　**Overall, the turnip — an unfairly maligned and often much despised above-the-ground developer — is in two types: the white turnip and the yellow. The white turnip matures some ten days in advance of the yellow. Its seeds are for sowing prior to and including July. The seeds of the yellow turnip are reserved for sowing in August and September, if it is decided to make a sowing as late as September.**

8 leave the turnip-section-to-be undisturbed and open to the skies until the start of the May moon's second quarter

9 at **the start of the May moon's second quarter**, peg a garden line across the 300cm length of the turnip-section-to-be. Position the line 20cm from and parallel to one of the two, adjacent temporary paths. Note that the line has an east-to-west orientation

10 inscribe a 250cm-long, 12mm-deep drill along the garden line. Do so with the edge of a hoe or with a suitable stick. Commence and end the drill 25cm from each of the two opposite sides of the permanent perimeter path

11 repeat the inscription with a second drill placed 30cm

from and parallel to the first drill

12 repeat the inscription with a third drill placed 30cm from and parallel to the second drill

13 note that the three drills fully occupy the 100cm width of the turnip-bed-to-be, leaving a 20cm-wide space between the first drill and its adjacent temporary path, and a 20cm-wide space between the third drill and its adjacent temporary path

14 remove the garden line. Clean it and return it to store

15 insert 30cm-long marker sticks 15cm into the ground at the ends of the three drills. Position each of the six marker sticks at the edges of the turnip-section-to-be, just clear of the permanent paths.

TURNIPS: sowing

Still at **the start of the May moon's second quarter** in the first year of the Year 1 Area

1 post 101 *Snowball* turnip seeds — "the earliest and fastest-growing of all of the turnips," comments Mr Harris — 25mm apart in the first drill. Do so with a seed dispenser, not by hand. Station the first seed at one end of the drill, and the final seed at the other end. [**Consideration:** *using a dispenser obviates the risk of the turnip seeds being crushed by the fingers. Crushed seeds are unlikely to germinate*]

2 reinstate the sown first drill with earth brushed carefully

from the surrounding bed surface by gloved hand and/or by the back of a rake

3 connect the sown drill's two end-of-row marker sticks with garden line placed at ground level and gently taughtened

4 at **the start of the June moon's second quarter**, repeat the May turnip-seed sowing and marker-stick/garden-line adjustment in its entirety. Sow *Early White Stone*

5 at **the start of the July moon's second quarter**, repeat the June turnip-seed sowing and marker-stick/garden-line adjustment in its entirety.

Repeat the *Early White Stone* sowing.

TURNIPS: managing

Moisture raising being of especial importance in respect of the turnip, instantly embark, after the first seed sowing, upon the weekly hoeing of the unemployed ground between and bordering the three rows. As the season progresses, be warned by the adjusted, ground-level garden lines of the presence of invisible seeds, and apply the hoe between the rows to within a couple of centimetres of the lines. Then

1 remove each garden line and its two marker sticks once seedlings appear above ground

2 clean the line and sticks, and return them to store

3 take care, when hoeing, not to make impact with the hoe's head upon the seedlings and, subsequently, the plantlets

4 choose a day as soon as possible after the turnip plantlets in a given row have grown between two and four leaves, and when, at the same time the top soil can be counted upon to be dry enough not to cling unduly to footwear when walked upon

5 stand upon the permanent path and place one foot upon the turnip section's surface at the beginning of, and alongside, a row of newly-developed, two-to-four-leafed plantlets. Align the foot with the row, position-ing it about 3cm from the row

6 permit the weight of the body to fall upon the positioned foot

75

Among his favourite turnips, the head gardener counts *Winter Golden Ball*, an horticul-tural curiosity which for a long period until recent times en-joyed the sobriquet *Orange Jelly* (which is still used by some seedsmen).

"This one," recalls the head gardener, "was probably deve-loped in Cheshire — hence its listing as a Cheshire variety — in the 1850s. It gives you a lovely round form, an admittedly small top, a skin of a pale orangey-yellow, and a truly beautiful rich, yellow, juicy and sweet flesh.

"It is very tender, and has almost no fibre.

"When boiled, it acquires the consistency of a jelly.

"Whe I was a lad, and for long before that, it was fed to invalids and to those recovering from ill-ness. This was because of its jelly-like consistency and its lack of fibre, which made it easy for the sick folk to swallow".

7 step off the permanent path and straddle the row, at the same time placing the other foot upon the section's surface on the other side of the row, at the beginning of the row. Align the other foot with the row, about 3cm from it

8 permit the weight of the body to impose upon the positioned other foot

9 pause, balancing upon soft, unstable top soil, and condition mind and body to this blatant breaking of one of the head gardener's cardinal rules: that a bed's prepared surface must never be trodden upon in any circumstances

10 slide the feet forward, one after the other, along the length of the row — slowly and carefully, still straddling the row and compacting the soil beneath foot impressions that follow one after the other without break: heel to toe; heel to toe

11 maintain the 3cm distance between the row of plantlets and the extending strip of compacted top soil that develops along each side of the row.
[**Considerations: 1** — *the turnip is an especially moisture-loving plant. It has to be, for it wants to develop the strongest possible root structure and most uniform, round shape and best possible colour speedily, and cannot do any of these things without plenteous moisture;* **2** — *this superfluity of moisture is provided, in important part, by ground from which evaporation is reduced to the minimum. Ground which is firmed by being walked upon is of this order;* **3** — *the turnip also benefits from the moisture that the firmed ground entraps close to its developing roots. This underlines the importance of maintaining the 3cm distance between each side of the affected row of plantlets and the walked-upon top soil. The 6cm-wide strip of loose soil encased by the two parallel lengths of compacted soil and harbouring the plantlets' roots becomes relatively highly moisture-charged, since its moisture has difficulty in escaping to the atmosphere ;* **4** — *the walked-upon, compacted soil sinks slightly, forming a shallow shoe- or boot-wide trough. The trough increases the conservation of moisture, for it collects rain and directs it down to the plants' roots systems*]

12 maintain the weekly hoeing of the turnip section's surface. Hoe from the temporary and permanent service paths. Avoid accidental footfall upon the section's surface and damage to the developing plants with the head of the hoe

13 repeat the row walking immediately after each weekly hoeing. Ensure that the hoe-removed weed growth is lifted from the section's surface, first of all, and placed in a receptacle. Later, dispose of it securely off site

14 begin thinning the plantlets as they begin to bear at least four leaves. Do so with minimal disturbance to the

TIP 82
➔ **It is received wisdom in horticultural circles that the turnip must not be sown in the months of May and June. The hot weather and consequently reduced rainfall of these two months, it is claimed, causes this highly water-demanding plant to bolt and to set seed, and, resultantly, to become unsuitable for the kitchen. R J Harris's experience is otherwise. This is not due to Cornwall's rainfall throughout the year being, comparatively, prodigious. It is due to the moisture-retentive properties of the spade's-blade-length-thick layer of animal manure that lies beneath the surface of his specially-designed, single-dug bed.**

76

The turnip is as effective as a catch crop as it is as a main crop, and, in this guise, can be every bit as useful as the lettuce or the spring onion. Indeed, there are gardeners — especially those with small vegetable gardens — who refuse to give it its own territory. They argue that if it can turn in-between-rows soil into a producer without harm being done to the affected rows, there is no profit in permitting it to commandeer space that is required for the less flexible or more demanding vegetables.

Managing it as a catch crop, repeat the July turnip-seed sowing and marker-stick adjustment in its entirety between the July and August cabbage-plantlet installations in the adjacent cabbage section (see *CABBAGES: planting out and managing*). Sow *Green Top Yellow* seeds. Position the turnip row centrally in the 30cm space that divides the July and August cabbage transplantations. Do so at the start of the August moon's second quarter.

Take care not to have an adverse impact upon the cabbage plantlets as the August turnip sowing is carried out.

Apply the weekly hoeing and the immediately succeeding weekly walk, which compacts the affected, turnip-plantlet-bearing soil

The August-sown turnip is installed as a catch crop not because it takes almost nothing from the soil, as is the case with the lettuce. It is closely related to the cabbage, being of the same family. Hence, it is able to meet its nutritional needs from the soil that has been prepared for the development of the cabbage.

Added to this, the cabbage and the turnip, both being brassicas, are compatible plants. For that reason, they co-exist successfully in shared top soil, and support each other.

soil Do so to relieve congestion as the plantlets' globes increase in girth

15 remove the weakest-looking plantlets first of all at each session of thinning. Place these initial thinnings in a small plastic bag as they are extracted. Later, transfer the bag's contents to the trench that awaits conversion into a deep-trench bed in the Year 2 Area-to-be

16 work from the temporary and permanent paths as the turnip section is managed, to avoid unwanted footfall upon the section's surface

17 donate the final extractions of young turnips to the kitchen as they become finger thick. [**Consideration:** *in the kitchen, grated, the young plants are useful for salad-making purposes. So are their green tops when shredded. Alternatively, the tops, if in sufficient number, can be lightly steamed and served as a side dish*]

18 thin until the maturing plants have a final spacing of 75mm

19 note that, as the turnip season progresses, opportunities must be found to move forward the conversion of the undeveloped Year 2, and the de-weeding of the Year 3 and Year 4 Areas of the garden.

TURNIPS: harvesting

It is of paramount importance, the head gardener is convinced, that the turnip be harvested, progressively, the moment that its size lies between that of a golf ball and a tennis ball. "Allow it to become bigger — as it will, given half a chance — and it will become coarse and less easy to process in the kitchen, and its flavour will diminish," he says. "And its top growth will toughen and become less suitable for the raw, mixed green salads and the steamer or saucepan.

"All of this," explains Mr Harris, "is because the turnip must be encouraged to be a very quick-growing crop."

To progressively harvest the turnips just short of full maturity (noting, at the same time, that, in ideal conditions, turnips of this quality are obtainable only sixty days or so after each of the three sowings)

1 insert a garden fork to the full length of its tines to loosen the soil well before removing the four or five turnips that normally equal the kitchen's current demand. This helps to secure unbroken, unbruised specimens

2 replace the lifted turnips immediately with catch-crop lettuce plantlets taken from the tray that is always on hand in the R J Harris style of garden. See *LETTUCES*

3 maintain the strictly-disciplined row structure of the turnip-planted section when inserting the lettuce plantlets, to aid and simplify the weekly hoeing

4 lift the whole of the turnip crop by no later than **the start of the September moon's fourth**

77

In cultivation, the turnip gets on as well with the broad bean as it does with the cabbage, being a companion plant to both. For that reason, try growing turnip tops — not turnips — as a catch crop along with the Autumn-sown broad beans in the first-year, single-dug bed in the Year 1 Area (see *BROAD BEANS: sowing*). The advantage is that nutritious, flavoursome green tops become available as from early February until the broad-bean section is emptied to make it ready for cabbage plantlets (see *CABBAGES: planting out and managing*). The tops fill the Winter-time gap that is left when the cabbage family is scarce or not available.

Once the broad-bean seeds have been sown at the start of the October moon's second quarter in the first year, place rows of 12mm-deep turnip seeds centrally between the broad-bean rows. Populate the rows as thinly as possible from a dispenser, and permit the seedlings and, subsequently, the plantlets, to develop without thinning and as Dame Nature dictates.

Harvest the leaves as they become takeable, sacrificing the parent globe in the process. Indeed, do not look for worthwhile globes; the overall conditions for turnip propagation could not be less friendly and less conducive to development.

Despite this, it must be said, as Spring approaches, it may be judged that some of the denuded globes are worth lifting and sending to the kitchen. In March/April, they could be more than welcome as additions to the casseroles, stews and roasts of late Winter/early Spring.

78

The winter turnip, known as swede, is not to be confused with the white and yellow varieties that are featured in this chapter. When being prepared as a solo dish, the swede, in most people's experience, can only be boiled or steamed and then converted into a watery, reddish pink slush. Its texture, flavour and smell when in this condition are not to everyone's taste; indeed, many, with memories of school dinners and iron-willed dinner ladies, so detest it that they refuse to countenance its presence either in the vegetable garden or on the table.

This is a very great pity, for — as Yorkshire, Lancashire and points north know full well — when steamed, mashed together with equal quantities of steamed carrot and steamed parsnip, and then creamed with old-fashioned butter and seasoned with sea salt and ground black pepper and served hot, it becomes, truly, a dinner-lady beater.

quarter. Do so, as far as is possible, without bruising or breakage.

[*Considerations: 1 — this moon quarter is when plants in general contain the least amount of moisture and, hence, are at their driest. This increases the length of their life during storage; 2 — the reduced moisture is caused by the falling water table. This falls during the moon's third and fourth quarters, reducing the pressure upon the top soil and, hence, the top soil's moisture content and the moisture content of all that is in it. A subsidiary benefit is*

that the lifted turnips bear dry earth, and are mud-free; 3 — this moon quarter also represents the last moment that the Year 1 Area — or any Year Area — may be permitted to remain in its first year. When the first year continues for very long beyond the end of September, with the commencement of the second year being delayed, there are likely to be unhelpful bed and Year-Area consequences. This is especially the case in a garden as small as the one under discussion in this manual]

5 clean the turnips by lightly brushing the earth from them with one hand. Do so the moment they are lifted. In doing so, take care not to break their skins. The turnip's quality declines when its outer surface is damaged. Subsequently, do not wash the lifted globes

TIP 83
→ **The swede is the odd man out among turnips, and, for that reason alone (although, there are others, among them being what many judge to be its foul flavour), is best not included in the sowing programme that is designed for the size of beds referred to in this manual. Sown late in the season, it stays in the ground until well into Winter before being harvested, making it difficult totally to empty the first-year single-dug bed before it progresses into its highly-important Winter dig prior to embarking upon its second year. The tidy gardener with the small R J Harris-style vegetable garden does not care for the vegetable that does not know how to say goodbye and take itself off.**

6 twist off the tops of the turnips immediately after lifting. Do not cut them off. In each case, leave some 5cm of the top growth attached to the parent globe.
[**Consideration:** *twisting off the tops, not cutting them off, eliminates bleeding and*

consequent loss of sap from the root. Bleeding results also in loss of flavour]

7 despatch the removed tops to the kitchen for use as a culinary ingredient in place of shredded lettuce or steamed cabbage.

TURNIPS: after harvesting

Immediately after harvesting, and without leaving the lifted turnips exposed upon the ground, isolate the damaged specimens, if any, and send them to the kitchen so that their usable parts may be rescued. Then, straight away

1 pack the perfect turnips — still hand cleaned, still unwashed — for storage in layers in timber boxes. Place a thickness of dry peat or dry sand between the layers. Note that it does not matter if the vegetables touch each other within the layers

2 lodge the filled boxes in a cold, dry, frost-free, easily-accessible place.
[**Consideration:** *of these conditions, that of ease of accessibility is the most significant, probably. Many a stored product has lain unused and, eventually, unusable, solely because extricating its container has become too energy- and time-consuming a task. Rules must be laid down and never broken. A helpful one is that nothing may be placed upon the top of the storage container, or in front of it, impeding or blocking access*]

3 expect the turnips to store throughout the Winter that introduces the second year of

the Year 1 Area, and into the following Spring until March or April. Begin to consume them without delay, to reduce the risk of loss due to deterioration

4 commit the sand or peat from the emptied storage container to other, non-storage tasks. Do not re-use it as an aid to storage. It is likely to be less than dry

5 fork over the surface of the emptied, ex-turnip section immediately after the harvesting. Do so at the same time as forking over the surface of the adjacent, vacated ex-cabbage section. Fork over, also, the surface of the Year 1 Area's emptied deep-trench bed

6 leave the two beds thus for a day or two, so that the birds may have an opportunity to investigate their insect life. Then, coarsely dig the two beds' surfaces with a sharpened spade, adding a ploughed field finish and texture to their top soil

7 leave the two emptied beds of the Year 1 Area fully exposed to Winter's worst, to await the second-year crop — the pot marigolds — in Mr Harris's moon-oriented, four-year, crop rotation programme

8 **by the end of the October moon's second quarter**, install in the Year 2 Area that Year Area's single-dug bed, and complete the Year 2 Area's deep-trench bed (*see Diagram 1, page 14, SINGLE-DUG BED and DEEP-TRENCH BED*). [**Consideration:** *the alternative is to commence installing the two new beds during unfriendly November by the start of the November moon's second quarter. At that time, the weather and ground conditions are likely to be inhospitable and uncomfortable*]

9 leave the surfaces of the new beds in the Year 2 Area roughly turned with a sharpened spade. Ensure that they acquire the ploughed-field appearance that now distinguishes the Year 1 Area's two beds, and that, thus, they are ready to receive Winter's cleansing, fertility-enhancing worst

10 note that the catalogues of the reputable seedsmen offer information on the available ranges of broad beans, cabbages and other first-year vegetables, soon to be required for the Year 2 Area during its first year of production. Autumn is the time to study them, for it provides the ideal moments in which to plan for what is to come and to make sowing/planting decisions.

11 review, also, the data recorded in the card-index system. Within the context of the present chapter they stem from a complete year of first-year vegetable production according to the head gardener's horticultural way. Note the lessons to be learned from them. Apply the lessons in the planning of the second year of the garden conversion project.

MOON

The moon month (or moonth) is made up of four quarters. These are referred to in this manual as the first, second, third and fourth quarter. In diaries — unhelpfully, so far as most urban dwellers are concerned, as well as the considerable majority who have no knowledge of traditional agricultural practices — they are referred to as 'new moon', 'first quarter', 'full moon' and 'last quarter'.

On the first day of the first quarter (new moon), the strength of the moon's gravitational pull upon Earth at the point at which the

Pressure and moisture content are the mechanisms that the Moon places in the aware gardener's hands

observer happens to be standing is at its weakest. The pull increases from that lowest point as the first quarter develops into and becomes the second quarter. At the end of the second quarter (full moon) and the start of the third, the gravitational pull is at its strongest.

When the third quarter begins, the strength of the pull starts to reduce. It goes on reducing through the third quarter and then through the fourth quarter. At the end of fourth quarter, the gravitational pull is once again at its weakest.

This is when the moon is once

79

'During the whole of my time with the walled kitchen garden and the estate at Tresillian — now almost twenty years — I have never had cause to instruct that water be applied to soil or plant for the purpose of irrigation," says head gardener R J Harris, speaking in 2002. "This has been during some of the driest spells that the British Isles has experienced.

"Water has been used only as an aid to feeding."

The statement expresses the reality that correctly-practised, moon-oriented management removes or considerably reduces what can be one of gardening's most wearisome and/or expensive chores.

This is true no matter what the water-applying gardener's method of gardening.

again new and at the start of the next first quarter.

Earth's water table responds to this unfailing, invariable phenomenon. It rises as the strength of the moon's gravitational pull increases. It falls back as that strength decreases.

As the water table rises, it exerts upward pressure. This causes the moisture beneath the garden soil to rise. This, in turn, results in concentrated moisture content at the level where gardeners do their gardening — which is to say that, for practical purposes, the top soil's moisture content increases, making increased moisture available to whatever grows in it.

As the water table falls back, released by the moon's weakening gravitational pull, the pressure decreases and the top soil's moisture content reduces.

This unfailing act of Nature — which is of greatest significance during Summer's diminished rainfall and increased activity in the garden — can be of help to the aware gardener in the following ways.

Pre-winter dig

Begin the soil manoeuvring that is the essence of R J Harris's fertilising Autumn dig at the start of the moon's fourth quarter. The fallen and still falling water table releases pressure upon the dug soil and causes it to be at its most receptive to the air and to the air-borne higher temperatures. This combination encourages increased vegetable-processing activity by the creatures of the soil and, thus, initiates, sustains and enhances the process that results in increased fertility.

A further benefit is that at the start of the moon's fourth quarter the top soil is at its least moisture charged and consequently, its lightest in weight. Hence, it offers least resistance to being dug with a garden spade or turned over with a garden fork, lightening the demand upon the spade- or fork-wielding gardener's physique.

Feeding

Add manure and fertilisers to the soil at the start of the moon's third quarter — on the first day, ideally, or as close as possible to that time. The falling water table

Simplifying the confusion	
as seen in most diaries	*as seen in this manual*
New Moon	**First Quarter**
First Quarter	**Second Quarter**
Full Moon	**Third Quarter**
Last Quarter	**Fourth Quarter**

80

A bonus of moon gardening is that fertiliser applied at the correct moon time — at the start of and during the fourth quarter — can be reduced by as much as 50% of the manufacturer's recommended volume or weight.

The moon's final phase is when its 'pull' on Earth diminishes to its weakest strength. In consequence, the water table beneath Earth's surface is permitted to slip back to its lowest level.

As the water table recedes, it draws to a deeper depth the fertiliser that is applied at the time. There is improved dispersal and, hence, there can be a reduction in the quantity used.

A consequently additional bonus is a reduction in the chemicals' build up that causes the now acknowledged problems to both wild life and mankind. For, every drop of run off created by fertiliser application (and *over-*application, of which many gardeners are guilty) adds to that build up.

In farming, this reality can be of significance — financially as well as environmentally.

releases pressure upon the dug soil and encourages the more thorough and deeper absorption of the additives.

Sowing the seeds of below-ground developers such as carrots

Sow at the start of the moon's first quarter. The following fortnight or so of gradually increasing moisture combines with the thoroughly absorbed feeds (applied at the start of the previous fourth quarter) to encourage the germination of these slow developers and, subsequently, enhance their ability to survive.

Sowing the seeds of above-ground developers such as cabbages

Sow at the start of the moon's second quarter. The following week or so of by now well-moistened growing medium combines with the thoroughly absorbed feeds (applied at the start of the previous fourth quarter) to create the conditions that encourage the rapid germination that these comparatively fast developers require. It also, subsequently, enhances their ability to survive.

Pruning

Perform surgical operations upon plants when there is the least resultant loss of sap. This is when the moon is in its fourth quarter. Then, being almost completely fallen, the water table exerts the least upward pressure. This, in turn, causes the least discharge of sap from the wound caused by the applied secateurs.

TIP 84

➔ Diaries and calendars indicate each month's new moon with a black disc. They indicate its full moon with an open circle. Their 'first quarter' — shown after the new moon — and their 'last quarter' — shown after the full moon — are presented graphically as slim crescents facing in opposite directions. Gardeners are advised to base their planning for gardening activity not upon this confusing presentation form but, simply, upon the first, second, third and fourth quarters of the moon.

81

The head gardener's belief in the efficacy of his design of underground 'sponge' (referred to throughout this manual whenever his way with preparation is under discussion) increases the significance of his statement of the moon's influence upon Earth's water table.

The 'sponge' is positioned beneath the inserted plant at an appropriate depth. It collects and conserves downward descending rain water. It acts as a reservoir from which the plant's roots draw moisture even during the driest of dry spells.

Crucially, it also collects and retains moisture that results from the rising water table — moisture that falls back and out of reach of plants' roots when there is no 'sponge' to trap it. Hence, the 'sponge' has a dual purpose and, thus, is doubly valuable to the gardener who makes it a feature of soil preparation.

Harvesting the above-ground developers such as cabbages

The ideal is to take leaves, or, much better, remove the whole plant from the soil, when one or the other is at its most juicy and, consequently, most flavoursome. This occurs during the moon's first and second quarter. At this time, the water table is at its highest level. Its increased pressure induces the greatest moisture content in the top soil and in everything that is in it.

Pragmatic considerations must over-ride this rule, of course. When, for example, a plant, such as the lettuce or the cabbage, is at peak quality for kitchen purposes, when it is just short of full maturity, it must be taken at that juncture no matter what is the prevailing moon quarter.

Harvesting the below-ground developers, such as carrots, that are to be stored

Remove these roots or tubers from the soil when the moon begins its fourth quarter. Then, the water table has almost completely fallen. It exerts the least upward pressure. This, in turn, results in the least moisture content in the top soil and in the targeted plants

growing in it. The plants are at their driest — the condition that enables the longest possible storage period. The drier the stored root or tuber, the more is rot held at bay. An improvement upon this result is won when two further steps are taken: 1) harvesting is done at the very end of the day; 2) the lifted roots or tubers are transferred immediately into store. By this means, the produce is not exposed to the sun and, hence, does not suffer drying caused by evaporation. When stored, it is as firm as when removed from the soil.

Harvesting the below-ground developers, such as carrots, that are to be consumed immediately

Harvest these roots or tubers when the moon is at the end of its second quarter or the commencement of its third. At this time the water table is at its highest level. Its pressure increases the top soil's moisture content to the maximum, inducing the maximum amount of sap — and, hence, flavour — within the individual units of the gathered crop. An improvement upon this is harvesting at this moon time in the cool of the end of the day or of the night. Then, there is a general reduction of evaporation. The harvested crops retain even more sap and, in consequence, even more flavour. Over-riding this general consideration is the need to remove the ready crop from the ground so that the correctly-timed renewal of the exhausted Year Area may be achieved — no matter what the extraneous conditions and targets.

Harvesting fruit

Allowing for the reality that all fruit is best picked the moment it is ripe, harvest soft and hard fruits when the moon is at the end of its second quarter or the commencement of its third. At this time the water table is at its highest level. It exerts the most pressure upon the plant's roots, inducing the maximum flow of sap within the plant and its fruit and, hence, the greatest amount of fruit flavour. An improvement upon this is harvesting in the cool of the end of the day. Then, there is reduced evaporation — from harvested crops as well as from soil.

Planting out

Insert plantlets, young bushes and young trees into the soil at the start of the moon's second quarter. The existing heightened moisture content — thanks to the rising water table — plus the following week or so of further moisture increase, encourages enhanced plant development. Improve upon this by planting in the cool of the end of the day. Then, there is reduced evaporation and, hence, greater retention by the soil of moisture. Added to this is the increased pressure upon the inserted plant's roots, exerted by the rising water table. It induces increased sap flow and, hence,

82

One of R J Harris's rules is that feeds must be added to the top soil ten days or so before the sowing of seeds or the insertion of plants. The result is that the new arrivals are received by a beneficial distribution of the supplements throughout the soil.

Carried out in accordance with the rules of moon gardening, the adding of feeds is done at the start of the moon's third quarter. This is when the soil begins to be at its most receptive to additives.

The moon's third quarter commences roughly fifteen days before the beginning of the ideal moon period during which to sow or to plant — the moon's first and second quarters.

This particular symmetry gives an indication of the overall symmetry and helpful discipline that is brought to gardening's ways and means by a practical observance of the moon's phases.

Arising out of this, a moon-oriented calendar drawn up by the gardener to cater for his or her horticultural needs and aspirations is extremely helpful.

more rapid, more thorough take-up and ingestion of nutrients. Overall, this combines with the increased moisture in the soil to maximise the benefits experienced by the plant during the traumatising days of its introduction to its new habitat.

Overall, the rising water table encourages growth because its upward pressure enhances the rising of the sap within the affected plant. Hence, it can be accepted that plants (and all

83

Some moon gardeners harvest their crops in the hours of darkness. "I know of a farmer in Somerset who swears by harvesting his potatoes and root vegetables by the tractor's headlights," comments Mr Harris. "He argues that the moon's gravitational pull is stronger by night than by day, and so puts more moisture into the crops. More moisture means more flavour, so he reckons he has an improved product that warrants a better price.

"Of course, he does this at full moon, which is the time of the highest level of the water table and the greatest amount of moisture in the top soil. And night time is the coolest time, with least evaporation, so everything — including his crops — retains more moisture than during the day."

The head gardener views the practice with uncertainty.

"There is a cost to be paid," he notes. "Night-time harvesting is harvesting by artificial light, and that is both anti-social and tricky. Also, how do you persuade staff to work that kind of overtime? — not to mention overtime rates of pay.

"Above all, is the slight improvement in flavour won by night-time harvesting — and it is only slight — worth all of that? And, in any event, the way of gardening I advocate brings so many improvements anyway, among them flavour improvement, so why go to all of that trouble?

"I have decided not to go down that road on a regular basis."

living things) are at their strongest and most desirous of survival when the moon is at the end of its second quarter and the start of its third quarter (when, in short, it is a Full Moon).

ROTATION

Correctly implemented, four-year crop rotation as designed by head gardener R J Harris ensures that a given vegetable, root, tuber, legume or annual flower is not grown in the same place twice until after an interval of three years and a renewal of the affected growing medium. The combination reduces considerably the risk of pest and disease becoming permanent residents where the affected plant is cultivated. It also reduces the burden that is imposed upon the given growing medium by the requirement that it produces the same crops, season after season.

Mr Harris's rules of crop rotation are his own. They combine with his rules of moon gardening and the traditional horticultural methods that he has revived. For as long as there is growing season in the year, these rules dictate what happens, and when and why, in the four 15m-wide, 34m-long crop-rotational areas that occupy approximately two-thirds of the three-quarters of an acre of space that is enclosed by the four tall, red-brick walls of Tresillian's kitchen garden.

Where no cultivated plant is to be found — due to current season or crop/bed management — the unemployed soil is kept in what the head gardener refers to as a naked

84

'Give serious thought," advises the head gardener, "to exactly what is and is not to be grown in the vegetable beds *before* drawing up the crop-rotation plan."

"If ever a matter called for a family discussion, it is this.

"If everyone hates cabbage, there is no point in growing cabbages — no matter how handsome and caterpillar-free they are.

"If everyone likes the idea of sweet-tasting sugar peas, make sure these are included.

"Equally, if the cos lettuce is preferred to the other types, note this and get the appropriate kind of seed."

Quantities is a related consideration.

"Too much of a given vegetable or salad crop is likely to lead to waste — of soil, seeds, feeds and effort," comments Mr Harris. "And of money."

They believed that it encouraged, maintained and enhanced soil fertility, and that it did so without the need to add fertilisers and manures.

"The modern approach," the head gardener notes, "is to cover unemployed ground with mustard or cress the moment its crops have been cleared, to dig this in as a green manure before it sets seed, and then to repeat the process, weather and season conditions permitting.

"It is a good way, too, and I recommend it to today's sparetime gardeners. They require such quick, safe, low-cost, undemanding solutions to the problem of restoring or increasing fertility — solutions, too, that demand little in the way of the appreciation of the basics of horticultural practice."

Mr Harris adds: "They *could* make this particular solution even more effective by sowing their green manure at the most beneficial moon time — which is at the start of, or during, the moon's second quarter.

"That is when there is maximum moisture and upward pressure within the top soil at the very moment when the sown seed tries to germinate."

state. This, in the growing season, is why, partly, vegetable beds mulched in the popular style — that is, with a thickness of homemade, waste-vegetable compost — are never to be found in the estate.

Maintained in its naked state, the top soil is hoed at programmed intervals to prevent weed germination and remove at the earliest moment the few weeds that manage, somehow, to germinate. Thus is subjugated the hidden army of weed seeds that awaits constantly the opportunity to invade, to occupy and to pillage nutrients and moisture.

The hoeing also revives and continues the ancient tradition of manual manuring. The old-time horticulturists knew this as 'manoeuvring'.

TIP 85

➜ A crop-rotation system is possible in the garden that is large enough to provide only one vegetable/annual flower production area. With meticulous planning and record keeping, the single area can be devoted to the head gardener's four-year regime. By these means, a set of crops returns to it only after the required three-year pause and bed renewal. The growbag can be added to extend the growing area (for strawberry production, for example). This can be converted into an organic aid by being moistened and fed only with comfrey solution.

Each of Tresillian's four highly-productive, crop-rotation-controlled areas incorporates traditional deep-trench beds and single-dug beds constructed according to this manual's *SINGLE-DUG BED* and *DEEP-TRENCH BED*. Elsewhere, inside and outside the kitchen garden, double-dug beds cater for specific needs arising and being met outside the crop-rotation system.

The crop-rotation beds are installed in a given Autumn by the start of the September, October or November moon's third quarter. They endure for four years. They are renewed at the commencement of the fifth year, after which another four-year cycle begins.

In design, they are the head gardener's versions of the beds of the ancient Romans and Greeks. Theirs were beds for their times. In particular, the trenches for the deep-trench beds were dug at least two metres deep, not a mere one metre, being excavated by an unlimited supply of cheap, low-maintenance, disposable, easily-replaced labour and being filled with the product of efficient sewage- and night-soil-collection systems, extensive animal-intensive farming and the ubiquitous horse and mule.

In two particular respects, the beds of those times were exactly as those of today's walled, kitchen garden at Tresillian: 1) they considerably reduced the need for water and watering; 2) they were reliant upon the availability of copious quantities of manure.

Tresillian's revival programme has occupied at least two decades. During that period each of the kitchen garden's four crop-rotation areas has been equipped successively several times with renewed beds, each renewed area marking the commencement of a fresh four-year life span and occupying the site of the area that it has replaced. From the start, for the duration of its four-year life span,

the individual year area has produced, and still produces, as follows

First Year: broad beans, broccoli, cabbages, cauliflowers, dwarf french beans, kale, kohlrabi, leeks, onions, peas, savoys, spinach, swedes and turnips, all grown in the single-dug bed that was created in the previous Autumn. Runner beans, climbing french beans, marrows, courgettes, pumpkins and sweet peas, all grown in the deep-trench bed that was created in the previous Autumn.

Second Year: all annual flowers, and flowers the tubers and corms of which are lifted annually to safeguard them. They are grown in both the single-dug bed and the deep-trench bed, and the intervening temporary paths, now all two years old.

Third Year: potatoes — grown in the single-dug bed, the deep-trench bed and the intervening temporary paths, all now three years old.

Fourth Year: beetroots, carrots, celery, parsley and parsnips, all grown in the single-dug bed, the deep-trench bed and the intervening temporary paths. These are now four years old and, after full harvesting, completely spent and fit for no further main-crop production.

In its fifth year, the Year Area recommences the four-year cycle that is itemised above. The single-dug bed and the deep-trench bed are renewed and in use for the first time. They were created in the Autumn at the end of fourth year.

The pattern is repeated as from the Year Area's ninth year, thirteenth year, and so on.

Presented diagramatically, the

four Year Areas of the total crop-rotational kitchen garden relate to each other as shown below.

Read vertically to find out how the Year 3 Area, for example, must stand sown at the start of the moon's first quarter. The above-the-surface plants such as the cabbage and the lettuce are sown/planted at the start of the moon's second quarter.

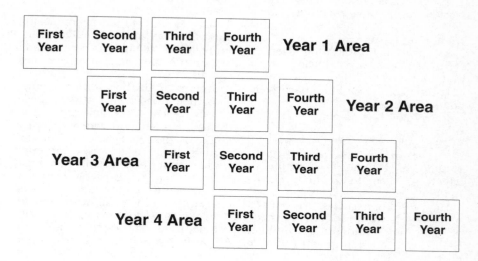

in relation to the Year 1 Area during the Year 1 Area's third year, and what must be happening elsewhere in the converted-garden-to-be at the time of the Year 2 Area's third year.

This four-year vegetable-product range is the product range for the four Year Areas that feature in this manual.

The below-the-surface plants such as the roots and the tubers are

SOIL

So far as head gardener R J Harris is concerned, the soil of Earth's crust is in two types: that which has been cultivated for more than one year by farmer or by gardener; that which, permanently, bears grass in the form of meadow, pasture or lawn.

"Fundamentally," says Mr Harris, "soil is the product of rock which has been broken down by weather

The sowing/planting is carried out in the appropriate month. Invariably, each follows a feed of a specific quantity of fish-blood-and-bone fertiliser applied some fifteen days beforehand at the start of the previous moon's third quarter.

TIP 86
➔ **A three-year/three-Year-Area rotation system utilising three vegetable-growing areas is almost as beneficial as a four-year/four-Year-Area system which includes flower production. Equally, advises R J Harris, in a four-area system the flowers can be omitted, with an area being given over each year to old-fashioned, fertility-enhancing 'manoeuvring' or, with much less physical effort, a cress or mustard green manure sown in Spring and turned into the soil in Autumn.**

activity during millions of years. In that time it has been augmented by the by-products of the growth and death of living creatures and vegetation."

Today's soil is in many types, worldwide, because rock has always existed in a similarly considerable number of types.

In practical, gardener-friendly terms, soil is in two categories: light and heavy.

Light soil has comparatively coarse particles.

Heavy soil has comparatively fine particles.

The difference accounts for the difference in weight between the two, volume for volume — a reality to which any spade-wielding, earth-hefting gardener can testify.

Heavy soil's particles are packed more closely together than are those of light soil, volume for volume. Heavy soil retains moisture more effectively than does light soil. It also, in given conditions, becomes more caked and sticky when wet than does light soil, and — with its greater concentration of particles — forms into harder lumps when dry than does light soil.

Light soil is more sand-laden than is heavy soil. Sand particles do not readily adhere to each other. As a consequence, moisture passes through light soil more readily than it does through heavy soil. That is why light soil requires to have moisture-retaining material added to it, such as heavy manure (preferably farmyard, not stable) or leaf mould.

Grit or sand — or horse manure containing much straw — opens up heavy soil's particles and, thus, reduces its tendency to retain moisture unhelpfully. These lightening additives are at their most effective when applied in Autumn. They then have time in which to penetrate the top soil and to become absorbed by it in readiness for the commencement of the following

growing season.

Chalky soils are limey soils. Usually, they are positioned above solid chalk, Their high lime content is counteracted by the addition of acid, organic matter such as fully-composted leaf mould.

Acid soils contain decomposing plant fibre and little or no lime. Natural conditions such as centuries of leaf drop or peat-marsh origins give rise to these soils. Their acidity is counteracted by the addition of lime.

In their uncorrected states, these two extremes — the lime-laden and the acidic — support widely differing kinds of plants. Hence, it can be argued that it is the wise gardener who finds out beyond question what is in his or her garden, does not devote resources to trying to alter its character, and is content to grow in it what it is best suited to grow in it.

Fortunately, the vast majority of gardens do not call upon their users to arrive at this kind of decision making. They possess the

---

TIP 87

➜ **"Get good soil in the garden,"** says R J Harris, **"by changing its colour to as dark a shade as possible. The darker the soil, the more warmth it retains. And warmth is the key to increased fertility and better plant life. Light soil loses its heat, which causes reduced bacteria activity and, hence, reduced fertility."** Added decomposed vegetable matter — as much as possible, and mulched on or turned in during the moon's third or fourth quarter — leads to a darkening **"and so does soot and ashes from the coal fire,"** adds the head gardener, **"which was one of the ways grandad achieved the lovely rich, dark-brown loam and tilth that enabled him to feed his large family right through the year."**

85

The traditional way to tame previously unused, unworked soil has not changed, notes Mr Harris. "Old-fashioned double digging — or bastard digging, as it was sometimes known — consists of trenching down as deep as twice the length of a spade's blade for the whole of the area that is to be turned into a bed.

"The trenches are dug right alongside each other, so that not one cubic inch of soil is unturned.

"The bottom of each trench is thoroughly loosened with a fork, and then the trench is reinstated with the earth from the next trench as that one is dug."

Traditionally, too, this preparatory work is done in the Autumn, so that the rains and the frost and the winds of Winter can have impact upon the deeply-turned soil and help to produce a generous depth of loosened, aerated, workable medium which features, eventually, a good surface tilth. It is done, too, during the moon's third and fourth quarters. This, thanks to the falling water table, is when the soil is at its lightest, being most devoid of moisture, and most receptive to air and rain thanks to the drawing-in effect created by the falling water table.

"Depending upon what is to be done with the completed bed, a depth of fully-composted manure is placed into each of the trenches before it is reinstated," says the head gardener. "So there are nutrients as well as enhanced drainage just where the plants' roots expect to find them.

"Indeed," he adds, "the other chief main reason for double digging is to cure drainage problems. Which it does, and very effectively."

medium that holds a co-operative balance of lime and acid. It responds enthusiastically to repeated, traditional deep digging plus the age-old way of making calculated, purposeful additions of manure. As a result, it converts itself into the holy grail of gardening, that which is known as loam or marly soil.

"Gardens which are kept alive with nothing other than artificial fertilisers are not gardens at all," comments R J Harris.

A feature of the healthy garden is a gardener-created, gardener-maintained combination within the soil of warmth, air and moisture. The combination provides the habitat in which beneficial bacteria turn decaying vegetable matter into the essential component, humus.

Overall, this ideal growing medium is seldom without its very minor disadvantages, but — again — it is the wise gardener who knows what these are and adapts to them.

MANURE

The more fertile top soil is, the better it enables plants to grow and to flourish, R J Harris points out. "As a matter of general truth, old-fashioned manure is the best at increasing top soil's fertility, and it does so by opening and keeping open the top soil's structure.

"It manages this in two ways: one, by being bulky, especially when it is mixed with straw; two, by feeding and, hence, increasing the top soil's worm and insect population."

The head gardener cannot emphasise sufficiently the importance of the worms and the insects of the soil.

86

Sub soil is an inferior growing medium principally (but not solely) because its dead vegetable- and animal-matter content does not decay.

This is due to the absence of bacteria, the soil-borne agent that causes decay.

Bacteria are not present because sub soil — due to its position deep beneath the top soil — is unable to receive air and warmth and — sometimes — moisture. These are the ingredients without which bacteria cannot exist.

"This is why the under layers of woodland soil form such an unsatisfactory growing medium," says Mr Harris. "They are rich in thicknesses of leaves — but they lack air, due to leaf compaction, and that lack of air results in a lack of warmth.

"Not until the gardener goes to work with spade and fork does air get in and, with it, warmth and moisture. These enable the bacteria to feed on the leaves, causing them to decay and, thus, create a medium for successful plant growth."

"They create an aerating structure within the top soil by tunnelling and forming passageways. The more of them that there are, the greater the number of these tunnels and passageways. And what really matters is that these three features of good top soil — tunnels, passageways and openness — admit air.

"The more of this infrastructure there is, the more air there is.

"Air draws in warmth and moisture, and the manure retains that moisture by virtue of its natural moisture retentativeness."

Air, warmth and moisture combine to make it possible for bacteria to be present in, and to thrive in, the top soil.

"The bacteria decompose the vegetable and the animal matter that is present in the top soil," continues the head gardener, "and the decomposed vegetable and animal matter — plus the air, the warmth, the moisture and the nutrients added to the top soil by the manure — create the environment that plants must have if they are to develop successfully from seed or plantlet to full maturity.

"And, of course," the head gardener adds, "don't forget the nutrients produced by the worms and the insects as, in Nature's way, they consume, digest, ingest and excrete their fellow creatures.

"These nutrients support the entire, complicated process.

"You can understand," Mr Harris comments, "why good top soil is the precious material it is, and why making it is not done overnight.

"It must be protected, especially from uninformed mankind. For those who are uninformed in these matters — and they are in the majority, sadly — can do only one thing to mankind's sole food provider, and that is spoil it."

R J Harris gives a reminder that the best time to insert manure and any other feed into the top soil is when the moon's third quarter begins: "When, in brief, the moon's gravitational pull upon the affected top soil begins to weaken, and begins to permit the level of the water table immediately beneath that top soil to fall," he says.

Nature notoriously abhorring vacuums, a drawing-in effect is a vital result. It encourages additives to be more deeply, more comprehensively absorbed into the top soil's highly receptive (at this moon time) structure.

Complementing the drawing-in process is the practical reality that

87

The garden spade and the garden fork offer the best form of manure, says R J Harris. "Understandably, very few sparetime gardeners know this. Professional horticulturists have known it for centuries.

"The word 'manuring' comes from the word 'manoeuvring'. And 'manoeuvring' was once a regularly-employed technique. Spade or fork dug into the soil, lifted it, turned it and replaced it in a broken form.

"The word 'manoeuvring' came from the ancient French 'maynoverer', which came from the Latin 'manu operari' or 'work by hand'.

'It just goes to show that turning the soil by hand — like so much in horticulture — goes right back to ancient times and has come to us in the form of an unchanged technique.

"Deep digging — or manoeuvring — or bastard trenching, as it was also once known — is by far the best way to enable essential air and, hence, warmth and moisture to get into the soil to encourage the bacteria that break down the dead animal and vegetable materials.

"This applies throughout the moon month," notes the head gardener, "but it applies especially during the moon's third and fourth quarters. This is when the sinking water table makes the top soil more ready to draw in whatever is applied to it, including air, warmth and moisture.

"The marvel of it is that manoeuvring increases soil fertility without the addition of any kind of plant food. That must make it the lowest-cost treatment, financially speaking."

the best time to apply feed is when the top soil is most charged with moisture.

This, again, is when the moon's third quarter begins.

Then, the previous fortnight's increasing gravitational pull has increased the upward pressure of the rising water-table level, concentrating and, thus, increasing the top soil's moisture content.

The process gathers pace until the next new moon, a fortnight or so later. Then, unhelpfully, the satellite planet's pull upon the top soil begins to strengthen, causing the water table's level to rise and, by its upward pressure, decreasing the top soil's receptivity.

The head gardener has evolved a way of making fresh mixed, farm-yard manure (not stable manure) suitable for use in the garden, and to minimise the smell arising from, and

caused by, the involved processes.

"Make a point of requesting the manure from the farmer or other supplier in sealed or tied-up plastic sacks," he advises. "That way, you avoid the shovelling and wheel-barrowing of delivered material from

TIP 88
➔ "Most gardeners know instinctively that animal manure is good for the soil," says Mr Harris. "The trouble is, some of them apply the 'more has got to be better' rule, and use far too much of the stuff. I have known cases where, ground area for ground area, up to five times as much has been applied as a farmer puts on his fields. This is a waste of effort as well as a waste of money and feed. And it does the soil no good at all."

88

"IT'S a fantastic job, of a cold, frosty morning, to get stuck in with a good fork and transfer the composting manure from one point to another to aerate it and thus increase its bacteria and insect population," says R J Harris.

"When I was an apprentice in the 1950s, it was standard practice for the young boys to go out once each month at the start of the day and turn a big heap of the stuff.

"We used to layer it with leaves and other waste vegetable matter."

Rain makes no difference to this ancient process. The farmers, indeed, tip cartloads of unprotected material into the corner of a field in the Spring and Summer and leave it there for twelve months to compost before spreading it.

"Years ago," recalls Mr Harris, "when it was all horse-and-cart work and everything was done manually, they used to dot large heaps from the cart all over the field and leave them to weather

"Then, later, the men would come in with forks, and spread it to where it was needed."

Wheelbarrow the plastic sacks to a timber bin of the kind that was once advocated as the best type for composting waste vegetable matter, the head gardener instructs, adding: "Needless to say, do not wear your Sunday best when doing this, because even bagged manure can be messy when lifted and handled.

"And sensible work gloves and rubber boots are a good idea, too."

Mr Harris's manure bins are a generous cubic metre in size. He suggests constructing the bin in the form of a Canadian log cabin, with notched, slotted-together timbers fashioned so that the bin's sides do not contain gaps.

"Apart from that," he notes, "this reduces the loss of moisture from the composting manure and serves to retain heat.

"And bear in mind," he adds, "that this kind of bin is without a bottom of any sort. Whatever you put in it rests directly upon the soil. That is a 'must'."

An alternative method, Mr Harris suggests, is to use one or more of the kind of black, plastic, bottomless, lidded, vegetable-waste composter that is available from most local authorities at a subsi-dised price, or from the garden centres. This type has the advantage of maximum moisture retention. It also possesses maximum heat at-traction and retention, due to its colour.

where it is tipped to where it is to be stored. You avoid, also, close proximity to a malodorous substance.

"In other words, listen hard and be alert when the supplier says, blithely, he'll drop off a load.

"Stop him right there, and revise his thinking.

"'Drop off a load' means just that, and a lorry load of loose, wet manure tipped onto the front drive at the front gates is not a thing to be welcomed."

TIP 89

➔ R J Harris: "Certainly, soil is bound to be fed and thus improved when stable or farmyard manure in its original, bulky state is applied to it in an unthinking manner. And results can be expected, of course. But, for truly splendid returns, and for truly improved top soil, it pays to compost correctly and to apply the correct amounts at the correct moon times."

89

'Know what you are buying when you buy in manure," cautions the head gardener.

"Stable manure — the product of the horse —must not have wood shavings in it. The shavings are detrimental when dug into the garden soil. And it *must* be straw based.

"Refuse pig manure if it is offered all by itself. It almost certainly contains toxic substances, which got into it from the feed that the pigs were given by the farmer. These substances are not wanted where food is grown."

Mr Harris suggests that some gardeners may prefer to buy commercially-produced, bagged manure.

"This is not the popular dried manure, which is poultry-based, usually, and seen as a feed, not a conditioner," he comments. "The bagged stuff from the garden centre is composted horse or farmyard manure. It is ready for use, it measures up to stated standards, and it is in a very convenient form for handling and storage.

"Its disadvantage is that it is not cheap."

Mr Harris parks the sacks at the bins or containers until the first day of the moon's first quarter, or as close to that day as can be managed.

On that day, he empties the plastic sacks into the bins or containers. As he does so, he mixes in with the manure as much waste vegetable matter as is available. If none is available, he has a bale of straw to hand, acquired in advance, and adds it in loosened form, until a strawy mix is arrived at.

"The first day of the moon's first quarter begins the fortnight or so during which the least loss of moisture into the earth from the stored manure can be expected," he explains.

"This is due to the rising water table, which exerts upward, repelling pressure."

Maximum moisture is a requirement in composting manure. It provides the all-important bacteria and insect life with one of the four elements that they need if they are to be able to live and to convert their habitat into a fertility-enhancing medium. The other three are air, warmth and vegetable matter.

"Stop the escape of odours from the filled timber bin by covering the surface of the manure with a 8cm-to-10cm thickness of leaf mould, top soil, peat, upside-down turfs, lawn mowings, weighted-down straw or gravel," Mr Harris concludes.

"Make sure that the lawn mowings are non-weed-killer-treated.

"With the plastic container, use its lid — but weigh it down firmly with something really heavy to secure a good seal and to stop the first winter wind from whipping it off."

Mr Harris leaves the binned/containered material to age for at least one year: "really," he points out, "two years is best, but that takes patience, and I know full well that today's life styles and pressures make patience a bit of a luxury for most hobby gardeners."

The two-year pause gives the bacteria within the manure ample

TIP 90
➜ **Compost stable manure by stacking it on the ground for a few weeks (no container is required, unless one happens to be available) and leaving it uncovered and undisturbed. It need not be turned. Ideally, make the stack on the first day of the moon's first quarter.**

opportunity to feed upon the vegetable matter that is present. This induces the process of decay that renders the manure beneficial when it is added to the garden's top soil.

During that time, the head gardener removes the capping or lid from the manure and transfers it to a similar container placed immediately alongside. He does so once per month, at the start of the moon's first quarter, thus adding air and, consequently, warmth to the material. This lends support to, and causes an increase in, the transforming activity of the bacteria.

Each time he makes the transference he replaces the top layer of non-manure material that protects the contents of the timber container.

"When you have made the switch once, you can expect the well-known odours of manure to have reduced almost to nothing at all."

The monthly removal highlights the advantage of the timber container over the plastic container.

"You see, after you have taken off the surface capping and put it tidily to one side, you simply de-assemble the timber bin from around the manure stack — remember, it is built like a Canadian log cabin — and begin to re-assemble it, only a few timbers high at first, immediately alongside.

"You then dig into the cube of composting manure and shovel it into its new home, raising the height of the sides of the timber bin gradually as the job goes along and the timbers are re-assembled.

"You finish off by replacing the top capping."

FERTILISERS

In Tresillian's Victorian walled, kitchen garden and elsewhere in the Tresillian estate in Cornwall, head gardener R J Harris applies in controlled, measured quantities seven organic fertilisers, two animal manures and one vegetable manure. His choice of organic fertilisers is

fish, blood &   **gypsum**
    bone   **hoof and**
bonemeal: **horn**
    sterilised   **seaweed:**
dolomite   **calcified**
limestone   **seaweed**
                     meal.

The two animal manures are

farmyard   **stable**
    manure (a   **manure**
    mixture of   **(solely**
    the prod-   **from**
    uct of all of   **horses).**
    the farm's
    creatures
    except
    horses)

The one vegetable manure is, with reluctance

    rotted vegetable waste, known
       as garden compost

with these feeds/conditioners being used at Tresillian as follows

FISH, BLOOD AND BONE

This fertiliser is applied at the rate of 115g to the square metre of bed surface for the hungry ones such as the cabbage and the other members of the brassica family. It is used at the rate of 60g-to-80g to the square metre for salad crops and generally, and at the rate of 115g to the square metre for potatoes. It is added at the rate of 60g-to-80g to the square metre when earthing up potatoes.

[*Consideration: fish-blood-and-bone fertiliser contains fast-acting nitrogen. It also has phosphates. These act to encourage strong root systems. It is for general-purpose use.*]

90

When received at the walled, kitchen garden, R J Harris's preferred fertilisers are emptied immediately into individual storage boxes: "made of wood, to keep the material dry," he explains. "Each has a tightly-fitting, shut-down lid and is marked with the fertiliser's name. Left in their plastic bags, the fertilisers deteriorate, either through sweating or through the bags eventually being accidentally punctured and the contents being at risk of contamination." The boxes are stored in the cool of the potting shed. They are replenished the instant they are empty. Thus, no detected deficiency in the soil has to await correction — and the execution of preparatory work does not have to be delayed — as a specific fertiliser's delivery is awaited. R J Harris's fertiliser policy is a pragmatic one: he causes a specific feed to be applied only when there is no doubt that a given lack is to be expected or has been established by a correctly-conducted test, the result of which is beyond question.

BONEMEAL: STERILISED

Used at the rate of 115g-to-145g to the square metre when planting new shrubs and trees.

[*Consideration: sterilised bonemeal slow-releases organic phosphates. It promotes strong root growth during a long period of time.*]

DOLOMITE LIMESTONE

Used at the rate of 200g-to-250g to the square metre to reduce the soil's acidity, the level of which is first ascertained by means of a soil-acidity testing kit.

[*Consideration: this fertiliser contains calcium and magnesium. pH-testing kits are sold widely. They are easy to use when the makers' instructions are followed.*]

GYPSUM

Improves the aeration and drainage of heavy clay soils. Makes them easier to work. Application: 250g-to-500g to the square metre.

HOOF AND HORN

Applied at the rate of 75g-to-130g to the square metre as a bed dressing for most green vegetables and the lawns that need to have their colour strengthened.

[*Consideration: it is a slow-acting source of organic nitrogen.*]

SEAWEED: CALCIFIED

The head gardener swears by this fertiliser for encouraging stone fruit such as plums. Applied in January at the rate of 115g-to-175g to the square metre, scattered around the affected trees onto the surface of the soil. "The turn-of-the-century way was

TIP 91

➔ **R J Harris: 'I know an old gravedigger who told me once that he dug an eight-foot-deep grave and found at the bottom of it the growing roots of the weed convolvulus.**

"That is a warning to those who put garden compost underground in their flower or vegetable beds.

"If there are living weed seeds in it, do not believe for one moment that they will be killed by depth."

91

Where to find the elements

calcium — in dolomite limestone

calcium — in seaweed: calcified

magnesium — in dolomite limestone

magnesium — in seaweed: calcified

nitrogen: *(high release)* — in fish, blood and bone or hoof and horn

phosphates *(quick release)* — in fish, blood and bone

phosphates *(slow release)* — in bonemeal: sterilised

potash *(unreliable source)* — in wood ash

trace elements — in seaweed: calcified

trace elements *(very slow acting)* — in seaweed meal

This table summarises FERTILISERS.
See specific descriptions in this section for specific guidance.

What to give the plants

apples — bonemeal: sterilised

apricots — seaweed: calcified

broad-leafed plants *(quick release)* — fish, blood and bone

cabbage family — fish, blood and bone or seaweed: calcified

courgettes — fish, blood and bone

cucumbers — fish, blood and bone

flower development — fish, blood and bone or bonemeal: sterilised

flowering shrubs — bonemeal: sterilised

fruit development *(slow)* — bonemeal: sterilised

grapes — fish, blood and bone

green vegetables — seaweed: calcified or hoof and horn or fish, blood and bone

lawn — seaweed: calcified or bonemeal: sterilised or fish, blood and bone

lettuces — fish, blood and bone

marrows — fish, blood and bone

nectarines — seaweed: calcified

peaches — seaweed: calcified

pears — bonemeal: sterilised

peas — fish, blood and bone

plums — seaweed: calcified

potatoes — fish, blood and bone

pumpkins — fish, blood and bone

quick-growing plants — fish, blood and bone

root growth: carrots, parsnips, turnips *(slow)* — bonemeal: sterilised

runner beans — fish, blood and bone

salad crops — fish, blood and bone

to grow these fruit trees on builders' rubble for the sake of the lime in the rubble's mortar," explains the head gardener. "Today, cement mortar does not contain the lime that the trees need, so builders' rubble is no longer used." Mr Harris comments: "The increased sweetness imparted to the soil by calcified seaweed creates a better stone. The better the stone, the better the fruit." It is also fed to the cabbages and the others of the brassica family. It is used for this purpose at the rate of 60g-to-80g to the square metre.

[**Consideration:** *calcified seaweed contains calcium, magnesium and trace elements. It is a very good soil conditioner.*]

SEAWEED MEAL

Applied as a lawn food. It gives strong growth and rich colour. It is also excellent as a general feed when applied to the surface of the soil at the rate of 60g-to-120g to the square metre three months before planting and lightly raked in. By planting time, the soil's bacteria have broken it down.

[**Consideration:** *seaweed meal is*

92

'Man-produced and 'man-managed', but not 'man-made', is the rule that R J Harris observes as far as possible when selecting the fertilisers that he applies in Tresillian's Victorian, walled, kitchen garden and elsewhere in the Tresillian estate.

"The animal manures," he notes, "are much more than solely feeds. They require different thinking and a different approach."

They are considered in separate sections in this manual.

93

The garden bonfire provides potash so long as only woody material or cut timber is burned upon it. The mineral is in the ash that is left over, which must be dry-stored the moment it is cold. Otherwise, atmospheric moisture and rain render it almost unusable.

Better is to save the wood for Christmas and then to enjoy an open fire for a day or two.

The wisest rates at which to apply wood ash in the garden cannot be suggested: the potash content varies with the type and age of the wood that is burned. A good rule is to apply it liberally, beng aware that thicknesses of it tend to cake on the soil when it is applied — especially after rain.

Roses love it.

The Tresillian project recently acquired a wood chipper and, for that reason, most of its timber is no longer burned. Instead, it is shredded and then heaped for about six months. "I like it to break down and neutralise itself by losing its sugar or acid content," says Mr Harris. "Its effect on soil pH is then negligible." It is applied as a moisture-retaining mulch around bushes, or as a mulch on the non-vegetable beds to subdue weeds. It is also applied as path surfacing.

---

a slow-acting, long-lasting plant food. It is rich in trace elements. It helps to build up the humus of the soil.]

ROTTED VEGETABLE WASTE, KNOWN AS GARDEN COMPOST

Arising out of the whole of the Tresillian estate, the mixed vegetable waste is so voluminous that,

94

The head gardener buys his fertilisers in 25-kilo bags: "the equivalent of the old half-hundredweight bag," he comments.

"Years ago, when I was a young man, we bought them in one-hundredweight bags — 50 kilos.

"That was when there was a fertiliser called guano.

"It was bird droppings from the Seychelle Islands in the Indian Ocean. It was packed in two-hundredweight hessian sacks.

"I can remember carrying many of those in my time as an apprentice."

often, not enough trenches for conversion into deep-trench beds are available to absorb it. A displeased R J Harris then has no choice but to compost it, doing so in uncontained heaps activated by the addition of composted animal manure. This is despite his view that such material has no place in his kind of garden, for the reasons that are presented elsewhere in this manual. The difficulty is further aggravated by the workload that is created by his determination that when this kind of material is rotted down it may include annual weeds that have not gone to seed plus their roots, but not annual weeds in seed and their roots. Also, it may not include perennial weeds and their roots. The entailed separation of material demands time and resources, the two equating to financial cost and impaired staff moral. Forced to do that which runs counter to his convictions, the head gardener has had no choice but to evolve a composting system. It is as follows

1 select a screened or otherwise unobtrusive site (for a compost heap is not a thing of beauty). Locate it, ideally, on ground that is unusable for cultivation purposes or is of poor quality

2 mark out on the chosen site two one-metre squares. Do so at any convenient time in the month (no moon-quarter is involved at this stage). Use capped (for safety's sake) garden canes and garden lines. [*Consideration: larger than this is better. The chosen size is determined by the size of the available site and the quantity of the available waste*]

3 position the two rectangles side by side and 30cm or so apart

4 ensure that their positions make available sufficient adjacent space for the manoeuvring of a wheelbarrow and the use of a garden fork

5 remove the turf from the two rectangles. Store it elsewhere

6 remove the top soil from the two rectangles. Dig down into each to a depth that equals the length of a spade's blade, or to

TIP 92
→ **The gardeners of old remembered in general terms which plants to feed with which fertilisers by repeating to themselves the Golden Triangle (so named for reasons that are now lost, even to the Cornish head gardener). The three points of the triangle, easily memorised, are**
   — nitrogen for leaf growth
   — phosphate for root growth
   — potash for flower and fruit growth.

95

The Tresillian design of compost heap is fully exposed to the air and to the rain. Hence, it always has the benefit of two of the essential ingredients for successful compost making. The other three — heat, minimal evaporation and regular turning to secure effective air distribution — are achieved by the heap's size and location, and the gardener's fork.

R J Harris agrees that in the average size of suburban garden, the compost bin brings the advantage of neatness and controlled containment.

sub soil level. Spread the excavated top soil thinly throughout the garden if there is no immediate use for it in connection with other projects

7 on **the first day of any moon's first quarter**, cut into short lengths the usable material that is dry, and immerse it in water in a large container. Leave it to absorb moisture for at least two hours

8 place a layer of usable, soft vegetable waste in the bottom of one of the excavated squares, whilst waiting. [*Considerations:* **1** — *this encourages hastened worm activity;* **2** — *the first day of the moon's first quarter marks the beginning of the fortnight during which there is the least loss of moisture into the earth from the composting vegetable matter. This is thanks to the upward pressure exerted by the rising water table. Maximum moisture retention within the compost heap aids and hastens the rotting of the vegetable matter*]

9 cut coarse, usable vegetable matter into short lengths. Layer it on top of the soft material in the excavation to encourage aeration from the bottom of the heap

10 layer on, next, accumulated vegetable waste in as premixed a condition as can be achieved. Include the presoaked matter. If wood ash is available, sprinkle it between the layers. Reject the whole of each perennial weed and the top growth of the annual weed that is in seed. Include the annual weeds' roots and the seedless tops of the annual weeds. Maintain the heap's rectangular shape

11 add a thin layer of any kind of composted or uncomposted animal manure from time to time. If this is not available, dust commercial dried manure such as 6X onto the heap as the vegetable waste is layered on

TIP 93
➜ **The vegetable waste that is perforce composted at Tresillian does not include kitchen waste and egg shells. Mr Harris agrees that this kind of material has a place in urban and suburban compost making, but not where he practices. "It attracts vermin," he says, "and that is a reality at Tresillian. In the town situation, it is less of a problem, perhaps. Even so, one should be alert. And beware of adding potato peelings to the compost," adds the head gardener. "Uncomposted, they can result in potato plants in unexpected places in the garden. The bonus of unplanned tubers is not always welcome."**

96

On the large estates of the wealthy Edwardians, garden compost was made in considerable volume by mixing rotting waste vegetable matter with hot stable manure — of which there was always an over-abundant supply — in metre-deep and at least metre-square pits in the ground.

The technique was modified to meet specific needs.

Out-of-season radishes and other salad crops, as example, were cultivated on the surface of such pits.

"Grape vines had their roots trained through gaps in the wall of the grape house into a brick pit built against the other side of the wall," Mr Harris recalls.

"Into the pit during the course of the year was tipped all of the waste vegetable matter that could be found, together with the small animals and the birds that died on the estate.

"Their blood content was reckoned to be one of the finest things to feed the grapes.

"You can image what sort of job some unfortunate apprentice had at the end of the year, having to remove most of that stuff because it was spent, and then having to replace it with more of the same.

"Then he had to spread the extracted matter onto the herbaceous borders — minus the bones, of course, which he had to bury.

"That was a very particular kind of compost pit, and not an item of loveliness."

12 move the completed heap from its rectangular depression to the other once per month, to aerate it. Do so on **the first day of the moon's first quarter**

13 commence the transferred heap with the matter that has not composted fully in the original excavation

14 begin, also, by moving the outer material of the original heap to the centre of the new heap

15 transfer the heap monthly in this way for twelve months. At the year's end, the heap is ready for use

16 apply the material in the required ways. Bear in mind that its first place in the R J Harris style of garden is at the very bottom of a deep-trench bed.

Note that Tresillian's heaps of composting waste vegetation are located — when they are unavoidable — outside the kitchen garden in the almost day-long shadow of the outward-facing, north-facing wall. This is where, typically, the offices, workshops and storage rooms are located. "Within the

TIP 94
➔ When cutting the two depressions into the ground for the heaping of the waste vegetable matter, stack the removed turfs neatly grass side to grass side. Leave the stack exposed to the elements for at least one year. Then pass it through a sieve with a 2cm-to-3cm mesh to remove the large stones and the surviving weed roots. Spread the resultant good-quality soil thinly throughout the garden, or save it in a suitable receptacle for dusting onto seed-sown drills.

97

When talking with dedicated waste-vegetable-compost makers and users the head gardener takes a pragmatic view both of the material and of its likely weed-seed content.

"I won't touch the stuff myself if I can avoid it," he reiterates, "but I agree that the annual weeds can be added into the heap or the container, roots and all, provided that no seeds are involved. Perennial weeds in their entirety are a "no, no", of course.

"You can be sure, though, that weed seeds of every kind will get in, no matter how many and what precautions are taken.

"After all, animal manure often comes with a corn- or a grass-seed content. That is inevitable, given the way that Nature works.

"The sensible philosophy," he says, "is don't worry about it if the reward is good, productive gardening, no matter how the gardening is done.

"The weeds that do manage to germinate when the compost is applied are all too visible, usually, and pulling them out is the work of a moment.

"And, of course, In compost, their roots have very little 'hold'. So they come out easily and, if they are suitable, can go straight onto the current compost heap."

Mr Harris insists, however, that the gardener's policy should be one of reducing the weed seeds in the garden, wherever they lurk, as much as possible.

"They steal the moisture and the nutrients that, by rights, belong to the developing plants not only in the vegetable beds, but in the flower beds, as well, and in the shrubberies.

"We should all remember the old saying that was drummed into me when I was an apprentice: one year's seed is seven years' weed, and that's a true saying if ever there was one."

garden should be a place of beauty," comments the head gardener, "where the lady of the house and her guests can smell the sweet peas and all of the other scented blossoms. They should not expect to have to encounter the aroma of rotting vegetable matter as they stroll and talk."

Remember that the external, north-facing domain is the least productive of the kitchen garden's areas, because the sun reaches it hardly at all. Its lack of warmth makes it ideal for the composting process, whether applied to vegetable matter or to animal manures, for the coldness reduces the resultant smell and induces the least amount of moisture loss from the composting heaps due to evaporation.

Bear in mind the head gardener's less demanding, more efficient, lower-cost way to use waste vegetable matter as it arises — and without composting the material. Always, somewhere in the walled, kitchen garden of the Tresillian estate, there are one or two extremely long, empty, metre-deep, metre-wide trenches with ready-loosened bases waiting to be converted into deep-trench beds. Into these goes as much as possible of the usable, redundant vegetable matter, to make the first of the several, varied layers that fill it completely before it is capped with a layer of top soil.

JOHN INNES COMPOSTS

R J Harris uses five of the John Innes composts, which are all manufactured commercially and are available at garden centres and other horticultural retail outlets. He considers them to be essential to his way of gardening. They are the

JI seed compost

JI No 1 potting compost

JI No 2 potting compost

JI No 3 potting compost

JI ericaceous compost

with Mr Harris sowing almost all of his seeds in the **JI seed compost**. It provides just enough goodness for germination and for the development of the seedlings' 'baby' leaves.

He uses it, also, for rooting soft cuttings.

It comprises, very approximately

— 2 parts of loam (sterilised soil)
— 1 part of sphagnum moss peat
— 1 part of coarse sand or grit
— fertilisers selected to ensure that the whole equals the nutritional standard that is authorised by the John Innes Manufacturers' Association

with, in general, Mr Harris transplanting seedlings and rooted cuttings from the seed compost to the **JI No 1 potting compost,** then on to the **JI No 2 potting compost**, and then on to the **JI No 3 potting compost**.

Some of his plants find a permanent place, in doors or out of doors, in containers filled with the **JI No 2** or the **JI No 3** potting compost. Others find a permanent home in the garden soil having completed the progression from the **JI No 2** or the **JI No 3** potting compost.

All depends upon the individual plant's appetite, identity and allotted place in the head gardener's overall horticultural plan.

For head gardener R J Harris, seeds in trays, pots, containers or modules develop most surely into seedlings, seedlings in trays, pots, containers or modules most surely into plantlets, and permanently-potted or containerised plantlets most surely into life-long healthy beings when they draw their sustenance from the commercially-manufactured medium that is known as growing compost — given, that is, the appropriate ambient tempera-ture, amount of sunlight, degree of moisture, location and overall management

The proprietory compost brings, also, an environment that is weed-free (until it is contaminated by exposure to uncontrolled conditions).

The Cornish head gardener's experience leads him to an even more specific conclusion: the most effective of what the uninitiated see as a confusion of branded, garden-centre-available composts are those that bear the name John Innes. These — to pinpoint but one of their many desirable features — are based upon what the professionals and refer to as loam and most non-gardeners as soil or earth.

In Mr Harris's view, the specially-treated loam/soil/earth that is a unique ingredient of the John Innes composts performs better than the peat that is the principal ingredient of the myriad of non-John Innes composts.

The **JI No 1**, **JI No 2** and **JI No 3** potting composts each consist, very approximately, of

'**B**ACK in the 1950s," recalls R J Harris, "when I was an apprentice and every major nursery made its own John Innes composts — and when today's peat-based composts were only just beginning to be heard of — I had to get to work at 5.30 every morning to start up a great big old horizontal boiler to get ready to sterilise the loam that was going to be used that day in the John Inneses

"First, I had to scrape the clinker out of the fire box, and then I had to light the fire with the kind of steam coal that was used for the railway steam engines of the time.

"It was not until after 8 o'clock that the fire was really going. That was when I took a long-handled, specially-polished shovel I kept for the purpose and put a couple of eggs and rashers of bacon on it and held it over the fire and that was my breakfast.

"The fire box was in two parts, so we could clear out and relight one part while the other was still burning.

"Steam at 180°F or 240 psi was required. Twenty minutes of this saw six level wheel-barrow loads of loam sterilised in a metal container that was attached to the boiler. There were several containers. We emptied one while two or three others were still operating."

The loam that the young Harris and his fellow apprentices barrowed and shovelled, paced by the boiler's demands, started out as turfs cut from a selected field of grass and stored in a rick. The rick stood for a year. It was then broken down and forced through a 12cm riddle to remove stones, hard material and surviving roots.

After sterilisation, the loam was combined with peat, sand or grit, lime and fertilisers and passed through a smaller riddle.

"Every single thing we produced each year— thousands of pot plants, tomato plants and cucumber plants, and a million lettuce plants — was grown in one form of John Innes compost or another.

"The sterilisation removed weeds, fungal diseases and soil-borne creatures — all those undesirables that make it impossible to guarantee cost-efficient plant operation and a perfect result in wholesale-trade volumes.

"It goes on today. You will not find anything growing in Nature's untouched soil wherever you go in commercial, greenhouse-based horticulture."

— 7 parts of loam (sterilised soil)
— 3 parts of sphagnum moss peat
— 2 parts of coarse sand or grit
— fertilisers selected to ensure that the composts equal the nutritional standard that is authorised by the John Innes Manufacturers' Association.

The presence of loam in Mr Harris's preferred John Innes composts must be emphasised. No other commercially-produced compost possesses this feature (in 2006).

The head gardener itemises as follows the advantages that spring from the loam's inclusion, and from the general character of the John Innes composts

— compared to peat (the main constituent of non-loam-based, non-John-Innes composts) loam has the better 'body'. For this reason, it provides a firmer

100

A Mr J Innes started it all. He lived in London in the 1800s, and became an extremely wealthy property developer and land speculator. When he died, he bequeathed everything he possessed to furthering the improvement of the horticultural practices of his day.

An horticultural research institute was the outcome of his generosity, named after him.

In the 1930s, the institute started out to rationalise and improve what was then an impossibly numerous and diverse range of manufactured composts — most of them, by today's standards, the product of inadequate horticultural understanding and undesirable manufacturing processes.

The John Innes loam-based composts resulted. They gained added significance in connection with food production during the war years of the 1940s. More than half a century later, the Institute, based, as it now is, at Norwich, continues to express its founder patron's belief in research and experimentation.

hold when the compost of which it is a part has a cane or a stick thrust into it to support a plant

— by the same token, loam's 'body' provides a more secure anchorage than does peat for the tall or big-waisted plant that has to spend its life in a container

— loam takes up water more readily than does peat, and so a container of loam-based compost that has dried out can be re-wetted more quickly and more thoroughly

— the peat content of the John Innes products combines with the loam and the grit content to give greater water-holding capacity and better drainage. Hence, with John Innes, under- or over-watering is not the calamity that it can be. "To the busy head gardener — who can be as forgetful or as distracted as anyone else — that can be both a reputation saver and a plant saver," comments R J Harris

— since the loam-based John Innes composts absorb liquids readily, there is either no run-off or hardly any at all when liquid is applied to them slowly and in a controlled manner. Thus, there is almost no loss of applied liquid and no accompanying wetted surface. In this, too, there may be a financial economy: the applied liquid may be an expensive liquid feed

— the loam-based compost is of help when feeding is delayed. It sustains plant life longer than does the peat-based compost, because the loam contains natural nutrients. It releases these as the plants rooted in the host compost require them

TIP 95
➔ **The John Innes No 1, No 2 and No 3 potting composts contain lime. Do not use them for lime-hating plants such as heathers, azaleas and rhododendrons. For this kind of plant, buy the compost the plastic-bag container of which bears the words John Innes Ericaceous Compost.**

101

The association that represents Britain's eight (at 2006) John Innes producers issues to garden centres, DIY and hardware stores and other retail outlets the following display and storage instructions

- *Keep the bags dry and cool*
- *Store them indoors*
- *If stored outside, keep them out of direct sunlight*
- *If stored outside, keep them sheltered from the rain — otherwise, they absorb the rain through their air holes*
- *If stored outside, site them against a north-facing wall*
- *If stored outside, keep them under a canopy or a roof*
- *Cover them with white or light-coloured plastic sheeting to keep them dry — not black sheeting*
- *Stack the bags on pallets or above ground level*
- *Stack them so that air can circulate within and between them*
- *Never stack new deliveries on top of old stock*
- *Rotate the stock*
- *Keep the bags at a distance from heat.*

Underlying these strictures is the association's awareness that as manufactured composts age they experience a natural and to-be-expected process of deterioration — all of them, not solely the John Innes composts.

This reality is not to be seen as a product weakness. Given the composition of composts and their purpose, there would be cause for concern if the opposite were the case.

— the loam that forms the greater part of the John Innes compost is heat-pasteurised. Thus, it is free from weeds, insects and disease.

The fertilisers with which the John Innes composts are enriched include

- phosphates, for root growth
- nitrogen, for top growth
- potash, for flowering and fruiting
- trace elements, for colour and flavour

with the John Innes numbers — **1, 2** and **3** — referring to the levels of the nutrients that are present in the composts. The **JI No 1** potting compost has the least amount, whilst the **JI No 3** potting compost has the greatest amount.

On average, each of the John Innes composts, used correctly, provides sufficient plant food to last for one to two months. After that, usually, a liquid feed is required. The head gardener's preferred feed for this purpose is his own make of comfrey solution, derived from his own make of comfrey stock, which is derived from his own cultivation of the herb comfrey.

In the garden centres and the other retail outlets for gardeners, the John Innes composts are available in plastic bags. These range from the easily-carried-in-the-one-hand, 5-litre pack to the largest 25-kilo pack, which is most sensibly moved on a trolley.

All manufactured composts are far from ever-lasting. In addition, they are in risk of being displayed for sale in conditions that do not maintain to the maximum their nutritional and other qualities.

102

The sparetime gardener might well wonder: "Why should I use a manufactured compost which costs good money when Nature has provided me with free top soil and a strong, trowel-wielding arm?"

"The answer, in the spirit of true horticulture, lies in the soil," comments R J Harris, "which contains just about every natural thing that sees sown seeds and potted/container-ised plants as its rightful prey."

Probably, also, the head gardener points out, Nature's loam does not offer the full complement of properties that protects and nourishes chosen seeds and plants. That is not the case with the manufactured, soil-based composts.

Used correctly, these can do nothing other than encourage germination, support seedling, plantlet and plant develop-ment and ensure maximum plant lifespan.

"The money spent on them is recovered in time and seeds saved, in flourishing plants and in protected reputation," says the head gardener.

For this reason, the association that represents Britain's John Innes producers, and imposes standards upon them, takes an undisguised interest in the retailers' storage and display conditions.

Arising out of this, it recommends for their use a well-publicised code of conduct.

Sell-by dates have not been adopted by the producers of the John Innes composts. It is left to the retail customer to make sure that a purchase is not a carry-over from a previous season's stock.

The association of John Innes compost makers requires that a batch number be shown on each bag of product.

With its help, a particular bag's history can be ascertained, should queries arise.

It is worth noting that there is no such thing as a standard, univer-sally-utilised John Innes compost recipe. This is despite the fact that the product is the same no matter where it is bought and which of the eight officially-recognised manufac-turers (see *SUPPLIERS*) produces it.

The key to this apparent contradiction lies in the product's loam content.

Loam varies in its properties according to where it is found.

This makes necessary a balancing variation in the quantities of peat, sand/grit and fertilisers that are mixed with it. In turn, this affects the amount of ground limestone that is added. The limestone counterbalances the acid nature of the peat, thus rendering the compost acceptable to most of plant life.

TIP 96

➜ **Whatever the type or grade of manufactured compost that is used, do as R J Harris does and close its plastic bag tightly to keep it moist and to prevent contamination. "Its soil sterilisation must not be lost," Mr Harris warns. "Equally, keep it inside and away from any source of heat, and away from weed killers. Do not keep it from one season to the next. Age is more than likely to disturb the balance of its nutrients. If out-of-season compost is on hand — no matter what its type and make — dispose of it by spreading it as thinly as possible on the garden's beds.**

103

At 2006, the member companies of the John Innes Manufacturers' Association, which produce the John Innes soil-based composts, were

Bulrush Hort Ltd, 16 Newferry Road, Bellaghy, Magherafelt, County Derry, BT45 8ND, *tel* 028-7938-6555, *fax* 028-7938-6741, www.bulrush.co.uk, amcc@bulrush.co.uk.

Eden Park Ltd, Crown Quay Lane, Sittingbourne, Kent, ME10 3JJ, *tel* 01795-471583, *fax* 01795 428011, www.edenpark.co.uk, sales@edenpark.co.uk.

Erin Horticulture Ltd, Derrinlough, BIRR, Co Offaly, Ireland, *tell* +353 5791 20161, *fax* +353 5791 33007, www.erinhorticulture.com, purchasing@erinhorticulture.com.

Gem Gardening, Brookside Lane, Oswaldtwistle, Accrington, Lancashire, BB5 3NY, *tel* 01254-356600, *fax* 01254-356677, www.gemgardening.co.uk, brianmetcalf@tiscali.co.uk, gem.technical@ntlworld.com.

The Scotts Co (UK) Ltd, Paper Mill Lane, Bramford, Ipswich, IP8 4BZ, *tel* 01473 202252, *fax* 01473 830386, www.scottsukonline.com, elaine.gotts@scotts.com, alan.shepherd@scotts.com.

Wm Sinclair Horticulture Ltd, Firth Road, Lincoln, LN6 7AH, *tel* 01522 537561 (s/b), *fax* 01522 513209, www.william-sinclair.co.uk, chris.turner@william-sinclair.co.uk.

Wessex Horticultural Products Ltd, Wessex House, Hill Top Business Park, 1-3 Devizes Road, Salisbury, Wiltshire, SP3 4UF, *tel* 01722-337744, *fax* 01722-333177, www.wessexhort.co.uk, stan@wessexhort.co.uk, rosemary@wessexhort.co.uk.

Westland Horticulture Ltd, 14 Granville Industrial Estate, Granville Road, Dungannon, Co Tyrone, BT70 1NJ, *tel* 028-8772-7500, *fax* 028-8772-3800, www.westlandhorticulture.com, jrobinson@westlandhorticulture.com, csutton@westlandhorticulture.com.

The John Innes Manufacturers' Association is at PO Box 8, Harrogate, HG2 8XB, *tel* 01423 879208, *fax* 01423 870025, info@johninnes.info, www.johninnes.info. Contact it for a helpful, illustrated brochure on the benefits and uses of the John Innes loam-based composts. The brochure is free in return for a stamped, addressed envelope.

COMPATIBLE and NON-COMPATIBLE PLANTS

Head gardener R J Harris's forty-five-plus years in horticulture (in 2007) have taught him that many vegetables help or harm each other when grown in each other's company. Equally, he has been shown that flowers and herbs have a beneficial or harmful effect upon other plants. In general, for improved results, he twins

all beans with asparagus, borage, buckwheat, the cabbage family, carrots, cauliflowers, celery, cucumbers, leeks, peas, poached egg flowers, potatoes, squashes, strawberries, sweet corn, sweet peas, turnips

all herbs except rue with the cabbage family

all peas with all beans, carrots,

104

In the plant world there are friends and enemies and, in R J Harris's opinion, allying knowledge of which is which to that of the moon's impact upon preparation, planting, feeding and harvesting — and applying that combination — can make the difference between adequate results and superlative results. This reality is demonstrated season after season at Tresillian.

For the individual applications of the laws of compatible and non-compatible planting consult this chapter's named plants.

celery, cucumbers, leeks, radishes, swedes, sweet corn, turnips

asparagus with all beans, parsley, tomatoes

basil with tomatoes

beans (all) with asparagus, borage, buckwheat, the cabbage family, carrots, cauliflowers, celery, cucumbers, leeks, peas, poached egg flowers, potatoes, squashes, strawberries, sweet corn, sweet peas, turnips

beetroots with kohlrabi

borage with all beans

buckwheat with all beans

cabbage family with all beans, most herbs, cucumbers, marigolds, potatoes

calendula (marigolds) with the cabbage family, carrots

carrots with all beans, chives, garlic, leeks, lettuce, marigolds, onions, parsley, peas, sage, turnips

cauliflowers with all beans

celery with all beans, dill, leeks, all peas, potatoes

chives with carrots, cucumbers

corn (sweet) with all beans, lettuce, peas, potatoes, pumpkins

cucumbers with all beans, the cabbage family, chives, peas, potatoes

dill with celery

garlic with carrots

herbs (all) with the cabbage family

horse radish with potatoes

kohlrabi with beetroots, onions

leeks with all beans, carrots, celery, lettuce, peas, turnips

lettuce with carrots, leeks, radishes, strawberries, sweet corn

marigolds (calendula) with the cabbage family, carrots

marigolds (Mexican) with potatoes

Mexican marigolds with potatoes

mint with the cabbage family

onions with carrots, kohlrabi

parsley with asparagus, carrots, tomatoes

peas (all) with all beans, carrot, celery, cucumbers, leeks, radishes, swedes, sweet corn, turnips

peas (sweet) with all beans

poached egg flowers with all beans

potatoes with all beans, the cabbage family, celery, cucumbers, horse radish, Mexican marigolds, peas, radishes, strawberries, sweet corn

pumpkins with sweet corn

radishes with lettuce, peas

radish (horse) with potatoes

sage with carrots

squashes with all beans

strawberries with all beans, lettuce, potatoes

swedes with peas

sweet corn with all beans, lettuce, peas, potatoes, pumpkins

sweet peas with all beans

tomatoes with asparagus, basil,

TIP 97

➔ **Plant mixed aromatic herbs in profusion around vegetable beds to confuse and thus discourage unwelcome insects — as well as to add colourful, decorative planting to the work-a-day kitchen garden.**

> **105**
>
> 'Beware the walnut tree," counsels R J Harris. "It is a wonderful tree, a most useful tree; there are several on the Tresillian estate. But be very, very careful where you plant it. It is the king of the 'non-compatibles'. The ground it grows in becomes sterile. Few plants thrive in its vicinity.
>
> "Even the oak would rather be somewhere else."

parsley
turnips with all beans, carrots, leeks, peas.

Certain plants fail to thrive in each other's company. When positioning plants that he wishes to see flourish, the aware gardener avoids such pairings. When his aim is natural weed control, he exploits them. In the Cornish head gardener's experience, the most common of these hapless pairings are

all beans and beetroots, garlic, kohlrabi, onions,
all peas and garlic, onions, shallots
asparagus and garlic, onions
beans (all) and beetroots, garlic, kohlrabi, onions,
beetroots and all beans
cabbage family and garlic, onions, rue, strawberries, vines

camomile and potatoes
couch grass and lupins, tomatoes, turnips
garlic and all beans, asparagus, the cabbage family, all peas, strawberries
ground elder and Mexican marigolds
ground ivy and Mexican marigolds
kohlrabi and all beans, tomatoes
ivy (ground) and Mexican marigolds
lupins and couch grass
marigolds (Mexican) and ground elder, ground ivy
Mexican marigolds and ground elder, ground ivy
mint and potatoes
oak tree and olive tree
olive tree and oak tree
onions and all beans, asparagus, the cabbage family, peas, strawberries
peas (all) and garlic, onions, shallots
potatoes and camomile, mint, pumpkins, rosemary, sunflowers, thyme, tomatoes
pumpkins and potatoes
rosemary and potatoes
rue and the cabbage family
shallots and all peas
strawberries and the cabbage family, garlic, onions
sunflowers and potatoes
thyme and potatoes
tomatoes and couch grass, kohlrabi, potatoes
tree (oak) and olive tree
tree (olive) and oak tree
turnips and couch grass
vines and the cabbage family.

COLD FRAME

In essence, the cold frame — without which R J Harris could not function as a professional horticulturist and could not achieve the results that he does on the Tresillian estate — is an unheated, bottomless box made of timber or brick. It is equipped with a sloping, glazed lid, which can be raised fully to admit access to the interior, or in stages to admit air. The frame rests upon the earth in an unshaded place and is angled so that the slope of its lid faces south. Usually, it is accompanied by an immediately adjacent area of hard standing for general work purposes. This area can also accommodate trayed, pot-

106

RJ Harris points out that a sound, redundant, newly-puttied casement window can be the starting point in constructing a cold frame. Its size dictates the size of the area of the frame's top. That dictates the length of each of the cold frame's four sides. Its height remains 40cm at the back and 25cm at the front.

If the window retains its original hinges, fasten them to the rear wall of the frame, at the top. Otherwise, the recommended cabin hooks and eyes (see 7 and 8), which provide the simplest 'hinging', are utilised.

gardener and his staff.

Each is brick-built. It is about 10m long and about 1.5m wide. Its sloping, glass-glazed lid comprises twelve, 75cm-wide sections, each of which is hinged to the back of the frame and can be raised independently of the others for ventilation or access.

The interior of the cold frame offers an uninterrupted area of ground for seed sowing, planting out, the parking of pots and containers, and cultivation for specific purposes and plant developments "bearing in mind," the head gardener points out, "that when using the frames for the development of rooted plants, I observe the moon's quarters in the correct manner."

The two Tresillian cold frames back onto the south-facing wall of the kitchen garden's heated greenhouse. In turn, this backs onto the south-facing, inner side of one of the garden's four perimeter walls.

ted or containerised plants when they are removed from the frame in a planned sequence to accustom them to open-air conditions before they are planted out permanently.

In a cold frame

— seeds sown in the earth base can be brought to seedling or plantlet stage prior to being planted out

— seeds sown in the earth base can be brought to maturity to provide a crop

— seeds sown in trays or pots can be brought to seedling or plantlet stage prior to being being planted out in the open garden

— plants not native to the British Isles and removed from the open ground at the end of the season and then potted can be protected from the elements during Winter.

At Tresillian, in the walled, kitchen garden, two cold frames are available to the head

To create a simple, low-cost, durable, cold frame, Mr Harris recommends

1 construct a four-sided, one-metre-square timber box. Give it a 40cm-high back and a 25cm-high front. Use exterior-quality ply wood, planking or planed- tongued-and-grooved boards obtained from a

TIP 98
➔ **The cold frame's contents are watered, as required, first thing in the morning — not in the coolness of the end of the day (as is good practice in the open garden). Watered at the end of the day, the plants inside the frame endure a night of unrelieved wet and cold, especially when the lid is closed. It does them no good at all, advises the head gardener.**

107

The head gardener favours a simple refinement to the home-made cold frame.

"Build a deep frame," he suggests, "and fill it with a depth of 30cm-to-45cm of home-made compost to within about 30cm of its top at the front."

He makes the compost by mixing together three parts of top soil from the garden, one part of sand and two parts of fully-composted leaf mould. First, he passes the top soil through a 6mm sieve, to remove the large stones, weed growth and rubbish. Then he rubs the leafmould through the sieve.

He stifles the weed-seed content of the garden soil by covering the mixture in the deep frame with a 10cm layer of John Innes No 2 potting compost.

Seeds can be sown directly into the John Innes.

Such a frame, Mr Harris believes, is of benefit especially to the gardener whose bending and stooping days are in the past. A very wide range of plants can be developed (albeit it in limited numbers), thanks to the controlled protection that the lid makes possible. Another advantage, he finds, is that — easily and at low cost — the John Innes compost can be replaced with fresh compost when necessary.

"Sprinkle the removed, rredundant compost as thinly as possible on the garden's beds," he advises.

2 use a sheet of translucent, rigid, plastic sheet for the cold frame's lid. Make it of a size to more than cover the cold frame's top by 5cm all round

3 screw four lengths of 5cm-wide, exterior-quality, timber-strip edging to the four edges of the perimeter of one face of the plastic sheet. Pre-drill the plastic sheet appropriately

4 join the timber-strip edging together at each of its four corners by screwing on a galvanised or brass flat, metal, L piece. Alterrnatively, fashion halving joints and affix each with a single screw

5 use galvanised or brass (preferably) screws throughout. Favour the Pozidrive screw with the Philips head over the old-fashioned, slotted-head screw. Use a manually-turned ratchet screwdriver

6 position the lid on the cold frame's top so that its timber-strip edging is underneath. [***Consideration:*** *thus, rain water runs off the plastic sheet without being impeded by — and, possibly, adversely affecting — the timber-strip*

builders' merchant. Use timber strip positioned internally to join together the ply wood, planks or boards of the four sides

TIP 99
➔ **Seen in a 'Yellow Book' garden: a timber-built cold frame made portable by the addition at its back and its front of carrying arms. These were two lengths of screwed-on timber strip the ends of which extended beyond the frame's sides by some 45cm. Thus, two people were provided with convenient handles. The owner claimed that a removable frame provided her with more scope in her very small garden.**

108

Mr Harris's lifetime in horticulture has taught him, among many things, that the places where plants are developed and managed can be places of unexpected and, sometimes, alarming hazards. The home-made cold frame offers a case in point.

"Glass *can* be used instead of rigid plastic for the lid," he notes. "In some places it is the more easily obtained of the two.

"I do not recommend it.

"It complicates the construction method. More seriously, imagine anyone being unlucky enough to fall upon the lid and to go crashing through it."

The head gardener suggests that if only glass can be used its external face be covered with fine-mesh wire netting.

"Stretch it tautly in both directions," he recommends. "Wrap it around the lid's edges and fasten it securely to the underneath of the lid's timber frame.

"In the event of the worst happening, it prevents the glass from caving in."

edging. Also, the edging forms a seal around the top of the cold frame]

7 'hinge' the lid to the cold frame's taller side with two galvanised or brass cabin hooks and eyes. Fasten the hooks to the timber edge of the lid. Screw the eyes into the timber body of the cold frame. Alterrnatively, but with greater complexity and expense, join the one to the other with a metre-long, brass or galvanised piano hinge

8 secure the lid at the front when it is fully closed by two more cabin hooks and eyes.

9 paint all of the timber surfaces before bringing lid and frame together with as many coats of exterior-quality, glossy white paint as patience and resources permit.
[**Consideration:** *this is both to preserve the timber and to concentrate and reflect as much light as possible within and around the cold frame*]

10 position the completed cold frame 1) in an unshaded place, with the downward slope of its glazed lid facing south, and 2) adjacent to the garden's greenhouse, if there is one. Do so on the greenhouse's south side.
[**Consideration:** *this results in the taking of plants over the shortest possible distance when they are transferred from cold frame to greenhouse, or from greenhouse to cold frame. The transferred plants suffer when removed from one level of ambient temperature to another. This kind of changed condition must be experienced*

TIP 100
➔ **Today's DIY materials, tools and skills render it possible for the cold frame to be made in any width, any length. Necessarily, the larger structure must have a larger lid requiring a stouter timber frame. The lid is, as a result, heavy. When very large, it can be too heavy for one person to raise. Also, as a result, it may be unsafe. This risk-incurring limitation must be borne in mind at the design stage.**

by them for the shortest possible time]

11 establish the cold frame upon a metre square framing of bricks set into the earth, so that the bottom edges of the cold frame's four timber sides are not in contact with the earth. Do not mortar the bricks together. Line them up lengthwise, so that they abut each other, and so that as little draught as possible can be admitted into the cold frame's interior. Use a spirit level, if possible, to establish a truly horizontal surface of the assembled framing of bricks

12 place a strip of damp-proof course material between the brick course and the lower edges of the cold frame's timber walls, if possible

13 provide props to support the frame's lid at its two front corners when it is raised. Cut them from exterior-quality strip timber. Devize a range of props making possible air-admitting openings beginning at 2cm wide and advancing in 2cm stages to 30cm wide.
[**Consideration:** *beyond the 30cm width, the lid is raised fully if hinged, or removed entirely if fastened with cabin hooks and eyes and then placed to one side. Facilitate access to the frame's interior by these means*].

'This is the cold frame for the gardener whose skills do not include brick laying," comments the head gardener.

"Most professional frames are of brick construction throughout. Brick provides the longer life and does not have timber's need for pre-use painting and sustained maintenance throughout the frame's life.

"As well as this, in most professional gardens, the greenhouse has a brick-wall base. That becomes the back wall of the brick-built cold frames when they are attached to it. So there is an economy as well."

In the days when the greenhouse was heated by water pipes, the attached cold frames were converted into hot frames by switching them, at will, into the heating system. This was achieved, simply, by directing the run of the pipes through the heated greenhouse's wall into the frames at ground level and then back into the greenhouse.

The head gardener recommends that when the home-made cold frame is in use — however it is constructed — the exterior of its body and both sides of its glazed lid be kept scrupulously clean.

"Equally," he adds, "always have a couple of clean sacks or a piece of redundant carpet ready to drape over the frame to guard its contents against the frost.

"Keep these where they can be found rapidly and with ease," he advises.

"Many a plant has been lost to Jack Frost because improvising or searching for coverings takes too long."

pH

The p in pH stands for potenz, the H for Hydrogen. Hence, pH stands for potenz of hydrogen, or, translated, the power of hydrogen. The term refers — not especially helpfully, so far as the practical, non-chemist gardener is concerned — to the presence of hydrogen ions in the soil. More usefully, when shown on a seed packet as a pH number, the term answers the gardener's question: May I or may I not sow these seeds at a given spot in my garden? — the pH of that spot being known to me because I have found out what it is.

R J Harris endorses this practical view of what very easily can become a horticultural mystery.

"Each plant has a pH preference," he says.

"That preference can be ascertained without difficulty.

"If it is not printed on the seed packet it is recorded in any number of manuals obtainable at the local reference library.

'So," states the head gardener, "when you find that the declared pH requirement of your chosen plant matches the pH of your soil, you know that you are off to a flying start."

No matter what a given plant's, shrub's, vegetable's or tree's role in the grand gardening scheme happens to be, its pH preference is bound to be in the range pH1 to pH14.

"Soil at pH1 is soil at its most acid," says Mr Harris. "You find it in bog conditions.

"Soil at pH14 has hardly any acid at all. You go to the beach to find it.

"The important one is pH7.

"This is the neutral level. It is the pH of most soils. Luckily, most plants prefer it."

The matter, R J Harris points out, can be finely balanced, and he offers, as example of this, the case of the potato.

Potatoes are at their best grown not in the more common pH7 but in the less common pH5-to-pH6. Growing in pH7 or over, they incur small warts on the skin known as potato scab.

"This is in no way detrimental, of course; it just affects the look of the tuber."

A pH soil-testing kit for general use has been a weapon in the head gardener's horticultural arm-

oury for many years.

"Any garden centre will sell you one," he says. "It is not expensive, and it is a very simple item.

"You are given a test tube. You put in it a pinch of the soil that you want to test. You add the liquid that is supplied with the test tube, you shake it all up and you leave the test tube to stand as directed by the kit manufacturer's instructions.

"In a short time, a colour appears in the soil in the test tube.

"You then hold the tube against a supplied chart of colours, find a colour match, read across a simple scale, and there you are, that is the pH of the part of the garden that the soil came from."

The head gardener stresses: "When all is said and done, pH identification using one of these kits cannot be established with pin-point precision — and, certainly, no research laboratory would be satisfied with it.

"Fortunately, most crops and plants grow in most pH conditions and produce some sort of a result, and I am the first to sympathise when the sparetime gardener decides that life is too short to fiddle about with testing and trying to find out why a small p stands alongside a capital H.

"In my experience, it is either the perfectionist or the one who has to feed a family through the year from an allotment who, before putting seed in ground, looks for an exact match between a plant's pH requirement and the growing medium's pH content."

SUPPLIERS

The suppliers and organisations with which Mr Harris deals for the resources that he applies on behalf of the Tresillian estate — and from which he receives advice — are listed in this chapter. Their products and services are indicated, as that information is required, elsewhere in the other chapters of the manual.

Chase Organics Ltd, Riverdene, Molesey Road, Hersham, Surrey, KT12 4RG, *01932 253666*, *richard. rixson@chaseorganics.co.uk*, *www.chaseorganics.co.uk.com.*

Edwin Tucker & Sons Ltd, Brewery Meadow, Stonepark, Ashburton, Newton Abbot, Devon, TQ13 7DG, *01364 652403*, *seeds@ edwintucker.com*, *www.edwintucker. com.*

Garden Organic Ryton, Coventry, CV8 3LG, *(024) 7630 3517*, *enquiry@gardenorganic.org.uk*, *www.gardenorganic.org.uk*, *www.hdra.org.uk.*

Heritage Seed Library, an initiative of Garden Organic Ryton, or HDRA.

HDRA, see Garden Organic Ryton.

Kings Seeds, Monks Farm, Coggeshall Road, Kelvedon, Essex, CO5 9PG, *01376 570000*, *sales@kingsseeds. com*, *www.kingsseeds.com.*

Peter Grayson, Sweet Pea Seedsman, 34 Glenthorne Close, Brampton, Chesterfield, Derbyshire, S40 3AR, *0124 627 8503* (also fax number).

Simpson's Seeds, The Walled Garden Nursery, Horningsham, Warminster, Wiltshire, BA12 7NQ, *01985 845004*, *sales@simpsonsseeds.co.uk*, *www.simpsonsseeds.co.uk.*

Suffolk Herbs, Monks Farm, Coggeshall Road, Kelvedon, Essex, CO5 9PG, *01376 572456*, *sales@suffolkherbs. com*, *www.suffolkherbs.com.*

The Organic Gardening Catalogue, Riverdene, Molesey Road, Hersham, Surrey, KT12 4RG, *0845 1301304*, *enquiries@haseorganics.co.uk*, *www.organiccatalog.com.*

The Seed Swap Register, an initiative of Garden Organic Ryton, or HDRA.

The Tomato Growers Club, an initiative of Simpson's Seeds.

Thomas Etty, 7 Coombe Close, Castle Cary, Somerset, BA7 7HJ, *01963 359202*, *sales@ thomasetty.co.uk*, *www.thomasetty.co.uk.*

THE GARDENER'S DAY

In the garden, so peaceful, nature takes its turn to awaken, while some must slumber.

The owl from lofty heights swoops silently upon its prey of mice and vermin, the hedgehog in the undergrowth seeks beetles, worms and slugs.

The new moon shines brightly, so that the gardener, when morn arrives, sees the plants with dew upon their leaves, it is the time to plant the seeds, for all good gardeners work by the moon, with all its phases it is a busy time.

Seed planting must take place, for when with the full moon, harvest will reap a bountiful reward.

The gardener's life is always a busy one, for during the early part of the day he is busy raking, tilling, weeding, pruning, and keeping everything in order, as the heat of the day takes its toll so the gardener finds a shady place to stand and think, more often or not it is under an old oak tree with so many tales it could tell.

The afternoon sun sees the gardener once more busy picking fruits and caring for his ways, for the gardener's life is a never ending toll of things that must be done, evening sunset is fast approaching and the beckoning of another day will soon arrive, so he must shut the door upon this day because his tomorrow will soon be another day.

R J HARRIS 1998

Tips and information-panel indexes, complementary moon-gardening discussion and a continuing report on R J Harris's horticultural methods and experimentations are available on *www.moongardening.fsnet.co.uk* or *www.moongardening.cwc.net*